GOD'S LOVE THROUGH THE SPIRIT

GOD'S LOVE THROUGH THE SPIRIT

The Holy Spirit in Thomas Aquinas & John Wesley

Kenneth M. Loyer

THE CATHOLIC UNIVERSITY
OF AMERICA PRESS
Washington, D.C.

The paper used in this publication meets the minimum
requirements of American National Standards for Information
Science—Permanence of Paper for Printed Library Materials,
ANSI Z39.48-1984.
∞

Cataloging-in-Publication Data available
from the Library of Congress
ISBN 978-0-8132-2599-9

For my parents,
Mary and Jim Loyer,
with love

CONTENTS

Four

AQUINAS ON THE HOLY SPIRIT AS MUTUAL LOVE

Five

GIFT OF THE SPIRIT: THE HOLY SPIRIT, LOVE, AND THE CHRISTIAN LIFE IN AQUINAS

Six

TOWARD GREATER LOVE: AQUINAS, WESLEY, AND LIFE IN THE SPIRIT

Conclusion

FURTHER PATHS TO MUTUAL THOMIST AND METHODIST ENRICHMENT

ACKNOWLEDGMENTS

I AM INDEBTED to a number of people whose influence has helped make the writing of this book possible. In particular, I gratefully acknowledge Bruce Marshall, under whose wise and generous guidance I wrote the dissertation on which this study is based; William Abraham, Rebekah Miles, Reinhard Hütter, Stanley Hauerwas, and Randy Maddox for their feedback on various chapters; Geoffrey Wainwright for introducing me to ecumenism; Edgardo Colón-Emeric for initial conversations on Aquinas and Wesley; and Richard Heitzenrater and Randy Maddox, coleaders of the 2007 Summer Wesley Seminar on History and Tradition in the Wesleyan Heritage at Duke Divinity School, during which I conducted research on chapters 2 and 6.

I also express my gratitude to my wife, Molly, whose love and encouragement are among God's greatest gifts to me; to the Catholic University of America Press; and to the people of Otterbein United Methodist Church of Spry in York, Pa., who have been understanding and supportive of my vocation to theological scholarship as well as pastoral ministry. Lastly, I would like to thank my parents, Mary and Jim Loyer, to whom I dedicate this book.

INTRODUCTION

Pneumatology has often been a neglected theme in Christian theology, perhaps especially in the modern West, but it was not always that way. In fact, the doctrine of the Holy Spirit, far from being disregarded, has been the subject of considerable attention and elaboration throughout the history of Christian thought. While scholastic theology is not normally championed as a high point in pneumatological reflection, some significant accounts of the Spirit's person and work originate from the theologians of that period. Among the scholastic doctors, St. Thomas Aquinas provides a particularly developed account of the doctrine of the Holy Spirit.

Aquinas offers a vibrant and sophisticated pneumatology in which the connection between the Holy Spirit and love is especially important. According to Aquinas, this connection is complex and multifaceted, touching on his account of the doctrine of the Trinity as well as his moral theology. It comes into play, for example, in his discussion of (1) the Spirit as personal love, (2) the Spirit as the mutual love of the Father and the Son, and (3) the implications of the Spirit as love for his soteriology. Taken together, these three headings represent a convenient way to approach the topic of pneumatology in Aquinas because of their scope, ranging from questions about the inner trinitarian life of God to questions about the shape of the Christian life. There is a need for more sustained reflection on Aquinas's pneumatology, as well as pneumatology in general, and a study of Aquinas on these questions contributes to the knowledge of his theology while establishing that he is an important source for contemporary efforts at pneumatological recovery—in other words, he is part of the solution and not the problem.

The pneumatology of Thomas Aquinas also has implications for Christian theology more broadly, including a certain theological strand in the Western tradition, namely, Wesleyan theology. To be sure, any direct influence of Aquinas on John Wesley would be extremely difficult to establish since Wesley cites Aquinas only a few times in his entire corpus, but there does exist a considerable, and even surprising, degree of pneumatological resonance and compatibility between these two figures. Of course, the differences between Aquinas and Wesley must be readily acknowledged. Not only did they occupy different historical locations, but also their basic understandings of the task of theology were not the same. Put somewhat simply, while Aquinas took a speculative approach to theology,[1] Wesley was driven by more practical concerns. Nevertheless, their interests were not foreign to one another. In each case, for example, there is a clearly operative pneumatology with emphasis on love and holiness in Christian living. This basic parallel between Aquinas and Wesley has been observed in Catholic-Methodist bilateral dialogue, and it can be developed further both for ecumenical purposes and for the enrichment of theological reflection today.

Chapter 1 diagnoses a vexing problem in contemporary Methodist theology, the widespread pneumatological deficit and typical reduction of the Spirit's work to political projects. In the process the claim is made that to a considerable extent Methodism's theological core has been obscured, and a key theme is introduced: the prospects for the retrieval and development of Methodist theology, specifically its traditional focus on sanctification.

Chapter 2 addresses the question of how best to interpret Wesley

1. Aquinas considered the task of theology to be speculative, but not in the modern sense of the term; for him, speculative theology was never disconnected from praxis. So he understood *sacra doctrina* to include both speculative and practical dimensions (*Summa theologiae* I, q. 1, a. 4; hereafter *ST* in the footnotes).

through an investigation of the problem of sanctification in his works. In particular, after outlining various proposals by other scholars, this chapter seeks to rediscover the implicitly trinitarian understanding of sanctification that animates Wesley's vision of the Christian life as one of participation in God through the Holy Spirit. In response to recent calls for Methodists and Wesleyans to describe sanctification in more compelling theological terms, such a rediscovery holds promise for advancing the constructive interpretation of Wesley's doctrine of Christian perfection or, as Wesley often called it, perfect love.

After two chapters on the Methodist side of the project (outlining contemporary Methodist theology's struggle to find relevance for its traditional interest in holiness, and analyzing John Wesley's view of sanctification, respectively), our attention turns to Aquinas for theological enrichment of Wesley's implicit trinitarianism and especially his intuitions about the doctrine of the Holy Spirit. The next three chapters consist of an inquiry into Aquinas's *amor*-based pneumatology. Chapters 3 and 4 consider the place of the Holy Spirit in the life of the Trinity. In his account of the trinitarian persons in the *Summa theologiae* (*prima pars*, qq. 33–43), Aquinas raises questions pertaining to the relationship between the Spirit and love, in this case in the inner life of God. Those questions include whether love (*amor*) is a name proper to the Holy Spirit, and whether the Spirit is the mutual love of the Father and the Son. Chapter 3 provides an exposition of the former question, on the Spirit as personal love or love in person, which is the central opening theme in Aquinas's account of the Holy Spirit as love.

Chapter 4 then extends the inquiry by way of a consideration of the latter question, exploring the significance of the Spirit as mutual love in Aquinas's mature thought. This account of Aquinas's pneumatology begins with such trinitarian questions in order to set his understanding of the person and work of the Holy Spirit in its proper trinitarian context, which not only is crucial for an accurate account of Aquinas but also represents a connection that can help to illumine Wesley's deepest insights into the doctrine of the Holy Spirit.

Chapter 5 further expands the scope of the study to what might be called a third phase in Aquinas's *amor*-based pneumatology, which concerns the soteriological ramifications of the Spirit as love in these two senses. In particular, picking up on the motif of gift that Aquinas introduces in q. 38 of the *Summa*, this chapter investigates the application of the title of "gift" to the Spirit as well as the works appropriated to the Spirit, specifically in regard to the infusion and cultivation of love and its centrality in Aquinas's vision of the Christian life.

Following an assessment of the problem of sanctification in contemporary Methodism and in Wesley in chapters 1 and 2, and the subsequent investigation of Aquinas's *amor*-based pneumatology in chapters 3 through 5, chapter 6 integrates various ideas gleaned from these chapters in the context of a closing constructive argument. That argument, in brief, is that while each figure's thought has its own particular nuances, the common theological ground between Aquinas and Wesley—in particular, the link between pneumatology and love that each thinker perceives and develops—makes them a noteworthy pairing in the ongoing effort of pneumatological retrieval. In other words, the recent interest shown in recovering a sense of the importance of the doctrine of the Holy Spirit in theological inquiry[2] can be informed by an appreciation of the pneumatological thrust found in the works of these two figures, especially given (1) the fervent concern for holiness in love typified by Wesley and (2) the substantive trinitarian doctrine presented by Aquinas, which gives holiness and love their depth and *telos*. Thus, this portion of the book will explore

2. As expressed, for example, in Clark Pinnock, *Flame of Love: A Theology of the Holy Spirit* (Downers Grove, Ill.: InterVarsity Press, 1996); Gary D. Badcock, *Light of Truth and Fire of Love: A Theology of the Holy Spirit* (Grand Rapids: Eerdmans, 1997); Eugene F. Rogers Jr., *After the Spirit: A Constructive Pneumatology from Resources Outside the Modern West* (Grand Rapids: Eerdmans, 2005); and Amos Yong, *Spirit of Love: A Trinitarian Theology of Grace* (Waco, Tex.: Baylor University Press, 2012).

how Aquinas's pneumatology can be appropriated and amplified by the kind of concerns about the Holy Spirit and sanctification that are evident in the Wesleyan tradition, with an eye toward new horizons in the study of Aquinas and of Wesley, the discovery of common ground between Catholics and Protestants, and a pneumatological *ressourcement* for the advancement of constructive theology.

Returning to the problem in contemporary Methodist theology identified in chapters 1 and 2, namely, the need for a deeper theological foundation for the doctrine of sanctification, the final section of this chapter applies to this problem the lessons learned from Aquinas and Wesley on the doctrine of the Holy Spirit. The reflections of Wesley and Aquinas on the Spirit show that the political relevance of the Trinity, and of theology as a whole, is grounded in nothing other than the life of God and our communal participation in this life. Such participation is made possible for us all by the personal indwelling and power of the Holy Spirit, through whom God's love has been shed abroad in our hearts (Rom 5:5).

Finally, the book's conclusion suggests further paths for mutual Thomist and Methodist enrichment, extending the work that has already been done both here and elsewhere.

One

METHODISM AND THE WORK OF THE SPIRIT

Making Good on the Deficit

JOHN WESLEY stressed "practical divinity."[1] As part of this practical approach, he directed his theological teachings *ad populum*.[2] Most Methodists, following Wesley, have typically devoted

1. E.g., Wesley described the 1780 *Collection of Hymns for the Use of the People Called Methodists* as "a little body of experimental and practical divinity" (Preface to *A Collection of Hymns for the Use of the People Called Methodists* [1780], in *The Works of John Wesley*, ed. Albert C. Outler, et al., 35 vols. [Nashville: Abingdon Press, 1984 ff.], 7:74; henceforth referred to as Wesley, *Works*, ed. Outler, et al.).

2. As Wesley explained in the preface to his *Sermons on Several Occasions*, he conveyed his theology "*ad populum*—to the bulk of mankind—to those who neither relish nor understand the art of speaking, but who notwithstanding are competent judges of those truths which are necessary to present and future happiness ... I design plain truth for plain people. Therefore of set purpose I abstain from all nice and philosophical speculations, from all perplexed and intricate reasonings, and as far as possible from even the show of learning, unless in sometimes citing the original Scriptures. I labour to avoid all words which are not easy to be understood, all which are not used in common life; and in particular those kinds of technical terms that so frequently occur in bodies of divinity, those modes of speaking which men of reading are intimately acquainted with, but which to common people are an unknown tongue" (Preface to *Sermons on Several Occasions*, §§1–3, Wesley, *Works*, Outler, et al., 1:103–04).

little time and energy to dogmatic theology, with some exceptions.[3] Methodism is generally not known for its theological rigor and depth.[4] In fact, a case can be made that contemporary Methodist theology suffers from a widespread pneumatological deficit, a deficit that ultimately leaves much of what counts for theology among Methodists today sounding as though it is more about us or the world *per se* than about God or about us or the world in relation to God.

Within the Christian heritage, both specifically in Methodism and in other Christian sources more broadly, there are vital resources on the doctrine of the Holy Spirit that have the potential to inform contemporary Methodist theology by strengthening its theological, and especially pneumatological, content, and thus making good on the deficit. A serious challenge now facing theologians in the Methodist tradition is the task of naming and critically retrieving such resources. For that task, the work of John Wesley, Methodism's founder, is, not surprisingly, thought to be important. What may be surprising to some readers, however, is the inclusion of the other central figure within these pages: Thomas Aquinas. In due time, Aquinas will come to figure prominently, starting in chapter 3. For now, we begin with a survey of contemporary Methodist theology to show the necessity of grounding sanctification in a more robust theology of the Holy Spirit as love. The primary argument advanced throughout this book rests on the assertion that apart from a massive retrieval effort supported by external assistance, the tradition of John Wesley is imperiled.

3. Perhaps the most notable exception is the eighteenth-century theologian John Fletcher. For a fresh assessment of Fletcher's life, work, and legacy, see Geordan Hammond and Peter S. Forsaith, eds., *Religion, Gender, and Industry: Exploring Church and Methodism in a Local Setting* (Eugene, Ore.: Wipf and Stock, 2011).

4. As a Methodist theologian, I make this assessment in an attempt to be honest and appropriately self-critical about the particular Christian tradition of which I am a part. My argument that Methodist theology needs to become more theological is based on a positive evaluation of the quality of resources for reclaiming a richer pneumatology that lie within Methodism as well as those from the wider Christian tradition.

THE SPIRIT OF METHODIST THEOLOGY: PNEUMATOLOGICAL DEFICIT AND REDUCTION TO POLITICAL PROJECTS

Many benefits have come from the emergence and development of the discipline of Wesley and Methodist Studies over the last sixty years.[5] Yet there still remains at least one significant oversight: for today's Methodists, theological reflection generally lacks a strong, sustained consideration of the person and work of the Holy Spirit. That is not to say, of course, that there are no references to the Spirit in contemporary theological inquiry within this tradition. Rather, the Spirit's work of sanctification is not stressed nearly as much as it could be, having been largely supplanted by attention to the human condition and its contextual complexities as the decisive so-called theological issue. In other words, contemporary Methodist theology runs the risk of so elevating the human spirit and the spirit of the times that a proper emphasis on the Holy Spirit is overlooked or recedes rather feebly to the background, instead of occupying its rightful position of prominence. Consequently, the spirit of Methodist theology—as in, its essence or heart—tends to end up reflecting the human spirit and its multifaceted quest for liberation more than it reflects the Spirit of God, who as the source of all life actually gives the human spirit its true freedom. This pneumatological deficit results from a preference for language about grace, sometimes in fairly generic terms, rather than about the Holy Spirit *per se*, and it often takes the form of a reduction of the Spirit's work to political projects.

5. As noted by William J. Abraham and James E. Kirby, "Methodist Studies emerged as a fresh academic venture in the 1950s with the decision to provide a proper edition of the works of John Wesley" (*The Oxford Handbook of Methodist Studies*, ed. William J. Abraham and James E. Kirby [Oxford: Oxford University Press, 2009], vi).

Grace over the Spirit and a Grazing over the Spirit

Contemporary Methodist theology has made much of Wesley's threefold doctrine of grace—prevenient, justifying, and sanctifying—and the *via salutis* in which it is situated. Grace and the way of salvation are indeed central to Wesleyan theology. In the process of highlighting and developing these themes, though, Methodist theologians have on the whole not tended nearly as closely to the related doctrine of the Holy Spirit, which was also crucial to Wesley's theology. As noted by Richard Heitzenrater, a historian of early Methodism, the Holy Spirit plays a key role in Wesley's theology of salvation. His soteriology

> is trinitarian, synergistic, dynamic, and perhaps above all a thoroughgoing theology of grace—God's presence-power-influence is the active initiating and empowering element at every stage. While his view is certainly christocentric in typically Protestant fashion, Wesley's position is also very trinitarian, as salvation is from God, in Christ, through the Holy Spirit. If anything, Wesley's theology has a stronger pneumatological emphasis than many other mainline Protestant positions.[6]

If Wesley's theology stands out for its pneumatological character, contemporary Methodist theology should be characterized in a similar way in so far as it is in keeping with the Wesleyan heritage. Yet it has largely failed to transmit that distinctive emphasis, in part because of a preference for language about grace that does not always make explicit the trinitarian content nor reflect the pneumatological prominence pointed out by Heitzenrater.

The tendency in contemporary Methodist theology to focus on grace sometimes without more specific language about the person and work of the Holy Spirit is exemplified in a recent essay by Mar-

6. Richard P. Heitzenrater, "God with Us: Grace and the Spiritual Senses in John Wesley's Theology," in *Grace Upon Grace: Essays in Honor of Thomas A. Langford*, ed. Robert K. Johnston, L. Gregory Jones, and Jonathan R. Wilson (Nashville: Abingdon Press, 1999), 87–109, in particular 97.

jorie Suchocki entitled "Wesleyan Grace."[7] In this article, Suchocki rightly states that Wesley's understanding of grace refers primarily to God's work of redemption, encompassing the three categories of prevenient, justifying, and sanctifying grace. She also indicates that her main concern is not to tease out the nuances of what she calls "redemptive grace" in Wesley, but to consider grace "as synonymous with all God's work, including creative as well as redemptive acts."[8] After a summary of Wesley's view with attention to certain suppositions by Wesley, she argues for "the necessity in the twenty-first century of broadening a Wesleyan understanding of grace to include the whole of God's activity, so that God's redemptive grace is seen to be but one form of God's all-encompassing creative grace."[9] While we should note Suchocki's intentions to recontextualize a Wesleyan understanding of grace, the fact remains that throughout this article she makes only a single reference to the Holy Spirit—a passing reference to the "witness of the Spirit"—and no references at all to the Trinity.[10] A number of times she refers to sanctifying grace, sanctification, and God's love, but the scarcity of language specifically about the third person of the Trinity, who in Wesley's view is the agent of holiness, suggests a preference for speaking of grace in more general terms, without necessarily denoting the Holy Spirit.[11] Lacking a specific and sustained stress on the Spirit's work in sanctification, and on the Spirit of sanctification—sanctification's pneumatological, and indeed trinitarian, basis and end—Suchocki's work is representative of much of contemporary Methodist theology, in

7. Marjorie Suchocki, "Wesleyan Grace," in Abraham and Kirby, eds., *The Oxford Handbook of Methodist Studies*, 540–53.

8. Ibid., 540.

9. Ibid.

10. Ibid., 544.

11. As discussed in the next section, Wesley makes clear the connection between holiness and the Holy Spirit in, for example, his *Letter to a Roman Catholic*: "I believe the infinite and eternal Spirit of God, equal with the Father and the Son, to be not only perfectly holy in himself but the immediate cause of all holiness in us," in *The Works of John Wesley*, ed. Thomas Jackson, 14 vols. (London: Wesleyan Conference Office, 1872; reprint, Grand Rapids: Zondervan, 1958–1959), 10:82; henceforth referred to as Wesley, *Works*, ed. Jackson.

which sanctification is not always clearly connected to the person and work of the Holy Spirit or to the doctrine of the Trinity.

The understanding of a priority of grace in Wesley's thought is also reflected in what is widely considered the standard text on Wesleyan theology, *Responsible Grace: John Wesley's Practical Theology* by Randy Maddox. More promisingly, Maddox ascribes a certain primacy to grace in Wesley's thought while relating in some detail the doctrine of the Holy Spirit to the doctrine of grace. Maddox calls Wesley's central orienting concern "responsible grace." This phrase underscores God's gracious initiative and the absolute necessity of grace for salvation in Wesley's thought. At the same time, salvation requires human participation as well, which this grace "inspires and enables" but does not coerce.[12] Because salvation for Wesley involves a divine-human relationship, Maddox understands grace as the presence of God through the Holy Spirit. In this way, Maddox situates the doctrine of the Holy Spirit under the larger heading of grace.[13]

Grace is surely essential to Wesley's theology, so the fact that the doctrine of grace has received ample attention among Methodist theologians is in one sense fitting. In another sense, however, with all the attention given to grace, even when the Spirit is at least implied in the language used about grace, we risk allowing the doctrine of the Holy Spirit to be to a considerable extent subsumed by the doctrine of grace, overshadowing the Spirit's primary appropriated activity of imparting the holiness without which no one will see the Lord (Heb 12:14). When our language about grace is not clearly connected to the Holy Spirit, the pneumatological accent that is so

12. Randy Maddox, *Responsible Grace: John Wesley's Practical Theology* (Nashville: Kingswood Books, 1994), 86.

13. Consider, for example, Maddox's chapter title on the Holy Spirit: "Holy Spirit—The Presence of Responsible Grace" (*Responsible Grace*, 119–40). While he goes on to describe the Holy Spirit more specifically as God's "renewed empowering Presence" (119), the chapter title is telling in the way it relates the Holy Spirit to the more determinative category of grace.

strong in Wesley's own theology becomes lessened if not muted altogether. The preference for language about grace over the Holy Spirit opens the way for a grazing over the Spirit in contemporary Methodist theology—for simply touching the doctrine of the Spirit lightly in passing, when the promise of deeper and more substantive theology of the third article, drawing in part from the resources of historic Methodism, remains largely unfulfilled.[14]

The Move to Political Projects: Toward a Secularization of the Doctrine of Sanctification

Nowhere is the pneumatological deficiency in contemporary Methodist theology more evident than in the common reduction of the Spirit's work to political projects. As a result, issues that certainly have theological implications, issues like poverty, power, and ethnicity, come to the forefront of consideration, but they are often approached in such a way that for all the justifiable concern about promotion of life, social context is magnified at the expense of theological content. Whatever the gains a focus on such projects may bring, this approach poses a theological challenge for Methodists because it constitutes a move away from a theological doctrine of sanctification and toward a secularization of the doctrine of sanctification.

14. Some might respond by asserting that what matters is not having correct insider vocabulary, but simply understanding that it is God's presence and power (and in that sense, the presence and work of the Holy Spirit) that enables Christians to love God and neighbor. Still, it is critical to name that reality with appropriate clarity. Even if we are describing the same reality, by moving too quickly to the more general language of grace we are one step removed from the more theologically precise language about the Holy Spirit. Greater specificity will contribute to a proper pneumatological focus and dynamism in our understanding of grace. Such precision is also important because it can help prevent Methodist theology from wandering off into indistinct generalities that lack the specific pneumatological connotation presupposed by Wesley (even if not explicitly developed by him). This basic point represents another way that Methodists can learn from someone like Aquinas, as I argue later.

While Wesley was keenly attentive to the social impact of faith, what he deemed of paramount importance was salvation, which he described in terms of the renewal of our souls after the image of God.[15] Contemporary Methodist theology, meanwhile, is marked increasingly by a broadening of the scope of inquiry to the salvation of society.[16] To be sure, a holistic understanding of salvation demands attention to wider social issues and context as well as appropriate action in response. The challenge facing today's Methodist theologians is that when it comes to this broader context, our doctrine of God is so thin that we have little to fall back on.

The difficulty of addressing questions of broader social and political renewal while retaining a sufficiently theological emphasis on sanctification is illustrated by Theodore Runyon's study, *The New Creation: John Wesley's Theology Today*. Here Runyon seeks to reclaim the notion of "new creation" as a foundational theme in Wesley's theology. He highlights the restoration of the divine image as crucial for Wesley, but he also claims for Wesley's theological vision of a new creation a wider context of cosmic renewal: "The cosmic drama of the renewing of creation begins ... with the renewal of the *imago Dei* in humankind. This is the indispensable key to Wesley's whole soteriology."[17] This wider context broadens the concept of sanctification in order for Runyon to engage the issues of human

15. Refusing to reduce salvation to an individualistic state of God's forgiveness of one's personal guilt as a sinner, Wesley understood salvation to include a spiritual transformation that has far-reaching social implications here and now through the renewal of our souls in God's image. "By salvation I mean, not barely (according to the vulgar notion) deliverance from hell, or going to heaven, but a present deliverance from sin, a restoration of the soul to its primitive health ... the renewal of our souls after the image of God in righteousness and true holiness, in justice, mercy, and truth" (*A Farther Appeal to Men of Reason and Religion*, Pt. I, I.3, in Wesley, *Works*, ed. Outler, et al., 11:106).

16. Andrew Thompson traces this change in perspective in his article "From Societies to Society: The Shift from Holiness to Justice in the Wesleyan Tradition" (*Methodist Review* 3 [2011]: 141–72).

17. *The New Creation: John Wesley's Theology Today* (Nashville: Abingdon Press, 1998), 12.

rights, poverty, the rights of women, care of the environment, ecumenism, and religious pluralism from a Wesleyan standpoint.[18] While Runyon applies certain aspects of Wesley's thought to questions of social, political, ecological, and ecumenical renewal, the doctrine of sanctification is only faintly present when he addresses these contemporary concerns, and in some cases it is noticeably absent. That this is so likely stems from the fact that this broader aspect does not figure prominently in Wesley's own writings. In fact, sanctification remains an underdeveloped theme throughout Runyon's book, misleadingly suggesting that holiness of heart and life is not directly pertinent to the new creation that God promises to bring about.

Where Runyon successfully uses the theme of new creation to elucidate instructive insights into Wesley's context and thought, he sets a compelling agenda for reclaiming and renewing the theological heritage of early Methodism and its founder. As will be discussed later, one valuable insight is Runyon's proposal to rethink Christian perfection as participating in and reflecting in our lives the perfect love that we receive from God. This suggestion points to the need to deepen Methodist theological reflection on the doctrine of God, and to the promise of such a pursuit. In the absence of a more robust doctrine of God and doctrine of the Holy Spirit, Methodist theologians will continue to struggle with the tendency to move toward a secularization of the doctrine of sanctification when doing the important work of addressing wider social and political issues.

One influential strand of Methodist theology that is especially keen on taking up such issues relates the thought of John Wesley to liberation traditions. This interest derives in part from Wesley's concern for the poor as well as his wider commitment to reforming society. Since the early 1980s, it has been the subject of significant attention at the Oxford Institute of Methodist Theological Studies, an event that meets every five years and brings together theologians

18. Ibid., chapter 6, "Wesley for Today," 168–221.

and scholars from the worldwide Methodist and Wesleyan family. At the 1987 Institute, M. Douglas Meeks noted the changes that were beginning to take shape in "the Methodist household," changes that dealt with the question "What should Methodists teach?"[19] One such change called for a new starting point for theological reflection:

> Many third and fourth world, black, and feminist theologians in this Institute have risked being strident and recalcitrant because they are convinced that Methodist theology cannot start with tradition or personal internal experience but with the experience of those who have been structurally and systematically shut out of the household, denied access to what it takes to live and work, to have a name and story.[20]

From this vantage point, experiences of the downtrodden take priority, and theology serves as a tool for criticizing the political, economic, racial, and sexual oppressions of our time.

Nearly three decades later, the appeal made in the 1980s to rereading Wesley with a strong contextual thrust has by now garnered numerous enthusiasts within Methodism. It is a move that has both strengths and weaknesses. Positively, in the spirit of the prophetic tradition it confronts us with the pressing moral issues facing the world today. In the process, it succeeds in raising good questions. Meeks lists a number of them, including the following:

> Why are the poor in poverty? Why does an eight-year-old girl get shot dead by a stray bullet of the security forces in South Africa? Why must peasants in Brazil plant soybeans in their fields rather than black beans on which they have subsisted for decades and so make themselves increasingly dependent on Northern markets? . . . Why are Blacks, Hispanics, Native Americans, and Asian Americans in the rich household of the United States still systematically excluded from what it takes to live and work?[21]

19. The title of the volume consisting of the major essays presented at that year's Institute is *What Should Methodists Teach? Wesleyan Tradition and Modern Diversity* (M. Douglas Meeks, ed. [Nashville: Kingswood Books, 1990]). Cf. Meeks's observation: "Things are changing in the Methodist household" (ibid., 138).

20. Ibid., 136.

21. Ibid.

All those questions, and others like them, are but forms of this one overarching question: In the face of suffering, does Christianity, and therefore Christian theology, have anything constructive to say? These are forceful questions calling for a response from theologians and from the church as a whole. Without attention to such matters, the disciplines of theology and theological ethics look much like the narrow, insulated, special-interest projects against which some rightly warn.[22]

Meeks proposes the possibility of investigating such issues alongside traditional theological categories: "These are questions that some in the Institute are convinced that we have to work at precisely as we work at pneumatology, sanctification, and evangelization."[23] Yet the idea of taking up these questions "precisely as we work at" classical doctrines can rather quickly become usurped by a vision that calls for recasting those doctrines in quite different terms. Since Meeks's report on the state of Methodist theology at the Oxford Institute of 1987, the balance has shifted so much that we seem to have lost our theological moorings. Meeks's own language later in the same address suggests that the turn away from theology proper and toward a pneumatological reduction to political projects had already begun, with his conceptualization of the Spirit's work in what he calls "the cruciality of socio-economic analysis for our life in the Spirit," according to which we are converted from "our fear of death and the self-possessiveness of life because of our fear of death."[24] Meeks claims, further, that such a conversion rests in a certain sense on God's distinctive agency through the experience of the poor: "only

22. For example, Joerg Rieger writes, "We can no longer afford to do special-interest theology for those who have made it, and who are by and large exempt from the more atrocious forms of pain and suffering that affect the rest of the world" ("What Do Margins and Center Have to Do with Each Other? The Future of Methodist Traditions and Theology," in *Methodist and Radical: Rejuvenating a Tradition*, eds. Joerg Rieger and John J. Vincent [Nashville: Kingswood Books, 2003], 29).

23. *What Should Methodists Teach?* 136–37.

24. Ibid., 138.

life at table with the poor is likely to cause us to break our present patterns of talking about and to God and living in God's presence."[25] Rather than an encounter with the living Christ in the Eucharist by the Spirit undergirding, shaping, and sustaining theological reflection, evangelism, and social action, the decisive moment becomes table fellowship with the poor.

Meeks admits that "a socio-economic analysis cannot bring God's redemption (any more so than theology)."[26] Nevertheless, while he encourages a social concern for the neediest of neighbors, his substantial rethinking of the work of the Spirit in primarily socioeconomic terms reflects certain tensions that are evident in this summary remark: "So, it seems to me, the path that lies ahead of us is the Wesleyan mediation, through the grace of the living Host who yearns for a new household, of the experience of the poor, the Spirit's conversion of our lives, and the Tradition."[27] Despite the stated goal of striking a posture of "Wesleyan mediation," several questions still emerge. Understood in this way, conversion by the Spirit is conversion toward what end? Is this language sufficiently theological, bearing continuity with the apostolic faith?[28]

These questions point to the weaknesses and limitations of this mode of theology that has become so influential in Methodism, and in wider theological circles, today. It gets at part of the Gospel but by no means all of it, and not even clearly the heart of the message of salvation in and by the triune God. Standing alone, such an approach may well turn theology into some other pursuit, gov-

25. Ibid.

26. Ibid.

27. Ibid., 139.

28. This last question reflects a concern raised by Geoffrey Wainwright: "We need to ensure that it is the *same faith* which is being confessed in the *various modes* of worship, mission and service." Fittingly, he concludes by highlighting the importance of "that proclamation and embodiment of the *one gospel* in *diverse cultural circumstances* which have been the aim of Christianity, and of Methodism, since their beginnings" ("Methodism and the Apostolic Faith," in *What Should Methodists Teach?* 117). Unless otherwise noted, all italics in quotations are original.

erned not by the norms of divine revelation through the historically unique person of Jesus Christ—God's eternal Word come to us in flesh and blood, in full identification with humanity, for our salvation—but by economics, sociology, or anthropology. For all the insights that can be provided by these and other disciplines, they are no substitute for theology proper; if the goal is in fact the fullest possible extent of God's reign on earth, an inherently theological goal, it cannot be achieved on insufficiently theological grounds. If the goal is anything else, then we encounter the problem that whenever a theological movement tries to recast the faith in order primarily to serve some social good, it not only distorts established Christian teaching but also fails to deliver on its promised utopia.

Issues of socioeconomic status and quality of life certainly cannot be ignored if we are to be faithful to the God incarnate in Jesus Christ, but in the end this kind of project must be part of a larger, more comprehensive system, rooted in the scriptural witness and the wider Christian tradition, in order to have an appropriate theological depth and *telos*. Otherwise we run the risk of minimizing the theological content and neglecting vital theological resources as if justice, for example, were a matter primarily about just us, a matter left for us to sort out ourselves, when in fact there are solid grounds for a theology of justice that can serve to strengthen and inform rather than weaken and obscure our efforts to "do justice" (Mi 6:8) in the name of the God of justice who establishes equity and executes justice and righteousness (cf. Ps 99:4). In this way, the development of a more theological theology, concerning God and the world in relation to God (and thus attentive to the realities of poverty and oppression), has the potential to deepen and enrich our efforts to enact the justice in which God's kingdom consists. Under the influence of liberation traditions, Methodist theology does not have sufficient theological content to stand on its own. It must be understood instead in a broader theological context where the end is more than socioeconomic liberation but in fact union with God.

Yet what is the theological content of this form of Methodist theology as it has developed over time? Two common themes are, first, the continuation of God's work in the world, and second, the promotion of teachings, practices, and social structures that give life. Typical among liberation theologians is a shift away from the person of Christ toward a stress on the work or offices of Christ. Christ describes his mission by drawing upon the prophet Isaiah: "The Spirit of the Lord is upon me, because he has anointed me to bring good news to the poor. He has sent me to proclaim release to the captives and recovery of sight to the blind, to let the oppressed go free, to proclaim the year of the Lord's favor" (Lk 4:18–19; cf. Is 61:1–2, 58:6). This mission has a clear orientation toward those at the margins of society. As two theologians interested in the relation between Wesley and contemporary forms of liberation theology, United Methodist Joerg Rieger and British Methodist John Vincent assert that "Like in Wesley's days, we will only come to know who God is by joining in God's work in community with others, particularly with those on the margins whom we often overlook."[29] In this way, they describe their perspective on the prospects of "rejuvenating" Methodism in terms of continuing God's mission in the world.[30] It is a mission, in their understanding, that hinges on the particularities of social location and context, to which priority is given.

Therefore, this approach to Methodist theology also shows great concern for the promotion of teachings, practices, and social structures that give life, as a way of seeking to address the pressing moral issues of our time. From this perspective, theology itself has sometimes been seen as part of the problem rather than the solution, but that view may be changing. Over against the common criticism of orthodox Christology as either morally irrelevant or morally objectionable, many liberation theologians have begun to revise their views on this point. Rieger, for example, suggests in his more recent study

29. Rieger and Vincent, *Methodist and Radical: Rejuvenating a Tradition*, 208.
30. Cf. the book's full title, *Methodist and Radical: Rejuvenating a Tradition.*

Christ & Empire: From Paul to Postcolonial Times an openness to a renewed understanding of the moral relevance of the person and work of Christ. After an account of how ecumenical creeds were a tool for maintaining unity and hierarchy in the Roman Empire, Rieger proposes that Nicaea and Chalcedon could serve as a means for resisting and challenging the powers of empire in our time, directing us, as he says, "beyond empire and closer toward God."[31] Considering the coequality of Christ's humanity and our humanity, Rieger writes: "But there is some surplus here that, if explored, pushes against the status quo, provided that the humanity in question is similar to that of Christ as reported in the Gospels—a humanity under pressure, suffering, struggling against the powers of empire."[32] Furthermore, Rieger concludes that in contrast to emphasis on the work of Christ in terms of sacrifice and submission, the Christology of the ecumenical creeds can "push us in new directions that emphasize what is life giving rather than death dealing."[33] Toward that end, as noted below, there may be an opportunity for more extended reflection on the Holy Spirit, who is identified in the Nicene-Constantinopolitan Creed as "giver of life."

Attention to quality of life here and now in its various dimensions, including social and material and not simply spiritual, has become characteristic of many of today's Methodist theologians. Especially significant in this regard is the work of those who have played leading roles in the various forms of liberation theology.[34] The recent receptivity among many liberation theologians to creedal christological claims may represent the start of a new chapter for this influential version of contemporary Methodist theology, a

31. Joerg Rieger, *Christ and Empire: From Paul to Postcolonial Times* (Minneapolis: Fortress Press, 2007), 70.

32. Ibid., 98.

33. Ibid., 100.

34. For example, in addition to Rieger (theology and economics, class, and empire), James Cone (Black theology), José Míguez Bonino (Latin American liberation theology), Harold Recinos (*Barrio* theology), and Rebecca Chopp (feminist theology) are all Methodists who have made significant contributions to their respective fields.

chapter that could both contribute to a renewed interest in pneumatology and aid in the effort to keep our language sufficiently theological.

PROSPECTS FOR RETRIEVAL AND DEVELOPMENT

In Methodist theology, there has been so much concern for social and political impact or relevance over the last century that the actual theological content has often been minimized or so dramatically reshaped that any substantial theological continuity can be hard to find.[35] The doctrine of the Spirit has been largely supplanted by fairly generic appeals to grace and by a deep and in many respects commendable commitment to the human condition and its complex contextual circumstances. As a result of this widespread pneumatological deficit, Methodist theology needs to become more theological and, in particular, more attentive to the person and work of the Holy Spirit. If present trends continue, the Methodist tradition is in danger of losing its distinctive message and collapsing into theological irrelevance.

What are the prospects for the retrieval and development of Methodist theology? That is a question that has given rise to this study in the first place. In certain respects, it is also a question to which a detailed answer will require the remainder of the work to provide.

35. For an attempt to make the most of what unity there is in this theological tradition, see Thomas A. Langford, *Practical Divinity*, vols. 1 and 2 (Nashville: Abingdon Press, 1998 and 1999).

Two

SANCTIFYING LOVE

The Holy Spirit and Sanctification in John Wesley

JOHN WESLEY would not fit neatly, or perhaps even at all, into the modern category of systematic theology. Wesley did not write sophisticated, sustained treatises on technical doctrinal problems. Rather, he conveyed his theological teachings through a variety of other means that were typically more occasional in nature, such as sermons, tracts, letters, journal entries, and hymns, the latter of which he often published in tandem with his younger brother Charles. Central to Wesley's "practical theology" is the doctrine of salvation, especially this soteriologist's deep-seated concern for holiness in love.[1]

While Wesley's thinking on the subject developed over time, one constant feature is that at its essential core his understanding of sanctification is an implicitly trinitarian one in which the Holy Spirit figures with particular prominence. The trinitarian foundation is not

1. Randy Maddox provides a comprehensive analysis of Wesley's theological works under the heading of "practical theology" in *Responsible Grace: John Wesley's Practical Theology*. The above designation of Wesley as a soteriologist represents a way of understanding his life's work that is complementary to the idea of practical theology but also slightly more focused in so far as it highlights the doctrine of salvation, which is a pervasive theme throughout Wesley's sermons and other writings.

systematically or exhaustively presented in Wesley's own work, but it remains clearly discernible in his vision of Christian existence. A rediscovery of this foundation can shed light on the theological essence of holiness according to Wesley, which is crucial for correcting perfectionist misreadings that have hindered the reception of this aspect of Wesley's thought virtually from its inception. In these ways, such a rediscovery holds promise for advancing the constructive interpretation of Wesley's doctrine of Christian perfection or, as Wesley often called it, perfect love. Viewing the doctrine through the lens of trinitarian theology clarifies its appropriately theological content and orientation while illuminating Wesley's emphasis on the immediate and ongoing work of the Holy Spirit sanctifying those in Christ so that the image of God is more fully restored in their lives.

A THEOLOGY OF CHRISTIAN PERFECTION

At the heart of historic Methodist teaching and self-understanding is the doctrine of Christian perfection or entire sanctification, the goal of Christian existence under grace. While the doctrine would find different interpretations throughout Methodist history, the essence of Christian perfection as expressed by Wesley is nothing else than loving God with all of one's heart, soul, and mind and loving one's neighbor as oneself in keeping with the two greatest commandments according to Christ (e.g., Mt 22:37–39). The doctrine pertains to the gift of God's grace filling the heart, taking up the whole capacity of the soul, and leading believers to perfect obedience to the commands of God. Wesley described Christian perfection as an instantaneous work of God in the soul that is both preceded and followed by a gradual work of grace.[2] Therefore this reality, while beginning at a particular moment in time, is not a static state or isolated momentary event but rather an experience of God's grace that Wesley

2. "Brief Thoughts on Christian Perfection," §2. Wesley includes this set of reflections at the end of *A Plain Account of Christian Perfection as Believed and Taught by the Reverend Mr. John Wesley, from the Year 1725, to the Year 1777* (Bristol, 1777; reprint edition, London: Epworth Press, 1952), 112.

situates in the broader context of the ongoing journey toward God. Wesley considered the propagation of this doctrine to be one of the chief purposes for which God had raised up Methodism. Indeed, he referred to entire sanctification as the grand *depositum* of Methodism to the world.[3] Although Wesley described the doctrine of Christian perfection as being foundational to the character of a Methodist, he understood it to be not uniquely Methodist in a strict or narrow sense but rather the mark of any genuine Christian.[4] In the midst of calls for contemporary Methodists and Wesleyans to reclaim and develop a more compelling theological account of Christian perfection, a possible way forward can be forged through emphasis on the theme of perfection as participation in God and a renewed appreciation for Wesley's trinitarian understanding of sanctification.

The Need for a More Compelling Theological Account of Christian Perfection

Numerous interpreters of Wesley's writings have recently pointed out the need for a more compelling theological account of Christian perfection. For example, Thomas Oord and Michael Lodahl claim that the "classical terms of holiness" such as Christian perfection and entire sanctification "no longer seize the imaginations of many people."[5] They argue that the traditional language of holiness must be updated in ways that can capture hearts and imaginations once more. Their own attempt, informed by a critical reading of Wesley, is to posit love as "the core of holiness" and to emphasize what they describe as the relational component of holiness.[6]

3. "This doctrine is the grand depositum which God has lodged with the people called Methodists; and for the sake of propagating this chiefly He appeared to have raised us up" (To Robert Carr Brackenbury, September 15, 1790, in John Wesley, *The Letters of the Rev. John Wesley, M. A.*, ed. John Telford, 8 vols. [London: Epworth Press, 1931], 8:238; henceforth referred to as Wesley, *Letters*).

4. *The Character of a Methodist*, §17, in Wesley, *Works*, ed. Outler, et al., 9:41.

5. Thomas Jay Oord and Michael Lodahl, *Relational Holiness: Responding to the Call of Love* (Kansas City, Mo.: Beacon Hill Press, 2005), 25.

6. Ibid., 70.

Joining Oord and Lodahl in identifying the pitfalls of a theologically insipid understanding of holiness and love and seeking to develop a more richly theological account is Kenneth Collins in *The Theology of John Wesley: Holy Love and the Shape of Grace.*[7] Collins, however, takes issue with the specific solution that Oord and Lodahl propose. Collins claims that in essentially equating holiness with love, they fail to discern the nuanced relationship between holiness and love in Wesley's thought. Love and holiness certainly share an intimate relationship according to Wesley, but they are not virtually identical as Oord and Lodahl seem to suggest. After all, Wesley considered the "essence of Christian holiness" to be simplicity and purity, not love.[8] Rather than a direct equation between the two, there is a "conjunction," and even some tension, in holiness and love as Wesley described them, with holiness entailing what Collins calls "a movement of separation for the sake of purity" and love, for its part, involving "a movement of revelation, engagement, and, at its highest levels, communion."[9] Cognizant of Wesley's own preferred vocabulary and usage, Collins carefully traces the nuances of his thought and proposes as "the best and most accurate summarizing word or phrase, and Wesley's ultimate hermeneutic," not "love" per se but "holy love."[10] Collins's reading of Wesley parses the key themes of holiness and love in a way that not only affirms the particular theological resonance of each concept but also constructively relates them to one another. The importance of such an association emerges from a consideration of the problem created by keeping them apart: "love apart from holiness is soft, naively wishful, and likely self-indulgent" while "[h]oliness apart from love is a

7. Kenneth J. Collins, *The Theology of John Wesley: Holy Love and the Shape of Grace* (Nashville: Abingdon Press, 2007).

8. "Always remember, the essence of Christian holiness is simplicity and purity; one design, one desire; entire devotion to God" (To a Member of the Society, April 4, 1771, in Wesley, *Letters*, 5:238).

9. Collins, *The Theology of John Wesley*, 8.

10. Ibid.

consuming fire."[11] By contrast, when holiness and love are held in creative tension, as in the phrase holy love, it represents the "artful balance" in Wesley's thought that "ably describes not only the divine nature but also the earnest Christian life."[12] This way of explaining how Wesley relates holiness and love is noteworthy for several reasons. First, it illumines the connection between Wesley's account of the Christian life and his understanding of the nature of God. Second, it underscores the significance of an appropriately theological foundation for the very concept of love. These are two topics that will receive greater attention later in this chapter. For now, it is sufficient to note the place of Collins among those interpreters of Wesley calling for greater attention to be given to a theology of holiness and perfect love in keeping with the insights of Wesley.

In addition to the constructive work of Oord and Lodahl and the closer reading of Wesley proffered by Collins, several other Wesley scholars have also pointed out of late the need for a more theologically substantial understanding of sanctification in general and perfection in particular in presenting and probing Wesley's thought. William Abraham makes the quite startling claim that "beyond vague platitudes and rhetorical flourishes [Wesley's] doctrine of Christian perfection is no longer operative" among contemporary Methodists and Wesleyans.[13] If this is indeed the case, the seriousness of the problem can hardly be overstated: "What is at issue is the unraveling of the very core of a tradition.... Something has gone seriously wrong at the very heart of Methodist doctrine; if the patient is not already dead, it will take strong medicine to effect a cure."[14] What is the "strong medicine" necessary to provide an antidote?

The solution proposed by Abraham arises from a critical analysis of Wesley's thought that is attentive to the complexities of the

11. Ibid.

12. Ibid.

13. William J. Abraham, "Christian Perfection," in Abraham and Kirby, eds., *The Oxford Handbook of Methodist Studies*, 587–601, in particular 587.

14. Ibid.

doctrine as well as the difficulties intrinsic to Wesley himself. The doctrine is a complex one in part because it consists of what Abraham describes as "an exercise in ascetic theology, a vision of realized eschatology, and a psychology of spiritual development."[15] Wesley's vision of Christian perfection is predicated on the idea that the goal of Christian existence—namely, to be made perfect in love—is actually attainable in this life by God's grace and involves the believer's coming to terms with the problem of guilt and separation from God; the atoning death of Christ; the nature of living faith, repentance, and the whole orientation of one's life to God; the assurance of forgiveness of sins; and holiness experienced in the new birth and continued growth in grace for daily life in Christ.[16] The complexity of the life of sanctification according to Wesley is further reflected in the far-reaching set of resources that he made available to those on the journey to holiness. Such resources included not only numerous sermons, tracts, and other writings in which Wesley explicated pertinent conceptual and theological issues from different angles but also his brother's hymns for the learning and singing of the faith, accounts of Christian experiences of sanctification that Wesley published in the *Arminian Magazine*, and recorded minutes of discussions over doctrinal nuances while in conference with Methodist preachers. Wesley also developed and oversaw an extensive system of societies, classes, and bands for spiritual direction and the promotion of communally accountable Christian discipleship as part of the quest for perfection in love.[17]

Nevertheless, whatever the merits of this complex view of perfection, there are inherent difficulties in Wesley's own account that complicate an attempt to appropriate it. Among the challenges is

15. Ibid.

16. Ibid., 590.

17. Cf. Abraham: "Once we locate entire sanctification in the full panoply of biblical exegesis, theological articulation, experiential testimony, and inventive spiritual and ecclesial practices, we can begin to see the massive experiment in the spiritual life that was at the core of Methodism" (ibid., 591).

overcoming the tendency toward anthropocentrism to which Wesley, with his insistence on holiness as the heart of Christianity, opens the door. While the sanctification of human beings in Christ is indeed intrinsic to the message of the Gospel, any claim about the centrality of sanctification in Christian teaching and practice must be made carefully lest a theocentric vision be supplanted by an anthropocentric one. Yet that is precisely what happens in Wesley's own sermons, according to Abraham, with the generations following Wesley taking an even further anthropocentric turn.[18] The deeper issue here is the problem of reducing the faith to a doctrine of the Christian life. Whether Wesley ultimately succumbs to this problem or not, he clearly heads in that direction at the very least, as in his description of the *analogia fidei*, which traditionally centers on the doctrine of God, in terms of his own more narrowly focused understanding of the way of salvation.[19] In short, Wesley's characteristic concentration on soteriology requires a deeper and broader theological vision than the one that Wesley explicitly articulated himself. Nowhere is this general principle more apposite than in regard to the interpretation of his doctrine of Christian perfection.

When it comes specifically to this doctrine, Abraham argues that the most promising way forward is through the work of grafting the doctrine more deeply into the faith of the church. As he explains, "indeed the history of Methodism shows that the doctrine of

18. Ibid., 593–94.

19. Wesley provides the most detailed explanation of what he means by the "analogy of faith" in his notes on Rom 12:6 in reference to the phrase "Let us prophesy according to the analogy of faith": "St. Peter express it, 'as the oracles of God' [1 Pt 4:1]; according to the general tenor of them; according to that grand scheme of doctrine which is delivered therein, touching original sin, justification by faith, and present, inward salvation. There is a wonderful analogy between all these; and a close and intimate connexion between the chief heads of that faith 'which was once delivered to the saints' [Jude 3]. Every article, therefore, concerning which there is any question should be determined by this rule; every doubtful scripture interpreted according to the grand truths which run through the whole" (*Explanatory Notes Upon the New Testament* [London: William Bowyer, 1755; reprint Epworth Press, 1954], Rom 12:6).

perfection cannot survive if its anthropocentric tendencies are not healed by radical immersion in the great sweep of Christian thinking embodied in creation, freedom, fall, and redemption."[20] The task at hand, then, is to enrich Wesley's discoveries and insights through a more robust theological account of perfection that draws from the riches of the Christian tradition and the faith of the church across time and space.[21]

Another scholar calling for a more theological understanding of sanctification in the retrieval and updating of Wesley is Theodore Runyon. In *The New Creation: John Wesley's Theology Today*, Runyon documents the problems of perfectionism, understood as a state of completed perfection, and spiritual elitism that have hindered the full reception of Wesley's doctrine virtually from the outset.[22] In response to these difficulties, Runyon suggests a reinterpretation of the doctrine of Christian perfection with additional emphasis on the perfection of God's love. According to Runyon, God's perfect love is "the most viable starting point" for such a project for two reasons: first, to begin with the perfection of God's love obviates the "preoccupation with self and perfect sinlessness" that has limited some prior interpretations and more closely reflects Wesley's careful avoidance of the phrase "sinless perfection"; second, it "opens" believers to "participation in the only source of genuine sanctification," namely, the grace and love of the triune God.[23] For these

20. Abraham, "Christian Perfection," 599.

21. Ibid., 597–98.

22. Theodore Runyon, *The New Creation: John Wesley's Theology Today* (Nashville: Abingdon Press, 1998), esp. 91–101, 222–33.

23. Ibid., 231–32. Wesley forcefully rejects claims to "sinless perfection" in *On Sin in Believers,* where he allows that believers are delivered from the guilt and power of sin but not the being of it (Sermon 13 [1763], IV.4, in Wesley, *Works*, ed. Outler, et al., 1:328). He offers more detail in *A Plain Account of Christian Perfection*, in which he quotes an earlier tract entitled "Thoughts on Perfection": "To explain myself a little farther on this head—(1) Not only sin, properly so called (that is, a voluntary transgression of a known law), but sin, improperly so called (that is, an involuntary transgression of a divine law, known or unknown), needs the atoning

reasons, Runyon concludes that to advance the interpretation of Wesley on perfection, Wesley's teaching can profitably be set against the theological backdrop of God's perfect love. Though this love is inexhaustible, God has made it truly accessible to human beings in the opening up of his divine life in Jesus Christ and the invitation for all people to participate in it through the sanctifying grace of the Holy Spirit.[24]

While some differences among the solutions recently proposed by these scholars are readily apparent, one common theme in the

---

blood [of Christ]. (2) I believe there is no such perfection in this life as excludes these involuntary transgressions, which I apprehend to be naturally consequent on the ignorance and mistakes inseparable from mortality. (3) Therefore, *sinless perfection* is a phrase I never use, lest I should seem to contradict myself. (4) I believe, a person filled with the love of God is still liable to these involuntary transgressions. (5) Such transgressions you may call sins, if you please: I do not, for the reasons above mentioned" ("Thoughts On Perfection" [1759], Q.-A. 6, included in *A Plain Account of Christian Perfection*, 45). Similarly, in a 1763 letter, Wesley writes: "What, then, does their arguing prove who object against *perfection*? 'Absolute and infallible *perfection*?' I never contended for it. *Sinless perfection*? Neither do I contend *for this*, seeing the term is not scriptural. A perfection that perfectly fulfils the whole law, and so needs not the merits of Christ? I acknowledge none such—I do now, and always did, protest against it. 'But is there not *sin* in those that are *perfect*?' I believe not; but, be that as it may, they feel none, no temper but pure love, while they rejoice, pray, and give thanks continually. And whether sin is *suspended* or *extinguished*, I will not dispute; it is enough that they feel nothing but love. This you allow 'we should daily press after'; and this is all I contend for. O may the Lord give you to taste of it to-day!" (To Mrs. Maitland, May 12, 1763, in Wesley, *Letters*, 4:213). Despite Wesley's care in avoiding the phrase himself, many of his followers understood his doctrine as implying "sinless perfection"; cf. John L. Peters, *Christian Perfection and American Methodism* (New York: Abingdon Press, 1956). Still, in the face of criticism that any notion of perfection, no matter how qualified, is misleading if not fundamentally erroneous, Wesley justified his use of the word "perfection" itself in, among other places, the aforementioned letter: "As to *the word*, it is scriptural; therefore neither you nor I can in conscience object against it, unless we would send the Holy Ghost to school and teach Him to speak who made the tongue" (To Mrs. Maitland, May 12, 1763, in Wesley, *Letters*, 4:212).

24. Throughout this book, masculine pronouns are used for God in the absence of a satisfactory alternative tradition. Rather than suggesting that God is male as opposed to female, such formulations simply reflect the inevitable limitations of human language for God.

secondary works cited above is the assumption that a more satisfying theological account of Wesley's doctrine of Christian perfection is needed. Picking up on several suggestions in the works of these and other scholars, we will seek in what follows to extend the conversation and contribute to a deep retrieval and constructive interpretation of Wesley's doctrine of Christian perfection. More specifically, following Collins, Abraham, and most directly Runyon in his concluding suggestions, a juxtaposition of the doctrine of God and holiness in Wesley's thought can shed new light on the themes of participation in God, the sanctification of those in Christ by God's love through the Spirit, and even the sanctification of the notion of love itself.

Perfection as Participation in God: The Love that Sanctifies and the Sanctification of Love

Considering perfection in terms of participation in God's perfect love, as Runyon particularly emphasizes based on his reading of Wesley, underscores the crucial theological point that the love that sanctifies is God's love. God's love is sanctifying in so far as it is this love, and this love only, that makes people holy. Through their participation in God's life by grace, Christians are renewed in the image of God and become holy as God is holy (cf. Mt 5:48). Wesley consistently propagated such an understanding of what might be called participatory sanctification, as explained more fully below. For now, it is enough simply to note that sanctifying love denotes, first of all, the love that sanctifies the faithful toward the goal of perfection or entire sanctification.

A second meaning of the phrase has to do with the sanctification of the very concept of love. In this sense, the idea of sanctifying love pertains to the identification and safeguarding of an appropriately theological understanding of love that is rooted in and shaped by the Trinity's economy of salvation. Simply put, if it is to be in keeping with Wesley (and, for that matter, with the historic Christian faith), then the way in which people understand love must itself be sanctified in order to ensure its properly theological focus and orientation. Otherwise the conception of love in question would become detached from true holiness and, as such, vulnerable to the kind of sentimentality, self-determination, and likely the self-indulgence against which Collins rightly cautions.[25] To speak of sanctifying love, however, is to illumine love in a distinct way, setting it apart from other uses, and to clarify that what is under consideration here is not a sentimentalized or self-determined notion of love but precisely the transforming love of God revealed in Jesus Christ and applied to human hearts through the Holy Spirit. This indeed is the love that so captivated the thought of Wesley and animated his vision of the Christian life.

Participation in God is a useful motif for interpreting Wesley on perfection, not simply because Wesley employs it in his own writings but also because it points to God as the boundless source of all perfection and sanctifies the very concept of love. Thus, this twofold meaning of the phrase "sanctifying love" resolves a major problem associated with the interpretation of Wesley's doctrine of Christian perfection—namely, perfectionism—while also securing a conception of love that is sanctified in the being and activity of God.

Regarding the former, perfectionism denotes the idea that once perfection is attained there is no room for additional growth; in this view the goal has been reached, and the finish line crossed. Yet Wesley taught that while Christian perfection is the work of God wrought in the faithful soul at a particular moment in time, it is not a static, completed state (perfect*ed* perfection) but an ongoing journey (perfect*ing* perfection), and that with continued growth in grace through faith perfection can always be experienced in higher levels of love.[26] In his commentary on Philippians 3:12 and 15, for example, Wesley points out a crucial distinction between being per-

25. Collins, *The Theology of John Wesley*, 8–9.

26. Cf. Outler's introduction to *Christian Perfection*, in Wesley, *Works*, ed. Outler, et al., 2:98.

fect and being perfected: "There is a difference between one that is perfect and one that is *perfected*. The one is fitted for the race (verse 15); the other, ready to receive the prize."[27] Wesley takes St. Paul's references to perfection here to mean being strong and mature in faith, and fit for the race that is not yet completed—hence the directive to press on toward the goal for the prize awaiting us at the end of our journey to God (Phil 3:12, 14). So in contrast to perfectionism, Wesley promoted a view of perfection that was dynamic and always remained open to the possibility of greater growth in love through the continuous activity of the Holy Spirit leading disciples of Jesus Christ toward the goal of eternal happiness in God. Wesley could readily affirm such an understanding of participatory sanctification because he taught that along the way of salvation the opportunities for growth are as limitless as the God who is the source, author, and perfecter of salvation. The participation in God's love that is possible here and now can always be deepened—even for those who have been made perfect in love, as God will then further expand their capacity to love. For Wesley, rather than being a static state, perfection is a never-ending aspiration to share in all of love's perfecting fullness.[28] Against any mistaken notion of perfectionism, the first meaning of the phrase "sanctifying love" denotes the Spirit's ongoing work of sanctifying those who are in Christ, of perfecting them in love as they continue, by grace, toward full and final union with God in glory.

27. *Explanatory Notes*, Phil 3:12, 15.

28. Cf. Outler's introduction to *Christian Perfection*, in Wesley, *Works*, ed. Outler, et al., 2:98. Thomas A. Langford expounds the idea of "perfection becoming more perfect" by referring to friendship: "The best illustration I can think of is a friendship which is complete and fully good (if there is such a friendship) which by its quality creates new possibility for more completeness" ("John Wesley's Doctrine of Sanctification," *Bulletin of the United Church of Canada Committee on Archives and History* 29 [1980–1982]: 63–73, in particular 69). This illustration expresses the deeply relational and dynamic features of Wesley's understanding of perfect love. Aquinas speaks similarly of God's work in expanding our ability to love and also, of course, utilizes the language of friendship (e.g., *ST*, I, q. 12; II–II, q. 23 and I–II, q. 114).

Meanwhile, the secondary connotation of sanctifying love is important for the sake of clarification because it calls attention to the theological content and context of love as found in the doctrine of God. What gives Wesley's notion of love its specific meaning, setting it apart from other conceptions of love, is its grounding in the nature and activity of the triune God and especially in the missions of the Son and the Spirit by which the faithful come to share in the life of God. The participatory component in Wesley's doctrine of perfect love, a fuller account of which will follow, ensures that the kind of love in question is precisely the love of God, a love richly shown in Christ and imparted to human lives in all its sanctifying grace through the Spirit.

Consequently, in response to recent calls from Methodist and Wesleyan theologians to rethink sanctification in more compelling theological terms, the study of Wesley can be advanced through a reappraisal of Wesley on sanctification, the interpretive problems that his approach poses, and its potential enhancement via a deeper and clearer grounding in the doctrine of God and the doctrine of the Holy Spirit in particular. Toward that end, a fresh consideration of Wesley's trinitarian understanding of sanctification is in order.

WESLEY'S TRINITARIAN UNDERSTANDING OF SANCTIFICATION

The essence of Wesley's approach to sanctification found articulation long before his time, in Scripture and ancient Christian writings.[29] Wesley, however, showed a measure of originality in the way he combined various strands of thought, along with several emphases of his own, to account for what he considered the overarching goal of the Christian life, perfection in love of God and neighbor.

29. On the scriptural and patristic influences on Wesley's view of Christian perfection, and on his theology as a whole, see Ted A. Campbell, *John Wesley and Christian Antiquity: Religious Vision and Cultural Change* (Nashville: Kingswood Books, 1991).

Wesley's views on perfect love have received no shortage of attention over the years.[30] Here, however, the aim is not to conduct a wholesale examination of this doctrine. It is rather to analyze and interpret his teaching in light of the doctrine of God, in order to explore the bearing of Wesley's understanding of God on his conception of perfection in love. An account of these two subjects will point to a crucial connection between them, a connection that seems intrinsic to Wesley's thought even if he does not provide a systematic or comprehensive explanation of it. That connection might be described in this way: Wesley's doctrine of Christian perfection is rooted in the God of perfect love and directed toward human communion with this God, which is to say that the doctrine has an implicitly trinitarian basis and end.

In order to examine the relationship among the Trinity, love, and sanctification in the theology of John Wesley, it is necessary first to consider Wesley's approach to the doctrine of God. Concerning this approach, two issues emerge as particularly important. The first is Wesley's soteriological trinitarianism, and the second is how he accounts for the means by which human beings come to know the triune God.

"The Root of All Vital Religion": Wesley on God the Holy Trinity

In keeping with classical Christianity, Wesley embraced and propagated the doctrine of the Trinity according to which the one

30. The classic study remains Harald Lindström, *Wesley and Sanctification: A Study in the Doctrine of Salvation* (Stockholm: Nya Bokförlags Aktiebolaget, 1946). Other noteworthy accounts include Matthew R. Schlimm, "The Puzzle of Perfection: Growth in John Wesley's Doctrine of Perfection," *Wesleyan Theological Journal* 38/2 (Fall 2003): 124–42; Leonard D. Hulley, "An Interpretation of John Wesley's Doctrine of Perfect Love," *Theologia Evangelica* 23 (March 1990): 21–29; William M. Arnett, "The Role of the Holy Spirit in Entire Sanctification in the Writings of John Wesley," *Wesleyan Theological Journal* 14/2 (Fall 1979): 15–30; and D. Marselle Moore, "Development in Wesley's Thought on Sanctification and Perfection," *Wesleyan Theological Journal* 20/2 (Fall 1985): 29–53.

God is Father, Son, and Holy Spirit. While Wesley rarely engaged in prolonged debates over this doctrine (although he clearly distanced himself from the anti-trinitarianism of his day, as shown below), it was nevertheless essential to his understanding of the faith. As he writes in his sermon *On the Trinity*, the truth of the Trinity "enters into the very heart of Christianity; it lies at the root of all vital religion."[31] Later in the same sermon he further emphasizes the central place of this doctrine in Christian life:

> I know not how anyone can be a Christian believer till he "hath" (as St. John speaks) "the witness in himself" [1 Jn 5:10]; till "the Spirit of God witnesses with his spirit, that he is a child of God" [cf. Rom 8:16]—that is, in effect, till God the Holy Ghost witnesses that God the Father has accepted him through the merits of God the Son—and having this witness he honours the Son and the blessed Spirit "even as he honours the Father" [cf. Jn 5:23]. Not that every Christian believer *adverts* to this; perhaps at first not one in twenty; but if you ask any of them a few questions you will easily find it is implied in what he believes.[32]

Here, Wesley focuses on the meaning of the doctrine of the Trinity for Christian existence and, characteristically, approaches the doctrine with an eye toward soteriology. More than simply an intellectual affirmation about God, this doctrine shapes Wesley's outlook on the Christian life. It is a matter of not just the head but also the heart, and indeed of personal communion both with God, which Christians experience by grace, and within God in the eternity of God's own being. While Wesley rarely speculated about God's inner life, some of his comments about the person of the Holy Spirit and the person of Christ, as we will see, explicitly affirm common Christian teaching about the unity and full equality of the three divine persons. Of more immediate concern to Wesley in this sermon is

31. Sermon 55, *On the Trinity* (1775), §17, in Wesley, *Works*, ed. Outler, et al., 2:384. Titles of sermons that were first published separately, before their inclusion in a collection, are italicized.

32. Ibid., §§17–18, in Wesley, *Works*, ed. Outler, et al., 2:385.

the fact that all Christians—regardless of whether they can articulate a formal account of the Trinity—are trinitarians in so far as the very God whom they know and love is triune. As Wesley observes, God reveals his tri-unity in his gracious actions toward the world, which means that God's actions in salvation history have a trinitarian shape. The Holy Spirit witnesses to and with each Christian's spirit that God the Father has accepted this human person through the merits of God the Son. Although not every Christian may use this very language, the reality of thus sharing in God's life is intrinsic to Christian faith according to Wesley.

In his *Letter to a Roman Catholic*, Wesley describes more fully his understanding of the person of the Holy Spirit and the Spirit's work in believers. His words not only reveal his essential trinitarian orthodoxy but also highlight a critical connection between pneumatology and sanctification in his thought.

> I believe the infinite and eternal Spirit of God, equal with the Father and the Son, to be not only perfectly holy in himself, but the immediate cause of all holiness in us: enlightening our understandings, rectifying our wills and affections, renewing our natures, uniting our persons to Christ, assuring us of the adoption of sons, leading us in our actions, purifying and sanctifying our souls and bodies to a full and eternal enjoyment of God.[33]

All this work can be attributed especially to the Holy Spirit, whose presence in the lives of Christians yields ever greater holiness and happiness in God. What is more, Wesley's understanding of the work of the Spirit is intelligible only in light of trinitarian doctrine, which confirms the Spirit's essential unity and full equality with the Father and the Son.

In Wesley's account of the doctrine of the Trinity, the soteriological and doxological dimensions neatly coalesce. Salvation is the work of the triune God, Father, Son, and Spirit; and the appropriate human response to God's saving work is worship. Having been adopted by the Father as daughters and sons in the Son, Christians

33. Wesley, *Letter to a Roman Catholic*, in Wesley, *Works*, ed. Jackson, 10:82.

worship God triunely, as it were, by honoring both the Son and the Spirit even while honoring the Father.[34] In highlighting the intersection between soteriology and doxology, Wesley is especially attentive to the catechetical and doxological thrust of trinitarian doctrine.

Such concern for the practical implications of the faith has led some of Wesley's interpreters to describe him as a practical theologian. Randy Maddox, for example, characterizes Wesley's thought in this way in *Responsible Grace: John Wesley's Practical Theology*. Maddox suggests that the doctrine of the Trinity served implicitly as a "grammar" of Wesley's theological convictions.[35] That is, this doctrine was for Wesley a way of speaking that expressed fundamental truths about the nature of God in relation to Christian living and served as the norm for proper belief in God. In addition to warning his followers against "practical atheism," Wesley was also concerned that they avoid doctrinal and practical unitarianism.[36]

Doctrinally speaking, he differentiated between himself and his fellow Methodists (and common Christians), on the one hand, and Socinian and Arian alternatives to the church's trinitarian doctrine, on the other, on the grounds that Methodists "believe Christ to be the eternal, supreme God; and herein we are distinguished from the Socinians and Arians."[37] In his sermon "Catholic Spirit," he categorically rejected doctrinal "latitudinarianism" and maintained that "a man of a truly catholic spirit . . . is as fixed as the sun in his judgment concerning the main branches of Christian doctrine."[38] In that same sermon he stresses the christological center of the faith, with the rhetorical use of questions to determine whether his interlocutor's heart is right with his. So, for example, he asks:

34. *On the Trinity*, §17, in Wesley, *Works*, ed. Outler, et al., 2:385.

35. Maddox, *Responsible Grace*, 140.

36. On "practical atheism," see Wesley, "Upon Our Lord's Sermon on the Mount, III," I.11, in Wesley, *Works*, ed. Outler, et al., 1:517.

37. *The Character of a Methodist*, §1, in Wesley, *Works*, ed. Outler, et al., 9:34.

38. Sermon 39 (1750), III.1, in Wesley, *Works*, ed. Outler, et al., 2:93.

Dost thou believe in the Lord Jesus Christ, "God over all, blessed for ever" [Rom 9:5]? Is he "revealed in" thy soul [Gal 1:16]? Dost thou "know Jesus Christ and him crucified" [1 Cor 2:2]? Does he "dwell in thee, and thou in him" [cf. Jn 6:56; 1 Jn 4:13, 15]? Is he "formed in thy heart by faith" [cf. Gal 4:19, Eph 3:17]?[39]

Wesley also sets out this faith in a trinitarian pattern, indicating that his conception of a "catholic spirit," along with the "catholic love" that proceeds from it, rests upon the foundation of such doctrinal essentials. Even at his most catholic spirited, Wesley repudiated doctrinal unitarianismin favor of the classical christological and trinitarian teaching that he had inherited from the Anglican theological tradition and the faith of the wider church.[40]

Seeking to promote in human hearts and lives nothing less than the very life of God, Wesley also eschewed a practical or functional unitarianism that did not reflect a truly trinitarian balance. Maddox pursues this line of inquiry by explaining that Wesley typically distinguished the persons of the Trinity in terms of the "most defining work" of each person, for it is on this basis that we know the distinctions among the persons: creation and providence (Father), redemption (Son), and sanctification (Holy Spirit).[41] Without a sufficiently balanced view of God and of God's saving works, there might arise at this point three versions of practical unitarianism, each resulting in a diminished understanding of Christian participation in the life of the triune God: (1) a "unitarianism of the Father," emphasizing the created abilities given to human beings without adequately acknowledging the reality of human sin and humanity's subsequent need for grace; (2) a "unitarianism of the Son," elevating Christ's

39. Ibid., I.13, in Wesley, *Works*, ed. Outler, et al., 2:87.

40. Geoffrey Wainwright, "Why Wesley Was a Trinitarian," in *Methodists in Dialog* (Nashville: Kingswood Books, 1995), 261–74, in particular 261–62.

41. That we distinguish the persons of the Trinity in this way pertains to our knowledge of the distinctions among the persons, but not to what actually makes them distinct—since the works of the Trinity are contingent and the Trinity is not. Aquinas clarifies this point in his treatise on the Trinity (*ST*, I, qq. 27–43).

provision of forgiveness while neglecting the Father's continuing will for human obedience and the Spirit's empowerment for it; and (3) a "unitarianism of the Spirit," so captivated by spiritual gifts and ecstatic experiences of the Spirit that one could forget the Spirit's purpose in effecting the renewal of the moral image entrusted to all persons by the Father and fully revealed by the Son.[42]

Wesley, however, did not settle for such functionally unitarian reformulations of the faith, despite the faint trinitarian vestiges they might contain, but instead promoted a more integrated, biblically based, and traditionally informed view of the place of the doctrine of God in Christian faith and life. What is at stake here, according to Wesley, is nothing less than "the very heart of Christianity"—namely, the believers' personal communion with God, in which salvation consists.[43] Maddox thus describes the importance of a holistic, balanced approach to the doctrine of God for both John and Charles Wesley, as well as those who might learn from them:

> By contrast with all such unitarianisms, the Wesleys sought to form in their Methodist followers a truly trinitarian balance of (1) reverence for the God of Holy Love and for God/Father's original design for human life, (2) gratitude for the unmerited Divine Initiative in Christ that frees us from the guilt and enslavement of our sin, and (3) responsiveness to the Presence of the Holy Spirit that empowers our recovery of the Divine Image in our lives. *There can be no better expression of Wesley's theology of* responsible grace *than Christians who preserve such a trinitarian balance as they proceed along the Way of Salvation.*[44]

This trinitarian balance, with its considerable soteriological import, lies at the center of John Wesley's theology in particular. His view of grace, faith, and the whole of Christian life is rooted in his understanding of the God who is Father, Son, and Holy Spirit. To anticipate, the holiness that Wesley sought and taught about—holiness

42. Maddox, *Responsible Grace*, 140.

43. *On the Trinity*, §17, in Wesley, *Works*, ed. Outler, et al., 2:384.

44. Maddox, *Responsible Grace*, 140, emphasis added.

that is accessible through human participation, by grace, in God—is intelligible only in light of the God whose nature is holy love. Hence the "one thing needful," as Wesley sees it, is precisely the Spirit's renewal of the divine image in human hearts and lives, restoring persons to holiness in the God of all holiness and love.[45]

"A New Class of Senses Opened in Your Soul": Wesley on Human Knowledge of God

Closely related to Wesley's soteriological trinitarianism is his way of accounting for human knowledge of God. Given Wesley's approach to the doctrine of the Trinity, a second question now comes to the forefront of this inquiry: According to Wesley, how do human beings come to know God? Attending to this question will shed further light on the relationship between the Trinity and sanctification in Wesley's theology.

Wesley believed that all human knowledge of God was derived from experience. Following the empiricist denial of innate ideas, Wesley maintained that there was nothing in the intellect that had not first been in the senses.[46] While Wesley readily asserted that knowledge must come through the senses, he differed from the empiricists of his era on the specific issue of the knowledge of God. The prevailing opinion among Wesley's contemporaries was that human

45. Cf. Sermon 146, "The One Thing Needful" (1746), in Wesley, *Works*, ed. Outler, et al., 4:351–59.

46. Wesley often cited or alluded to the scholastic maxim derived from Aristotle (*De Anima*, III.7) and explicated by Aquinas in *ST*, I, q. 84, aa. 1, 7: *nihil est in intellectu quod non fuit prius in sensu* (e.g., Sermon 117, "On the Discoveries of Faith" [1788], §1, in Wesley, *Works*, ed. Outler, et al., 4:29; Sermon 119, "Walking by Sight and Walking by Faith" [1788], §7, in Wesley, *Works*, ed. Outler, et al., 4:51; Sermon 130, "On Living without God" [1790], §§3–4, in Wesley, *Works*, ed. Outler, et al., 4:170; Sermon 132, "On Faith, Heb. 11:1" [1791], §18, in Wesley, *Works*, ed. Outler, et al., 4:200). In terms of Wesley's own sources, Rex Matthews shows his epistemological indebtedness to the Oxford Aristotelian logical tradition, which Matthews argues was more influential on Wesley's thinking than were the ideas of Peter Browne, Cambridge Platonism, Malebranchean Platonism, and even John Locke ("'Religion and Reason Joined': A Study in the Theology of John Wesley," Th.D. diss., Harvard University, 1986, 259).

beings could only attain knowledge of God by inference from their experience of the world or by assent to the external testimony of Scripture, as expressed by Peter Browne in his *Limits of Human Understanding*.[47] Wesley allowed a role for this indirect knowledge of God but also sought knowledge of God, and specifically of the operations of the Holy Spirit, that was of a more immediate nature—or, technically, knowledge that was *supra* nature. To account for such knowledge, rather than claim that the work of the Spirit is perceptible through the five natural senses, Wesley posited instead the concept of special spiritual senses, which he believed gave human beings supernatural access to the things of God. Browne, meanwhile, rejected this notion of spiritual senses in *Limits of Human Understanding*, and for that reason Wesley's omission of these sections in his abridgement of Browne is not surprising.[48] In *An Earnest Appeal to Men of Reason and Religion*, Wesley describes the spiritual senses by way of analogy to the physical senses:

> It is necessary that you have *the hearing ear*, and the *seeing eye*, emphatically so called; that you have a new class of senses opened in your soul, not depending on organs of flesh and blood, to be "the evidence of things not seen" [Heb 11:1] as your bodily senses are of visible things; to be the avenues to the invisible world, to discern spiritual objects, and to furnish you with ideas of what the outward "eye hath not seen, neither the ear heard" [1 Cor 2:9, Is 64:4].[49]

According to Wesley, God establishes this "new class of senses" through the operations of the Holy Spirit on the soul. In this way God provides spiritual senses to sense spiritual realities, just as physical senses sense physical realities.[50]

47. London: William Innys, 1728. Wesley provides an abstract of this work in *Survey of the Wisdom of God in Creation*, in Wesley, *Works*, ed. Outler, et al., 5:149–96.

48. Browne, *Limits of Human Understanding*, 94–96, 111. Cf. Wesley, *Survey*, in Wesley, *Works*, ed. Outler, et al., 5:157–59.

49. *An Earnest Appeal to Men of Reason and Religion*, §32, in Wesley, *Works*, ed. Outler, et al., 11:56–57.

50. Mark Mealey shows that Wesley's understanding of spiritual senses does not

Wesley's notion of a spiritual sensorium would become a recurring point of emphasis in his thought, as reflected in a number of his sermons. He develops the idea in "The Great Privilege of those that are Born of God."[51] In this sermon, Wesley claims that being born of God implies not simply an outward change but "a vast inward change . . . wrought in the soul by the operation of the Holy Ghost, a change in the whole manner of our existence; for from the moment we are 'born of God' [1 Jn 3:9] we live in quite another manner than we did before; we are, as it were, in another world."[52] The spiritual senses awaken those who believe to the reality of this other world. In keeping with the biblical imagery, the result is a new birth, a spiritual birth analogous to the physical one. Prior to the physical birth, a child lacks sensual perception. At the moment of birth, however, the baby's senses become fully operative through direct contact with the physical world. The baby then goes on to acquire more and more knowledge of sensible things. So it is, Wesley says, with those who are born of God; prior to the change of spiritual birth they are not yet sensible of God, but through the Spirit's work their manner of existence is changed, the senses of the soul having been awakened, and they are capable of perceiving God, hearing God's voice, and knowing—through direct experience of God—God's peace, joy, and love shed abroad in their hearts.[53]

In his sermon "The New Birth," Wesley further explains his understanding of the spiritual senses and how they make possible Christian participation in God.[54] Spiritually reborn to new life in Christ, the believer "feels, is inwardly sensible of, the graces which

---

refer to a natural human capacity such as affection or imagination (the referents for this language commonly cited by Wesley's interpreters), but to a supernatural capacity made possible by the believer's experience of God ("Taste and See That the Lord Is Good: John Wesley in the Christian Tradition of Spiritual Sensation," Ph.D. diss., University of St. Michael's College, Toronto, 2006).

51. Sermon 19 (1748), in Wesley, *Works*, ed. Outler, et al., 1:431–43.

52. Ibid., I.1, in Wesley, *Works*, ed. Outler, et al., 1:432.

53. Ibid., I.1–10, in Wesley, *Works*, ed. Outler, et al., 1:432–35.

54. Sermon 45 (1760), in Wesley, *Works*, ed. Outler, et al., 2:186–201.

the Spirit of God works in his heart."[55] As a result, the person's spiritual senses are piqued so as to discern the presence and power of God. Through the use of these senses, it is possible for the newborn Christian, eyes now opened and heart full of life and love, to increase daily in the knowledge of God. Wesley equates this state of existence with true and abundant life, for now may this person

> properly be said *to live*: God having quickened him by his Spirit [cf. 1 Pt 3:18], he is alive to God through Jesus Christ [Rom 6:11]. He lives a life which the world knoweth not of, a "life" which "is hid with Christ in God" [Col 3:3]. God is continually breathing, as it were, upon his soul, and his soul is breathing unto God. Grace is descending into his heart, and prayer and praise ascending to heaven. And by this intercourse between God and man, this fellowship with the Father and the Son [1 Jn 1:3], as by a kind of spiritual respiration, the life of God in the soul is sustained: and the child of God grows up, till he comes to "the full measure of the stature of Christ" [Eph 4:13].[56]

Here again Wesley stresses the theme of communion with God, this time couched in terms of a spiritual respiration that sustains the life of God in the faithful soul all the way to the point of maturity in Christ. Through the grace of the Holy Spirit filling believers' hearts, they come into fellowship with the Father and the Son. Awakened to God by virtue of the Spirit's influence on and through the spiritual senses, those in Christ are thereby drawn ever more deeply into God's triune life of communion and love.

Wesley's chief interest in discussing the spiritual senses was to explicate the way in which they serve to facilitate the Christian's awareness of and personal fellowship with the Holy Trinity. In particular, Wesley employed his conception of spiritual senses in order to account for the human knowledge of God conveyed by the work of the Holy Spirit, teaching the truth about Christ the Savior and leading Christians to a deeper and more perfect union with God. Once made operative by the Spirit's enlivening power, the spiritual senses become

55. Ibid., II.4, in Wesley, *Works*, ed. Outler, et al., 2:193.

56. Ibid.

what Wesley called "the ground of all spiritual knowledge."[57] Yet for all that Wesley says kataphatically about the spiritual senses, elements of mystery and apophaticism still remain, specifically in regard to the Spirit's direct witness to believers. Wesley readily admits that the precise manner of how "the divine testimony is manifested to the heart" is a matter that he cannot sufficiently explain, nor can one who has this witness fully explain to another who does not.[58] As to the fact, however, Wesley shows no hesitation in affirming the Spirit's operation, which establishes as it were a new category of senses facilitating among the faithful their personal communion with God.[59]

Wesley's account of the spiritual senses affirms the basic principle that human knowledge of God is ultimately a matter of divine revelation. Knowledge of God is possible for human beings only through a disclosure of saving truths by God and about God, truths that are accessible through actual human experience of God under grace. For Wesley, God's definitive revelation is given in Christ to whom Scripture bears witness, and it is confirmed by God's direct address to Christian believers through their spiritual senses, which are awakened and sustained by the influences of the Holy Spirit. Given his religious empiricism, Wesley believed that all human knowledge of God was gained through experience. He could therefore maintain that it is through their experience of God that human beings come to know the God revealed in Jesus Christ, since human knowledge of God is fundamentally experiential.

57. *Explanatory Notes*, Phil 1:9.

58. Sermon 10, "The Witness of the Spirit, I" (1746), in Wesley, *Works*, ed. Outler, et al., 1:276. This latter point raises certain problems about the linguistic limitations of conveying theological truths apart from the knowledge gained by personal experience of those truths. Although this is not the place to solve such difficulties, one example that Wesley surely faced in his evangelical work was the problem of how human language can communicate the faith to those who do not have it, that is, to those who, not having had the right experience, are simply unable to understand the reality to which these words refer.

59. Cf. Collins, who presents Wesley's distinction between fact and manner regarding both the spiritual senses and the doctrine of the Trinity (*The Theology of John Wesley*, 143, 146–48).

Another way of describing such knowledge is to say that it is experimental, a term that recalls Wesley's designation of the 1780 *Collection of Hymns for the Use of the People Called Methodists* as "a little body of experimental and practical divinity."[60] In keeping with this language, a classic example of the experimental nature of human knowledge of God is found in hymns. Of course, hymns have long represented one of the primary means through which Christians have proclaimed and taught the truths of their faith. Theology comes to life, in a certain sense, through the singing of hymns in worship to God. As Wesley recalls in his letter of April 17, 1776 to Mary Bishop, the "application" of the doctrine of the Trinity to "our hearts" and "lives" is "abundantly supplied by my brother's *Hymns*."[61] He is here referring, primarily at least, to the *Hymns on the Trinity*, a noteworthy example of traditional trinitarian orthodoxy and piety at a time when both had come under attack through a resurgence of deism and unitarianism in eighteenth-century England.[62]

Published by Charles Wesley in 1767, this collection is structured in its first four parts ("The Divinity of Christ," "The Divinity of the Holy Ghost," "The Plurality and Trinity of Persons," and "The Trinity in Unity"), according to a tract written by Jones of Nayland, *The Catholic Doctrine of the Trinity, proved by above an hundred short and clear arguments, expressed in terms of Holy Scripture* (1756).[63] To these one hundred thirty-six hymns in sections one through four Charles then adds fifty-two more "Hymns and Prayers to the Trinity."[64] It is these final fifty-two hymns which J. Ernest Rattenbury

60. Preface to *A Collection of Hymns for the Use of the People Called Methodists* (1780), in Wesley, *Works*, ed. Outler, et al., 7:74.

61. Wesley, *Letters*, 6:213.

62. Facsimile of the first edition (Bristol: Felix Farley, 1767), Madison, N.J.: The Charles Wesley Society, 1998.

63. Wesley composed the *Hymns on the Trinity* as what Wilma J. Quantrille calls "a lyrical endorsement" of Jones's tract ("Introduction" to *Hymns on the Trinity* [Madison, N.J.: The Charles Wesley Society, 1998], vii–viii).

64. Wainwright, "Why Wesley Was a Trinitarian," 262.

calls "much the best hymns in the book."[65] In them, the experiential or experimental approach to the doctrine of the Trinity receives the greatest emphasis. Rattenbury further claims that this approach "is in its own way unique and of the highest value to the doctrine [of the Trinity]."[66] Here Charles gives poetic expression, with John's enthusiastic endorsement, to the vital experience of the Holy Trinity through the spiritual senses that is the privilege of every Christian:

> The Father, Son, and Spirit
> Himself to me makes known,
> And I in him inherit
> One God, for ever One:
> Jehovah's purest essence
> My raptur'd spirit seals;
> And all his blissful presence
> In all his people dwells.[67]

The self-revealing God makes his triune identity known and abides in all his people. They, in turn, are given a share in the life and love of God.

> Begotten again,
> And born from above,
> We join in the plan
> Of infinite love;
> Son, Father, and Spirit
> Our Saviour we see,
> And glory inherit
> Thro' faith in the Three.[68]

65. J. Ernest Rattenbury, *The Evangelical Doctrines of Charles Wesley's Hymns* (London: Epworth Press, 1941), 139.

66. Ibid.

67. *Hymns on the Trinity*, "Hymns and Prayers to the Trinity," 42:3. In citing these and other hymns, I list the hymn number and, in cases where only a portion of the hymn is quoted, a colon followed by the relevant stanza number(s).

68. Ibid., 21:3.

Christians receive new life in God and "see" the author of their salvation through the eyes of faith. Moreover, with their spiritual senses piqued by God in the economy of salvation, the lives of those in Christ come to reflect the character of God:

His Son on us bestow'd
The Father hath reveal'd:
  The Son his Father show'd
From mortal eye conceal'd;
Th' indwelling Comforter attests
That One is Three, in faithful breasts.

  Thrice holy God, in whom
We live, and move, and are,
  To do thy will we come,
Thy glory to declare,
By all our converse here to show
That God is manifest below.

Baptiz'd into thy name,
Mysterious One in Three,
  Our souls and bodies claim
A sacrifice to Thee:
We only live our faith to prove
The faith which works by humble love.

  O that our light may shine,
And all our lives express
  The character divine,
The real holiness!
Then, then receive us up t'adore
The Tri-une God for evermore.[69]

This hymn weaves together the themes of divine revelation and worship, with attention to both the extent and implications of participation in God made available to Christians in this life. In the economy of salvation, the Son shows the Father and the Spirit confirms that

69. Ibid., 8:3–6.

the one God is triune. Claimed by God in baptism, Christian believers are drawn into God's life. Through faith that works by love, their lives bear witness to the glory and presence of God in the world, even to the point of Christians expressing by their holiness the very character of the holy God.

John's observation that the doctrine of the Trinity is applied to faithful hearts and lives through such hymns confirms that, like Charles, he also believed human knowledge of God to be by nature experimental and in fact fundamentally participatory.[70] For both John and Charles, knowing God requires more than merely intellectual assent to correct notions about the nature of God. Human beings come to know God through the vibrant, heartfelt faith acquired in their experience of the God whose saving actions are recounted in Scripture and summarized in creedal form.[71] Knowledge of God is therefore gained through direct experience of the living God by means of the spiritual senses, to the end that the Christian life—as participation in God—expresses something of God's own holiness and love. For this reason, Christians should immerse themselves as a matter of profound spiritual discipline in the "exercise of the pres-

70. For more on Wesley's participatory trinitarianism, see Elmer M. Colyer, "Trinity," in Abraham and Kirby, eds., *The Oxford Handbook of Methodist Studies*, 505–21. This theme will be revisited in chapter 6 below.

71. On Wesley's theory and practice of the Scriptures, see Scott J. Jones, *John Wesley's Conception and Use of Scripture* (Nashville: Kingswood Books, 1995). As for creeds, Wesley exposits the Nicene Creed in his *Letter to a Roman Catholic*, and in his sermon *On the Trinity* he calls the explication of the doctrine of the Trinity in the Athanasian Creed "the best I ever saw"—although it should be noted that Wesley qualifies his approval of the creed's positive statement on the Trinity by admitting that "I am far from saying, he who does not assent to this [particular formulation of trinitarian faith] 'shall without doubt perish everlastingly'" (§3, Wesley, *Works*, ed. Outler, et al., 2:377). In addition, Wesley records in his journal entry for July 31, 1737 that "having long been in doubt concerning the principles of the Moravian Brethren," he asked them a number of queries, including one that suggests on Wesley's part the conviction of creedal and scriptural complementarity: "Do you believe those called Athanasian, the Nicene, and the Apostles' Creed to be agreeable to Scripture?" (Wesley, *Works*, ed. Outler, et al., 18:532). For more on the place of early Christian creeds in Wesley's thought, see Campbell, *John Wesley and Christian Antiquity*.

ence of God."[72] Elmer Colyer is correct to assert that "[t]he Trinity in early Methodism was not simply a doctrine affirmed, but *the* vibrant Divine Source, Agency, and Telos of all Christian faith, life, and practice, crucial to the vitality of the Methodist movement."[73] Two indications of the importance of the doctrine of the Trinity in historic Methodism are John's reflections on the Trinity and Charles's hymns on the Trinity, both of which highlight the gracious reality of personal communion with the God who is the subject of this doctrine.

So far this chapter has addressed the elder Wesley's understanding of God with attention to his soteriological trinitarianism and his conception of the spiritual senses. A survey of Wesley's writings has shown that his approach to the doctrine of the Trinity was soteriologically concentrated, marked by a particular emphasis on the work of the Holy Spirit, and that he understood knowledge of God to come through human experience, specifically through what he termed the spiritual senses. By now it should be clear that the idea of a spiritual sensorium was important for Wesley not simply as an end in itself but rather as a means to a larger end, namely, the Christian's actual participation in God by grace. The next step is to consider, in light of Wesley's views on the Trinity and experiential knowledge of God, the doctrine of Christian perfection or perfection in love. In short, Wesley's conception of perfect love is rooted in God and in human knowledge, which is to say experience, of God.

Wesley's Implicitly Trinitarian Doctrine of Christian Perfection

The doctrine of Christian perfection is, at its very core, about love. Yet the subject of this doctrine is not some vague or abstract

72. Sermon 79, "On Dissipation" (1784), §19, in Wesley, *Works*, ed. Outler, et al., 3:123. Wesley also uses this phrase in the "Large" *Minutes* (1763), §40.7, in Wesley, *Works*, ed. Outler, et al., 10:857.

73. Colyer, "Trinity," 505.

notion of love. Rather, Wesley's understanding of love has a particular theological focus and finds tangible expression in the life of faith. It deals specifically with the twofold love of which Christ himself speaks, love of God and neighbor (Mt 22:36–40, Mk 12:28–31, Lk 10:25–28). According to Wesley, Christian perfection is perfection in love, though not as in a static state of perfected spiritual completion—the primary misinterpretation that has hindered the reception of this doctrine, as pointed out earlier—but, instead, as denoting the perfect Christian obedience to the commands of God that is made possible by the gift of God's love continually filling the heart. As a result of the ongoing work of the Holy Spirit, the human capacity for love is enlarged; hence growth in grace toward a more perfect knowledge and love of God is an ever present possibility. Perfect love involves, in other words, an active, dynamic holiness of heart and life that is embodied in the grace-enabled, wholehearted fulfillment of the two greatest commandments, to love God with one's entire being and to love one's neighbor as oneself, and that can always be experienced in higher levels through the sanctifying grace of the Spirit.[74]

This love-based description is one of three ways in which Wesley summarizes the doctrine in *A Plain Account of Christian Perfection*, a synopsis of his views from 1725 until the time of its composition in 1765. The other two explanations that he provides express the same basic idea of full submission, in love, to God. In another view, Christian perfection is "purity of intention, dedicating all the life to God."[75] It is a matter of devoting "not a part, but all our soul, body, and substance" to God.[76] Wesley also describes the doctrine

74. In his sermon of the same title, Wesley says that Christian perfection is "only another term for holiness." As he goes on to clarify, there is always room for growth in grace toward a more perfect knowledge and love of God; hence the dynamic quality of Christian perfection in his understanding (*Christian Perfection*, I.9, in Wesley, *Works*, ed. Outler, et al., 2:104–05).

75. *A Plain Account of Christian Perfection*, 109.

76. Ibid.

in terms of renewal in the image of God. From this perspective, Christian perfection is a renewal of the heart in "the full likeness of Him that created it."[77] It entails having the mind that was in Christ (cf. Phil 2:5ff.) and thereby walking as Christ walked. While each of these summaries has its own nuances, Wesley maintains that there is no material difference among the three.[78] In fact, all three point to the proper backdrop against which perfection becomes intelligible, the doctrine of God.

Although Wesley's decidedly practical focus did not compel him to outline in systematic fashion the relationship between trinitarian theology and his conception of holiness, given the inalienably theological content of his account of perfection he seems to have assumed this backdrop.[79] Christian perfection or perfection in love has a trinitarian basis and end, each of which is intrinsic to Wesley's thought. Even if this trinitarian content is not exhaustively developed in his own writings, it can be unearthed and put to a constructive purpose.

That the doctrine of Christian perfection has an implicit trini-

77. Ibid.

78. Ibid.

79. That Wesley seems to have assumed a trinitarian grounding for his conception of holiness is an example of what John Deschner describes as Wesley's "presupposed theology." In his study of Wesley's Christology, Deschner observes that Wesley expressed his theology "on several levels." Deschner classifies these levels in a threefold manner: "the articulated theology of [Wesley's] writings, the presupposed theology behind the writings, and the enacted theology of his praxis." As Deschner goes on to explain, Wesley's "presupposed theology is for the most part the source-theology which underlies the Sermons: especially the ecumenical traditions of the Articles, but also to some degree the patristic, Anglican, puritan, pietist, and mystical influences which shaped his mind. It is important to recognize that this presupposed theology is not Wesley's unconscious theology, or some speculation on our part about what he might have thought, but a quite intentional level of Wesley's considered and settled theological understanding: the level of his Trinitarianism, of his christology, of his ecclesiology—themes which were absolutely fundamental in his theology, but which he did not emphasize when he preached at street corners" (*Wesley's Christology: An Interpretation*, second edition [Grand Rapids: Zondervan, 1988], xii).

tarian basis and end is indicated by two crucial themes in Wesley. The first is God's action in salvation history, which establishes the basis of the doctrine, and the second is the human communion with God made possible by this action, a communion that constitutes the doctrine's end, or more precisely our end as described in the doctrine. In order to explore the connection between Wesley's understanding of God and his conception of perfection in love, each of these themes will now be scrutinized in turn.

God's Saving Action: The Trinitarian Basis of Christian Perfection The doctrine of Christian perfection or perfection in love is firmly founded upon the economy of God's salvation, and thus grounded in God's saving actions in and for the world. Wesley provides one of the clearest and most comprehensive accounts of his vision of salvation in the sermon *The Scripture Way of Salvation.*[80] In specifically trinitarian fashion he explicates his understanding of salvation, which encompasses

> all the "drawings": of "the Father" [Jn 6:44], the desires after God, which, if we yield to them, increase more and more; all that "light" wherewith the Son of God "enlighteneth everyone that cometh into the world" [Jn 1:9], *showing* every man "to do justly, to love mercy, and to walk humbly with his God" [Mi 6:8]; all the *convictions* which his Spirit from time to time works in every child of man.[81]

For Wesley, salvation is the differentiated but united work of the three persons of the Godhead.[82] This work sets us into proper relationship to each of the three persons and, to anticipate the next main heading, effects our participation in their divine communion. Through the drawings of the Father, the illumination of the Son, and the convictions of the Holy Spirit, we come by grace to experience God's salvation. As Wesley goes on to explain, the salvation of which Paul speaks in the focal verse of the sermon (Eph 2:8) is a matter of

80. Sermon 43 (1765), in Wesley, *Works*, ed. Outler, et al., 2:152–69.
81. Ibid., I.2, in Wesley, *Works*, ed. Outler, et al., 2:156–57.
82. Wainwright, "Why Wesley Was a Trinitarian," 269.

both justification and sanctification. Justification, or pardon through the blood and righteousness of Christ, denotes (as Wesley elsewhere describes) "what God *does for us* through his Son," while sanctification, the inward renewal produced by the Holy Spirit, signifies "what [God] *works in us* through his Spirit."[83] Justification restores us "to the favour, [sanctification] to the image of God."[84] In a slight elaboration, Wesley explains in another sermon that such a renewal in the divine image involves holiness and deliverance from bondage to sin: "By justification we are saved from the guilt of sin, and restored to the favour of God: by sanctification we are saved from the power and root of sin, and restored to the image of God."[85] In regard to both justification and sanctification, the action of God is central and, indeed, pervasive. It is in such action on our behalf, as well as actually within our hearts and minds, that human salvation chiefly consists.

Having laid the foundation of his soteriology, Wesley builds upon this foundation at the end of the first section of the sermon. There he refers to entire sanctification or the "full salvation" for which Christ's followers wait.[86] Closely related to these terms is the Pauline directive to go on to perfection (cf. Phil 3:12), that is, to perfect love—the love that excludes sin, fills the heart, and takes up "the whole capacity of the soul."[87] Christian perfection for Wesley is the consummation of salvation, the culmination of God's saving work in and for us. As such it is the goal toward which all the faithful are called to strive.

In *The Scripture Way of Salvation*, Wesley identifies faith as the one condition for salvation. Wesley's conception of faith is linked

83. Sermon 5, "Justification by Faith" (1746), II.1, in Wesley, *Works*, ed. Outler, et al., 1:187. Cf. *The Scripture Way of Salvation*, I.3–4, in Wesley, *Works*, ed. Outler, et al., 2:157–58.

84. "The Great Privilege of Those That are Born of God," §2, in Wesley, *Works*, ed. Outler, et al., 1:432.

85. Sermon 85, "On Working Out Our Own Salvation" (1785), II.1, in Wesley, *Works*, ed. Outler, et al., 3:199–209, in particular 204.

86. *The Scripture Way of Salvation*, I.9, in Wesley, *Works*, ed. Outler, et al., 2:160.

87. Ibid.

to his notion of the spiritual senses through which human beings come to know God. Faith implies, Wesley says, "both a supernatural *evidence* of God and of the things of God, a kind of spiritual *light* exhibited to the soul, and a supernatural *sight* or perception thereof."[88] Through the operation of the Holy Spirit, opening and enlightening the eyes of the soul, Christians are able to see things that the natural eye cannot see. The illuminating work of God opens up a whole new world, "the *spiritual world*, which is all round about us, and yet no more discerned by our natural faculties than if it had no being."[89] In an even more particular sense, Wesley describes faith as a divine evidence and conviction of the saving grace of Christ, not only for the world as a whole but also for the individual believer.[90] Their spiritual senses having been stimulated, those in Christ come by faith to know God themselves, to see, touch, hear, and taste the salvation made possible by the gracious action of the triune God. That is, they are thus able, first of all, to discern that in Holy Scripture God has promised salvation to its fullest, to perfection in love; second, to trust that what God has promised he is able to perform; and third, to believe that perfection in love is possible, through God's grace, even now.[91]

Wesley's discussion of Christian perfection is predicated upon the understanding of salvation that he sets forth in *The Scripture Way of Salvation*, and that understanding is itself shaped by God's saving acts in and for the world. Christian perfection therefore assumes, and certainly relies upon, the prior and enabling work of the triune God in salvation history. It is only because of the Father's sending of the Son and the gift of their common Spirit to the church at Pentecost that such a notion as Christian perfection is even conceivable. In other words, only through the manifestation of God's love to the world in Christ, and the outpouring of his love into the

88. Ibid., II.1, in Wesley, *Works*, ed. Outler, et al., 2:160.

89. Ibid.

90. Ibid.

91. Ibid., III.14–16, in Wesley, *Works*, ed. Outler, et al., 2:167–68.

hearts of the faithful through the Holy Spirit, is it possible for human beings to come to the saving knowledge of God and so to share in the life of divine love.[92] God's decisive action in the economy of salvation is the sole foundation of Christian perfection.[93] The basis of this doctrine is found in the triune God and in his saving work.

Wesley gives concise expression to the trinitarian basis of love in one of one his final sermons, "The Unity of the Divine Being."[94] There he writes, "It is in consequence of our knowing God loves us that we love him, and love our neighbour as ourselves."[95] Wesley grounds the idea of love of God and neighbor, which is one of the most recurring themes in his writings, in God's prior and enabling love for the human family. In the Christian life, our love for God is rooted in God's love for us, as that love is revealed through God's gracious actions in salvation history. The same is true of our love for neighbor, which also follows from the knowledge of God's love for us. As Wesley sees it, the love of God is so strong and dynamic that the true knowledge of it produces in faithful hearts genuine love for God and for their neighbors in God and because of God; and this knowledge is gained through one's experience of God.[96] Wesley's

92. In *Christian Perfection*, Wesley asserts that the miracle-working power of the Holy Spirit was given when Jesus first sent the apostles to preach the Gospel (cf. Mt 10:1, 8), but that "the Holy Ghost was not yet given in his sanctifying graces, as he was after Jesus was glorified." It was on the day of Pentecost that those who "waited for the promise of the Father" (cf. Acts 1:4) were made "more than conquerors over sin by the Holy Ghost given unto them"; so "this great salvation from sin was not given till Jesus was glorified" (II.11, 12, in Wesley, *Works*, ed. Outler, et al., 2:110–11).

93. Perceiving the significance of the economy of salvation in Wesley's theological teaching and preaching, Jason Vickers claims that "in the light of his doctrines of the atonement and the work of the Holy Spirit, Wesley is rightly viewed as a theologian of the economic Trinity" (*Wesley: A Guide for the Perplexed* [London: T&T Clark, 2009], 84).

94. Sermon 120 (1789), in Wesley, *Works*, ed. Outler, et al., 4:60–71.

95. Ibid., §17, in Wesley, *Works*, ed. Outler, et al., 4:67.

96. The question of the accuracy and sufficiency of Outler's so-called "Wesleyan quadrilateral" remains a contested issue among Wesley's interpreters. While this is not the place for a detailed engagement with that debate, to the extent that experience had any theological significance for Wesley, it was not experience of the world

conception of love for God and neighbor, and therefore his understanding of perfection in love, is grounded specifically in the triune God. The foundation of Christian perfection is the one, true God who has opened his life to us in Christ and renews his own loving image in human hearts by the indwelling Spirit such that we are to become "Transcripts of the Trinity."[97] That last point, suggestive of the communion with God that is made possible by grace, introduces the next stage of this inquiry, the end of Christian perfection.

Communion with God: The Trinitarian End of Christian Perfection The end of Christian perfection is a matter of communion with God, personal union with the three-person God. As Wesley writes in his sermon "Spiritual Worship," on 1 John 5:20, in this epistle John treats directly "the foundation of all, the happy and holy communion which the faithful have with God the Father, Son, and Holy Ghost."[98] This communion is, for Wesley, the orienting vision of life. Alluding to the Augustinian dictum, he recalls that God has made human beings for himself, and that their hearts cannot rest until they rest in God.[99] Through his saving work, the God who has created us for communion with himself draws us into his own life so that we become partakers of the divine nature (2 Pt 1:4).

The connection between happiness and holiness runs deep in this sermon, as it does elsewhere in Wesley's writings.[100] The pursuit

---

in general but precisely experience of God—especially the experience of God's grace in regeneration and sanctification—that was of greatest importance. For more on this topic, see W. Stephen Gunter, Scott J. Jones, Ted A. Campbell, Rebekah L. Miles, and Randy L. Maddox, eds., *Wesley and the Quadrilateral: Renewing the Conversation* (Nashville: Abingdon Press, 1997).

97. *A Collection of Hymns for the Use of the People Called Methodists*, 7:3, in Wesley, *Works*, ed. Outler, et al., 7:88.

98. Sermon 77 (1780), §2, in Wesley, *Works*, ed. Outler, et al., 3:89–90.

99. Ibid., III.1, in Wesley, *Works*, ed. Outler, et al., 3:97. Cf. "The Unity of the Divine Being," §9–10, in Wesley, *Works*, ed. Outler, et al., 4:63–64; Sermon 3 (a sermon by Charles Wesley that is largely similar in content to many of John's sermons), '*Awake, Thou That Sleepest*,' II.5, in Wesley, *Works*, ed. Outler, et al., 1:148.

100. E.g., Sermon 59, "God's Love to Fallen Man" (1782), I.1–10, in Wesley,

of happiness, like the pursuit of holiness, is one that finds fulfillment in God: "In this alone can you find the happiness you seek—in the union of your spirit with the Father of spirits; in the knowledge and love of him who is the fountain of happiness, sufficient for all the souls he has made."[101] According to Wesley, this union, knowledge, and love consist in the indwelling of God in the hearts of Christian believers. Happiness, like holiness, begins and ends in God. It begins "when it pleases the Father to reveal his Son in our hearts; when we first know Christ, being enabled to 'call him Lord by the Holy Ghost' [1 Cor 12:3]; when we can testify, our conscience bearing us witness in the Holy Ghost, 'the life which I now life, I live by faith in the Son of God, who loved me, and gave himself for me' [Gal 2:20]."[102] It is then "that heaven is opened in the soul, that the proper, heavenly state commences, while the love of God, as loving us, is shed abroad in the heart [cf. Rom 5:5], instantly producing love to all mankind."[103] The God who freely pours his love into faithful hearts through the Holy Spirit is also the end of happiness, the one toward whom Wesley's account of the Christian life is irrevocably directed. As those who believe advance in the knowledge and love of God, they reach maturity in Christ, to the point of being filled with him, of being completely happy through God's indwelling in them and their continual rest in God:

> when "Christ in us, the hope of glory" [Col 1:27], is our God and our all; when he has taken the full possession of our heart; when he reigns therein, without a rival, the Lord of every motion there; when we dwell in Christ, and Christ in us, we are one with Christ, and Christ with us; then

---

Works, ed. Outler, et al., 2:425–31; Sermon 6, "The Righteousness of Faith" (1746), I.2, in Wesley, *Works*, ed. Outler, et al., 1:209; *A Plain Account of Christian Perfection*, 73. Cf. Rebekah L. Miles, "Happiness, Holiness, and the Moral Life," in Randy L. Maddox and Jason E. Vickers, eds., *The Cambridge Companion to John Wesley* (Cambridge: Cambridge University Press, 2010), 207–24.

101. "Spiritual Worship," III.8, in Wesley, *Works*, ed. Outler, et al., 3:101.

102. Ibid., II.5, in Wesley, *Works*, ed. Outler, et al., 3:96.

103. Ibid.

we are completely happy; then we live all "the life that is hid with Christ in God" [Col 3:3]. Then, and not till then, we properly experience what that word meaneth, "God is love; and whosoever dwelleth in love, dwelleth in God, and God in him" [1 Jn 4:16].[104]

The happiness for which God has made all human beings becomes a reality through the mutual indwelling between God and the faithful. By means of this personal communion, those who are in Christ learn the meaning of the biblical teaching that "God is love" (1 Jn 4:16). Indeed, they learn God's love and come to abide in it even as they abide in God. For Wesley this is the way to true happiness and holiness; the path to perfection is one of participation in God—a life of constant communion with the Father, the Son, and the Holy Spirit.

The idea of constant communion has decidedly eucharistic overtones in Wesley's thought, due in large part to a discourse that he published in 1787 entitled "The Duty of Constant Communion."[105] The sermon is based on an extract of Robert Nelson's *The Great Duty of Frequenting the Christian Sacrifice* (1707) that Wesley had produced in 1732 for use with his pupils at Lincoln College; and although in the published version Wesley claims the text as his own, the extent of his originality is not entirely clear. As Albert Outler observes, "there is too much of Nelson here for it to be acknowledged as truly 'original' [to Wesley] and too much of Wesley for it to be labelled as wholly 'borrowed.'"[106] What is certain, however, is that the sermon represents Wesley's most complete statement of his eucharistic doctrine and praxis.

104. Ibid., II.6, in Wesley, *Works*, ed. Outler, et al., 3:96–97.

105. Sermon 101 (1787), in Wesley, *Works*, ed. Outler, et al., 3:428–39.

106. Outler, "An Introductory Comment" to "The Duty of Constant Communion," in Wesley, *Works*, ed. Outler, et al., 3:427. Cf. Wesley's preface to the sermon: "The following discourse was written above five and fifty years ago, for the use of my pupils at Oxford. I have added very little, but retrenched much; as I then used more words than I do now. But I thank God I have not yet seen cause to alter my sentiments in any point which is therein delivered" (Wesley, *Works*, ed. Outler, et al., 3:428).

Wesley shifts the emphasis from Nelson's "frequenting the Christian sacrifice" to his preferred phrase "constant communion" as a way of stressing the importance of Christians receiving the sacrament not just frequently but, as it were, constantly—that is, as often as God provides them the opportunity.[107] One reason is because during his institution of the Lord's Supper Christ plainly commands all his followers, "Do this in remembrance of me" (e.g., Lk 22:19). While this is reason enough for God's people to obey constantly as Wesley sees it, he also cites as a second reason why every Christian should receive the Eucharist as often as possible the benefits of doing so, namely, "the forgiveness of our past sins and the present strengthening and refreshing of our souls." God's grace conveyed in this sacrament confirms to Christians the pardon of their sins because, as Wesley asks rhetorically, "what surer way have we of procuring pardon from [God] than the 'showing forth the Lord's death' [cf. 1 Cor 11:26], and beseeching him, for the sake of his Son's sufferings, to blot out all our sins?" The Lord's Supper also nourishes the soul; it is "the food of our souls," which "gives strength to perform our duty, and leads us on to perfection." A gift of God's mercy, this sacrament is a means to "obtain holiness on earth and everlasting glory in heaven" for those

107. In "The Duty of Constant Communion," Wesley focuses entirely on the physical act of receiving the sacrament (that is, what Aquinas calls eating sacramentally [*ST*, III, q. 80, a. 1]). Aquinas also speaks of "spiritual communion" as a second way of eating Christ's body, which can take place without reception of the sacrament itself (ibid.). While nowhere in his writings does Wesley write explicitly of such spiritual communion, the idea of the Christian life as a kind of spiritual communion with God pervades his writings, even if an overt eucharistic reference is lacking. Recall, for example, this description of a person "born from above" (Jn 3:3) in his sermon "The New Birth": "God having quickened him by his Spirit [cf. 1 Pt 3:18], he is alive to God through Jesus Christ [Rom 6:11]. He lives a life which the world knoweth not of, a 'life' which 'is hid with Christ in God' [Col 3:3]. God is continually breathing, as it were, upon his soul, and his soul is breathing unto God. Grace is descending into his heart, and prayer and praise ascending to heaven. And by this intercourse between God and man, this fellowship with the Father and the Son [1 Jn 1:3], as by a kind of spiritual respiration, the life of God in the soul is sustained: and the child of God grows up, till he comes to 'the full measure of the stature of Christ' [Eph 4:13]" ("The New Birth," II.4, in Wesley, *Works*, ed. Outler, et al., 2:193).

who are baptized.[108] Through their communion with God in the life of faith and especially in the Eucharist, Christians grow in grace and are strengthened to live in obedience to God as they continue their journey toward perfection.[109]

The sanctifying benefits of the sacrament find poetic articulation in a collection of hymns published jointly by John and Charles Wesley, *Hymns on the Lord's Supper* (1745).[110] Inspired by Daniel Brevint's treatise *On the Christian Sacrament and Sacrifice* (1672), which the Wesleys "extracted" in order to form a preface to the collection, these hymns are one sign of the efforts of the Wesley brothers to revitalize the eucharistic life of the Church of England.[111] The hymns celebrate the sacramental presence of Christ, the sacrificial character of the Eucharist, and its threefold temporal reference.[112] In addition, an-

108. The idea of "Open Communion" in the United Methodist Church, when taken to the extreme of meaning not simply ecumenical openness but the communing of nonbaptized persons as a purportedly evangelistic measure, represents a departure from both Wesley and the broader Christian tradition. Wesley's reference to the sacrament as a "*converting* ordinance" denotes conversion from one degree of faith in Christ to another, higher degree, not from no faith to faith (*Journal*, June 27, 1740, in Wesley, *Works*, ed. Outler, et al., 19:158). Cf. "there are *degrees in faith*, and *weak faith* may yet be *true faith*" (*Journal*, June 22, 1740, in ibid., 19:155).

109. "The Duty of Constant Communion," I.1–3, II.5, in Wesley, *Works*, ed. Outler, et al., 3:428–29, 432.

110. In his introduction to the facsimile reprint, Geoffrey Wainwright observes that, as in other such cases, it is very likely that Charles was the principal author of these hymns, and John the editor (*Hymns on the Lord's Supper* by John Wesley and Charles Wesley [hereafter *HLS*], with introduction by Geoffrey Wainwright, facsimile of the first edition [Bristol: Felix Farley, 1745], Madison, N.J.: The Charles Wesley Society, 1995, vi). Still, the significance of the joint publication should not be overlooked: even though John's contribution in all likelihood came not as author but editor of these hymns, the fact that they are published in his name as well as in Charles's indicates that they are clearly representative of his thoughts on the matter.

111. The preface is entitled "The Christian Sacrament and Sacrifice," and is said to be "extracted from Dr. Brevint" (preface, 3).

112. On the Wesleys' understanding of the intersection of past, present, and future in the Eucharist, see Kenneth M. Loyer, "Memorial, Means, and Pledge: Eucharist and Time in the Wesleys' *Hymns on the Lord's Supper*," *Proceedings of The Charles Wesley Society*, vol. 11 (2006–2007): 87–106. This article also explores the conver-

other prominent theme in this collection of hymns is the purpose of the sacrament, including its role in the promotion of holiness among and within believers through a sharing in God's perfect love.

O Rock of our Salvation, see
The souls that seek their rest in thee,
Beneath thy cooling shadow hide,
And keep us, Saviour, in thy side,
By water and by blood redeem,
And wash us in the mingled stream.

The sin-atoning blood apply,
And let the water sanctify,
Pardon and holiness impart
Sprinkle and purify our heart,
Wash out the last remains of sin,
And make our inmost nature clean.

The double stream in pardons rolls,
And brings thy love into our souls,
Who dare the truth divine receive,
And credence to thy witness give,
We here thy utmost power shall prove
Thy utmost power of perfect love.[113]

In this sacrament Christ nourishes the members of his body the church with the gifts of his own body and blood. By receiving these gifts, Christians receive nothing less than the life of God.

Now, Lord, on us thy flesh bestow,
And let us drink Thy Blood,
Till all our souls are fill'd below
With all the life of God.[114]

---

gence of a Wesleyan perspective with the thought of Thomas Aquinas and suggests that this topic has ecumenical potential for Methodists and Roman Catholics.

113. *HLS*, 31.

114. Ibid., 30:8.

Christ's eucharistic presence constitutes the ground of the deepest possible union that his people can enjoy with him, and they are thereby given access to his life-giving wounds, to the atoning blood that flows from them, and even to his very flesh made sacramentally present. As a result, faithful communicants grow in the likeness of their Savior, his image impressed upon their hearts.

> From thy blest wounds life let us draw,
> Thine all-atoning blood
> Now let us drink with trembling awe;
> Thy flesh be now our food.
> Come, Lord, thy sovereign aid impart,
> Here make thy likeness shine,
> Stamp thy whole image on our heart,
> And all our heart is thine.[115]

Striking a familiar soteriological theme, the Wesleys in their eucharistic hymns describe the sacramental bond in terms of participation in the divine nature. These outward signs effect an inward union between believers and Christ.

> Saviour, thou didst the mystery give
> That I thy nature might partake,
> Thou bidst me outward signs receive,
> One with thyself my soul to make,
> My body, soul and spi'rit to join
> Inseparably one with thine.[116]

Deeply united to Christ in this sacrament, his people are thereby fed spiritual food, sustained by God's grace, and trained for heaven, where faith shall become sight.

> Author of life divine,
> Who hast a table spread,
> Furnish'd with mystick wine
> And everlasting Bread,

115. Ibid., 83:3.

116. Ibid., 54:3.

Preserve the life thyself hast given,
And feed, and train us up for heaven.

Our needy souls sustain
With fresh supplies of love,
Till all thy life we gain,
And all thy fulness prove,
And strength'ned by thy perfect grace,
Behold without a veil thy face.[117]

The eucharistic union with God is one in which human souls receive God's life in this sacramental gift, which strengthens them in the journey to heaven.

The explicit trinitarian content found in many of the hymns in this collection further illustrates the connection discerned by the Wesleys among the Eucharist, love, and the doctrine of God. As an example, hymn seventy-five follows a trinitarian pattern emphasizing the benefits of the sacrament, namely, pardon, grace, and the genuinely heartfelt association between God and perfect love.

Father the grace we claim,
The double grace bestow'd,
On all who trust in him that came
By water and by blood.

Jesu, the blood apply,
The righteousness bring in,
Us by thy dying justify,
And wash out all our sin.

Spirit of faith, come down,
Thy seal with power set to,
The banquet by thy presence crown,
And prove the record true.

Pardon, and grace impart:
Come quickly from above,

117. Ibid., 40.

And witness now in every heart
That God is perfect love.[118]

As shown by these excerpts, in *Hymns on the Lord's Supper* the Wesleys affirm with considerable zeal the significance of the Eucharist for sanctification. The fellowship with God realized in this sacrament has important implications for daily Christian life and the journey toward perfection in love that is ultimately perfection in God.

While continued growth in communion with God is possible for believers at present, as John Wesley in particular tirelessly asserts throughout his writings on perfection, he also maintains that its full manifestation will come eschatologically. Wesley expresses this hope in trinitarian fashion at the close of his sermon "The New Creation": "And to crown all, there will be a deep, an intimate, an uninterrupted union with God; a constant communion with the Father and his Son Jesus Christ, through the Spirit; a continual enjoyment of the Three-One God, and of all the creatures in him!"[119] When it is viewed in eschatological perspective, the trinitarian end of Christian perfection comes clearly into focus. Wesley's emphasis on continued growth in grace gives his conception of perfection a dynamic quality, ensuring that his teaching on perfection includes the present but always points beyond it to even higher levels of holy love that can be experienced by God's grace. Ultimately, it points toward the consummation of God's saving purposes in the sealing of the union between Creator and creature in glory. While this doctrine calls Christians at present to press on in grace toward ever deepening embodiment of love for God and neighbor, for God's own sake, it is also an anticipation of that perfect communion with the God of perfect love that all who dwell in God by grace will forever enjoy.

Therefore, the above outline of Wesley's doctrine of God and the

118. Ibid., 75.

119. Sermon 64 (1785), §18, in Wesley, *Works*, ed. Outler, et al., 2:510. For a study of Wesley's holistic trinitarian account of the new creation, see Kenneth M. Loyer, "'And to Crown All': John Wesley on Union with God in the New Creation," *Methodist Review* 1 (2009): 109–25.

exploration of the doctrine of Christian perfection indicate a vital connection between the two. Implicitly, Wesley's conception of perfect love can be said to have a trinitarian basis by virtue of its firm grounding in God's saving action in and for the world. The end of this doctrine is found to be equally trinitarian, for although the connection between trinitarian theology and perfection is not thoroughly explicated by Wesley, upon analysis of his thought one can justifiably conclude that Wesley's vision of perfection derives its dynamism from the doctrine of God and the reality of Christian participation in God by way of the indwelling and operations of the Holy Spirit. As Christians experience God through their spiritual senses, they come to a deeper knowledge of God and a greater love for God and neighbor, unto the perfection that is attainable by God's grace. In other words, through the work of the Holy Spirit they are renewed in the divine image and drawn increasingly into the life of the God whose "darling attribute" is love: Father, Son, and Holy Spirit.[120]

CONCLUSION

This analysis of Wesley on love, sanctification, and perfection shows that his thought is animated by a participatory understanding of the doctrine of God in which the Holy Spirit is central. That Wesley's implicitly trinitarian account of sanctification has a vigorous pneumatological component is indicated by his conception of the spiritual senses through which human beings come to experience God, his attention to the soteriological theme of renewal in God's image, and his characteristic emphasis on love and holiness in the Spirit. It is for such reasons as these that Wesley is recognized as one who accentuates the activity and personhood of the Spirit more than many Western thinkers.[121] Although Wesley did not synthesize his insights

120. Commenting on 1 John 4:8, Wesley referred to love as God's "darling, his reigning attribute, the attribute that sheds an amiable glory on all his other perfections" (*Explanatory Notes*, 1 Jn 4:8).

121. Cf. F. LeRon Shults and Andrea Hollingsworth, *The Holy Spirit* (Grand Rapids: Eerdmans, 2008), 62. One can say that Wesley stands out in this regard without

into a comprehensive system of thought, this pneumatological component provides resources for the development of a theology of holiness and love that is truly Spiritual, which is to say, related especially closely to the Spirit of holiness and love. While that line of inquiry will be pursued more fully in chapter 6 below, the above inquiry confirms that the sort of more robust theological account of Christian perfection called for by a number of Wesley's interpreters can indeed be developed with considerable support from Wesley.

It is also possible, of course, to go further by building on Wesley and the trinitarian "grammar" implicit in Wesley's thought.[122] With its pneumatological focus, this "grammar" can profitably be made more explicit and be expanded in a way that locates love and holiness even more deeply in God, further underscoring their proper depth and *telos* in relation to the doctrine of God and to the doctrine of the Holy Spirit in particular. The spiritual and theological insights and intuitions of Wesley can be affirmed and advanced by more clearly connecting sanctification to God.

These two claims—that Wesley provides resources for the development of a pneumatological theology of holiness and love, and that the implicitly trinitarian basis and end of Wesley's doctrine of Christian perfection can be given greater clarity and depth—pave the way for the next section, which turns to the theology of Thomas Aquinas for theological enrichment of Wesley's implicit trinitarianism and especially his intuitions about the doctrine of the Holy Spirit. As we will see in the following chapters, despite the differences between Wesley and Aquinas, a constructive assessment of their views on sanctification reveals considerable pneumatological resonance and compatibility.

having to accept the dubious notion that Western theology as a whole suffers from a pneumatological deficiency. In fact, the conclusions reached in chapter 6 concerning Aquinas and Wesley as possible sources for the task of recovering a richer doctrine of the Spirit directly challenge this latter claim.

122. Maddox, *Responsible Grace*, 140.

Three

THE HOLY SPIRIT AS PERSONAL LOVE IN THOMAS AQUINAS

WHILE JOHN WESLEY primarily used such works as sermons, tracts, and hymns to communicate his theological teachings, Thomas Aquinas is perhaps best known for his sustained, rigorous inquiry into the more technical points of Christian doctrine. To be sure, Aquinas also expressed his theology through sermons and hymns, but his primary mode of theological reflection was the kind of comprehensive, orderly, and intricately reasoned exposition that Wesley, the Oxford don turned leader of a grassroots movement of evangelical and ecclesial renewal, so rarely composed. In short, Aquinas's writings on the Holy Spirit display a carefully delineated structure as well as his characteristic dogmatic precision.

Their differences in method and proportion aside, however, like Wesley, Aquinas is also notable for having discerned profound connections among love, sanctification, and the person and work of the Holy Spirit. The result is an understanding of soteriology that, while having its own particular emphases, is largely complementary to that of Wesley, with certain points of contact that will be explored in chapter 6. So after beginning with Wesley and the question of how best to read him, we now turn to Aquinas and his pneumatology, which is among the lesser appreciated aspects of his thought.[1] Nevertheless, a careful account of it can not only contribute to the knowledge of the theology of Aquinas but will also allow us to relate his pneumatological insights to the study of John Wesley and the possible advancement of theology in Methodist studies.

The next three chapters consist of an inquiry into Aquinas's *amor*-based pneumatology. In particular, we will begin with an assessment of his understanding of the person and work of the Holy Spirit that gives special attention to the crucial and evocative association that Aquinas discerns between the Spirit and love (*amor*). This association represents a significant point of contact between Aquinas's trinitarian theology and his moral theology, and an examination of three distinct but related topics will shed light on Aquinas's view of the Holy Spirit

1. One of the very few book-length studies on the Holy Spirit in Aquinas is a dissertation by Anthony Keaty in which he investigates the relationship between the Holy Spirit as love and the economy of salvation ("The Holy Spirit as Love: A Study in the Pneumatology of Thomas Aquinas" [Ph.D. diss., University of Notre Dame, 1997]). While Keaty illumines certain aspects of the connection between Aquinas's trinitarian theology and his account of the Christian life, he limits his study to Aquinas's treatment of love as a name proper to the Holy Spirit in the *prima pars* of the *Summa theologiae* and his discussion of *caritas* in the *secunda pars*. There is more work to be done on Aquinas's teaching on the Holy Spirit as love, particularly by including in more explicit ways other primary sources, such as *Scriptum super libros Sententiarum Magistri Petri Lombardi* (hereafter *In I Sent.* in the footnotes, *Scriptum* in the text above) and *Summa contra Gentiles* (*ScG* in the footnotes, *Summa contra Gentiles* in the text above), in so far as they facilitate a greater understanding of the rather compressed account in the *ST*. On the whole, Keaty makes little use of Aquinas's writings beyond the *ST*, and he does not even include the *ScG* in his bibliography. The value of his dissertation lies in his close and integrative reading of portions of the *ST*. With the focus still on the *ST*, as this is Aquinas's *magnum opus*, here the scope of the inquiry will be expanded to include other texts that clarify or amplify what Aquinas writes in the *ST*. The concerns addressed by Keaty are also of interest in the present study, but they are approached from a different perspective (one that has the benefit of the recent groundbreaking work on the Trinity in Aquinas by Gilles Emery in particular) and in view of a different end (the exploration of pneumatological resonance and compatibility between Thomas Aquinas and John Wesley and, on that basis, between Catholics and Methodists).

and the Christian life: first, the Spirit as personal love in Aquinas; second, the Spirit as the mutual love of the Father and the Son; and third, soteriological implications of the Spirit as love. This chapter will investigate Aquinas's understanding of the Holy Spirit as love in person or personal love.

Aquinas inherits from Augustine a problem concerning the identification of the Holy Spirit as love.[2] The problem is that in the Trinity love sometimes refers to the divine essence, which is common to the three divine persons, and sometimes refers especially to the Holy Spirit. How can love or charity denote both God's essence as Trinity and in a special way the Holy Spirit in particular? Augustine maintains that each usage is legitimate and seeks to resolve the difficulty by appealing to the name of wisdom, which is in one sense common to the whole Trinity and in another sense proper to the Son. In so far as it is a name common to the whole Trinity, each divine person can be called wisdom, although there are not three wisdoms but one:

> I do not know why, just as the Father and the Son and the Holy Spirit are called wisdom and all are together not three wisdoms but one wisdom, the Father and the Son and the Holy Spirit should not all be called charity and all together be one charity. For in this way the Father is God and the Son is God and the Holy Spirit is God, and they are all together one God.[3]

2. Jaroslav Pelikan identifies Augustine as the authority for naming the Holy Spirit love ("The Doctrine of *Filioque* in Thomas Aquinas and Its Patristic Antecedents: An Analysis of *Summa Theologiae*, Part I, Question 36," in Armand A Maurer, ed., *St. Thomas Aquinas, 1274–1974: Commemorative Studies*, vol. 1 [Toronto: Pontifical Institute of Mediaeval Studies, 1974], 315–36, in particular 331). Augustine's influence on Aquinas is clear on this point, as elsewhere. Such influence can be seen, for example, in Aquinas's commentary on the *Sentences* by Peter Lombard. Lombard also follows Augustine, and indeed quotes him extensively, on the identification of the Holy Spirit as love. Similarly, Aquinas follows this Augustinian line of inquiry in his commentary on Lombard (e.g., *In I Sent.*, d. 10). For more on Aquinas as an interpreter of Augustine, see Michael Dauphinais, Barry David, and Matthew Levering, eds., *Aquinas the Augustinian* (Washington, D.C.: The Catholic University of America Press, 2007).

3. *De Trinitate*, XV, 28, translated from *De Trinitate libri XV*, Cura et studio

The fact that the Father and the Son can also be called charity does not render it unfitting to call the Holy Spirit charity any more than calling the Holy Spirit charity renders it unfitting to call the Father and the Son charity.[4] Three are called charity and yet there are not three charities but one, just as three are called wisdom and yet there are not three wisdoms but one. Even though all three persons are wisdom, however, the title "the wisdom of God" belongs in a special sense to one of the three in particular, the Son who is God's Word (cf. 1 Cor 1:24). Just as the Word of God can be called distinctively the wisdom of God, although both the Father and the Holy Spirit are also wisdom (and are no less wise than the Son), so the Holy Spirit can be distinctively named charity, although both the Father and the Son are also charity (and are no less loving than the Holy Spirit). Augustine considers the name charity most suitable for the Holy Spirit even as the divine substance common to the three persons of the Trinity is itself charity.

> If therefore any of these three can properly be named charity, who more aptly than the Holy Spirit? So that, namely, in that most high and simple nature substance is not one thing and charity another, but the substance itself is charity and charity itself is the substance, whether in the Father or in the Son or in the Holy Spirit, and nevertheless the Holy Spirit is properly named charity.[5]

In these passages, then, Augustine deduces that as wisdom is in one sense common to the whole Trinity and in another sense proper to the Son, in a similar way the divine substance is charity while the Holy Spirit is properly named as such. With regard to the Trinity as a whole, love denotes the divine essence common to Father, Son, and Holy Spirit. With regard to the Holy Spirit in particular, love denotes the special sense in which the Spirit is love.

W. J. Mountain, auxiliante Fr. Glorie, Corpus Christianorum Series Latina, vol. LA, Aurelli Augustini Opera, Pars XVI, 2 (Turnholti: Typographi Brepols Editores Pontificii, 1968), 503. Unless indicated otherwise, all translations throughout are my own.

4. Ibid., XV, 30.

5. Ibid., XV, 29.

Yet in what sense is the Spirit distinctively love? Augustine's answer to this question is that the Spirit is the love proceeding from God and within God. Augustine reaches this conclusion in large part based on his exegesis of 1 John 4, especially verses seven to eight, thirteen, and sixteen.[6] Augustine interprets the phrase *dilectio ex Deo* in verse seven to mean "love is from God" in the sense that love proceeds from God precisely as God, for Augustine observes that the Apostle John equates love, which he had just said was from God (v. 7), with God (v. 8): *Deus dilectio est.* Therefore, since love is from God and, as Augustine perceives, this love from God is equated with God, "love is God from God" (*Deus … ex deo est dilectio*).[7] The Holy Spirit is love in a special sense because of the Spirit's inward procession as love.

Augustine further notes that in verses thirteen and sixteen a connection is made between the Holy Spirit and love in the Christian life. The faithful abide in God, and God abides in them, through God's gift of the Holy Spirit.[8] Moreover, to abide in love is to abide in God who is love.[9] Since the mutual indwelling, in love, of God in the faithful and the faithful in God occurs through the gift of the Holy Spirit, Augustine comes to understand that the Holy Spirit, who proceeds inwardly as love in the life of God, is given in love and indeed as love to the Father's adopted daughters and sons in Christ: "it is the Holy Spirit, of which [God] has given us, that makes us abide in God and him in us. But love does this. He is therefore God

6. The translations of Augustine's citations of these biblical passages are as follows: "Beloved, let us love each other because love is from God, and everyone who loves is born of God. Whoever does not love does not know God, because love is God" (4:7–8). "In this we know that we abide in [God] and he in us, because he has given us of his Spirit" (4:13). "God is love, and whoever abides in love abides in God, and God abides in him" (4:16). Edmund Hill translates Augustine's citation of the phrase *Deus dilectio est* (4:8, 16) as "love is God," which differs from the more common rendering "God is love" (*The Trinity*, trans. Edmund Hill, OP [Hyde Park, N.Y.: New City Press, 1991], 420–21). In both cases, however, the association between love and God is clear. That theological association is essential to Augustine's interpretation and, as will be shown, to Aquinas's account as well.

7. Augustine, *De Trinitate*, XV, 31.

8. 1 Jn 4:13.

9. 1 Jn 4:16.

who is love."[10] In turn, this gift, which the Holy Spirit is, produces in Christ's disciples the spiritual fruit of love. "Therefore God the Holy Spirit who proceeds from God ignites a human being in the love of God and neighbor when he has been given to him, and [the Spirit] himself is love."[11] In this way, Augustine understands the phrases "God is love" and "love is from God" to signify in a special way the person of the Holy Spirit, through whom the mutual indwelling between God and faithful in the life of grace occurs.[12] Thus, according to Augustine, Scripture teaches that the love who is God is also from God, which is to say that the Holy Spirit, while being God, is God's own gift of love.[13] While in a general sense the whole Trinity is love, the Holy Spirit is distinctively called love because it is the Spirit who proceeds as love from God and within God; and what is more, this same Spirit is given freely to God's people as the gift that brings them through to God.[14]

Following Augustine, Aquinas takes the name "love" (*amor*) as a central pneumatological theme. Like Augustine, Aquinas speaks of love in God in two distinct but related ways, sometimes rather generally to signify the divine essence and other times more specifically to indicate the distinctive place and importance of the Holy Spirit within the divine Trinity (in Aquinas's technical term, to indicate a *proprium* of the Holy Spirit). Rather than simply repeating Augustine's solution, however, Aquinas attempts to provide one of his own, which in some ways bears the imprint of Augustine but ultimately shows independent and innovative thinking on Aquinas's part. Precisely how Aquinas seeks to resolve that problem will be a focal point of the following inquiry. To anticipate, in various writings, and most notably in the *Summa theologiae*, Aquinas teaches that the Holy Spirit is the love proceeding from the Father and the Son.[15] As the

10. *De Trinitate*, XV, 31.
11. Ibid.
12. Ibid., XV, 31.
13. Ibid., XV, 30–31.
14. Ibid.; cf. Keaty, "The Holy Spirit as Love," 10.
15. E.g., *ST*, I, q. 27, a. 3c and q. 36, a. 2c.

term or expression of the love between Father and Son, the Holy Spirit is love in person.[16] The Spirit, in other words, is personal love, which is the central opening theme in Aquinas's account of the Holy Spirit as love. While it is not without its problems or difficulties, this way of understanding the Holy Spirit allows Aquinas to illumine the deep trinitarian basis of pneumatological affirmations as he clarifies the Spirit's authentic personal identity.

THE TRINITARIAN BASIS OF PNEUMATOLOGY

Before examining Aquinas's exposition, it is worth observing at the outset its prominence and specific location in his work as a whole. On this point the structure of the *Summa* is telling, for Aquinas sets his initial discussion of the Holy Spirit in a trinitarian context. Questions thirty-six to thirty-eight of the *prima pars* on the Holy Spirit constitute part of Aquinas's mature doctrine of the Trinity, as presented in questions twenty-seven to forty-three. The treatise on the Trinity, which Gilles Emery calls at once one of the most difficult and most important in the entire *Summa*, conveys in rather technical language Aquinas's insight into the specifically Christian understanding of God and of the world in relation to God.[17] The opening questions of this treatise introduce many of the themes that go on to figure prominently in Aquinas's discussion of the Holy Spirit in particular. The doctrines of processions (q. 27), relations (q. 28), and persons (qq. 29–32) are especially crucial for understanding Aquinas's teaching on the Holy Spirit as love. So too, of course, is his subsequent discussion of the missions (q. 43), which will be integral to chapter 5 below.

16. Ibid., I, q. 37, a. 1c, ad 3. Cf. the use of the phrase "Die Heilige Geist—Liebe in Person" in the article of the same title by Christian Schütz (*Internationale katholische Zeitschrift "Communio"* 34 [2005]: 333–40). In his careful exposition of Aquinas, Gilles Emery also describes the Holy Spirit as "love in person" (*The Trinitarian Theology of Saint Thomas Aquinas*, trans. Francesca Aran Murphy [Oxford: Oxford University Press, 2007], 225ff.).

17. Emery, *Trinity in Aquinas* (Ann Arbor, Mich.: Sapientia Press, 2006), 121.

The main point for now is that the location of the pneumatological questions in the *prima pars* is itself theologically significant.[18] Aquinas does not pursue the subject of the Spirit's person and work in a kind of theological—or to be more precise, pneumatological—isolation. While pneumatology is a critical topic in and of itself, it is best approached in view of the essential doctrines to which it is fundamentally related. As Aquinas shows, those include the doctrines of processions, relations, persons, and missions, all of which are subsets of the larger doctrinal heading under consideration at this point in the *Summa*, the doctrine of the Trinity. Rather than draw a distinction between trinitarian doctrine and pneumatology, Aquinas places his inquiry into the person of the Holy Spirit in an explicitly trinitarian context. In doing so, he demonstrates that the proper basis of pneumatology is the doctrine of the Trinity.

This doctrinal basis is further solidified, of course, by the actual content of Aquinas's exposition. In naming the Holy Spirit as love (*amor*), Aquinas assumes and then builds on the trinitarian foundation laid earlier in the *prima pars*, for the Holy Spirit is not some generic or vague love but precisely the love proceeding from, and thereby uniting, the Father and the Son.[19] As the third person of the Trinity, the Holy Spirit is personal love within God's own triune life. This name for the Spirit is a theme that Aquinas develops in question thirty-seven in particular.

18. For a more thorough analysis of the structure of Aquinas's treatise on the Trinity in the *ST*, see Paul Vanier, *Theologie trinitaire chez Saint Thomas D'Aquin: évolution du concept d'action notionnelle* (Montreal: Institut d'Études Médiévales, 1953), 55–60; and Emery, *Trinity in Aquinas*, 121–64.

19. The connection between procession and union is expressed early on in Aquinas's thought, as in *In I Sent.*, d. 10, q. 1, a. 3 ad 1, where Aquinas says of the Holy Spirit "ex modo processionis habet quod sit vinculum vel unio amantis et amati." While the *Sent.* is an important source for Aquinas's theology, this early text should be read carefully and in light of his more mature reflections, especially since his teaching on the way in which love is a *proprium* of the Spirit develops from the *Sent.* to the *ST*. It is for this reason that the account above focuses on the *ST*, where Aquinas presents his most advanced exposition, with occasional reference to the *Sent.* in order to show connections in his thinking as it developed over time.

THE HOLY SPIRIT: LOVE IN PERSON

The two articles of question thirty-seven correspond to what Emery, developing an observation made by Jean-Pierre Torrell, identifies as the first and second phases of Aquinas's account of the Holy Spirit as love: the procession of the imprint of love that comes about in the will of the lover, as in article one on love as a proper name of the Holy Spirit; and the Holy Spirit as the mutual love of the Father and the Son, as in article two on whether the Father and Son love one another by the Holy Spirit.[20] Here the focus will be on the first of these points, and the second will be taken up in the next chapter. Aquinas seeks to disclose that the Holy Spirit's procession is an inward or immanent procession of love while affirming the Spirit's consubstantiality with the Father and the Son.

In article one, Aquinas considers whether love is a name proper to the Holy Spirit. His affirmative answer distinguishes between the use of this term with regard to God in an essential sense, to denote the divine essence, and the use of the term in a personal sense, signifying a proper name of one of the three persons in particular: "It must be said that the term 'love' can be used of the divinity essentially and personally. And as it is used personally it is a proper name of the Holy Spirit, as 'Word' is a proper name of the Son."[21] Used essentially, the term "love" is not a name proper to the Holy Spirit, but a name proper to the entire Godhead because of the single divine essence common to Father, Son, and Holy Spirit. Used personally, however, the term is a name proper to the Holy Spirit, and in this respect it is the pneumatological equivalent of the term "Word," which is a name proper to the Son. In a way not unlike Augustine, Aquinas employs this basic distinction in his account, but it is still necessary to explain the way in which love, an essential name, can be used personally as

20. Emery, *The Trinitarian Theology of Saint Thomas Aquinas*, 236–37. See also Jean-Pierre Torrell, *Saint Thomas Aquinas*, vol. 2: *Spiritual Master*, trans. Robert Royal (Washington, D.C.: The Catholic University of America Press, 2003), 184–86.

21. *ST*, I, q. 37, a. 1c.

well. Precisely how can love denote in one sense the divine essence and in another sense a particular divine person? In other words, how can love by accommodation mean a relation (the relation of mutual indwelling among the three divine persons in their substantial unity) as well as a person (the Holy Spirit)?

To elucidate his position, Aquinas draws insights from three doctrines that he has addressed in detail earlier in his treatise on the Trinity: the processions, the relations, and the persons.[22] These doctrines help to lay the foundation not only of his trinitarian theology in general, but also of his pneumatology in particular. They are essential to a proper understanding of the Holy Spirit as personal love, since grasping love as an immanent procession makes it possible to perceive a relation subsisting in God, and that relation is the person of the Holy Spirit.[23]

22. John F. Boyle cites these three doctrines in his description of the principles of Aquinas's teaching on the Trinity in the *ST*, and characterizes them in the following manner: "procession as divine operation, divine relation founded upon the two processions, [and] divine person as subsisting relation" ("The Ordering of Trinitarian Teaching in Thomas Aquinas' Second Commentary on Lombard's *Sentences*," in *Thomistica*, ed. E. Manning, Recherches de Théologie ancienne et médiévale, Supplementa 1 [Leuven: Peeters, 1995], 127). Boyle proceeds in this article to compare the account of the doctrine of the Trinity in the *ST* with the so-called "Roman Commentary" on Lombard's *Sentences*, which he attributes to Aquinas as his allegedly second commentary on the *Sentences*, believed to have been written in Rome in 1265–66. This manuscript was first attributed to Aquinas in Leonard E. Boyle, "Alia lectura fratris Thome," *Mediaeval Studies* 45 (1983): 418–29. The authorship of this text, however, has been disputed by H. F. Dondaine, who before L. Boyle's examination reached a negative conclusion about the Thomistic authenticity of the manuscript (cf. Dondaine, "'Alia lectura fratris Thome'? [Super I Sent.]," *Mediaeval Studies* 42 [1980]: 308–36). This is not the place to attempt to settle the dispute, but what is worth noting is that at the very least the text in question addresses Lombard's work in a way that seems largely consistent with the spirit of Aquinas. For that reason alone, it is striking to compare this text with others that can be without doubt attributed to Aquinas. The complete edition is now in print as *Lectura Romana*, and Mark Johnson has provided a list of the incipits and the explicits of the document in "'Alia lectura fratris Thome': A List of the New Texts of St Thomas Aquinas found in Lincoln College, Oxford, MS. Lat. 95," *Recherches de Théologie ancienne et médiévale* 57 (1990): 34–61.

23. Emery provides a rather succinct explanation of this principle and rightly

The Procession of the Holy Spirit

As Aquinas shows in question twenty-seven, there are two processions in God, one by way of the intellect, which is the procession of the Word, and the other by way of the will, which is the procession of love.[24] Because of the nature of human language, the procession of the intellect is better known to human beings than the procession of the will. More suitable terms have been designated to describe the procession of the intellect than are available to explain the will's procession—terms like "word," "to speak," and "to understand."[25] In the case of the procession of the will there is simply not as much that can be said, due to what Aquinas calls "a poverty of vocabulary" (*vocabulorum inopiam*).[26] This is another difficulty that he encounters and must overcome. How can theologians speak accurately of the Holy Spirit when the right words to describe the Spirit's procession simply do not exist?

Aquinas, of course, does not think that this difficulty is insurmountable. The limitations of human language pose a certain problem, which emerges at various points throughout Aquinas's account, but he maintains that even at their worst these limitations are not so severe as to prohibit further penetration of the mystery of the Holy Spirit's procession. Rather, the task of the theologian as Aquinas sees

observes that it is the point of departure that Aquinas takes in his account of the Spirit as love (*The Trinitarian Theology of Saint Thomas Aquinas*, 236). The detailed exposition of Aquinas's argument that follows will allow us to build on Emery's foundational insight.

24. *ST*, I, q. 27, aa. 2–5. The idea of the Holy Spirit as love in question thirty-seven must be read in light of the trinitarian principles set forth earlier in the *prima pars*. As Keaty points out, Aquinas's exposition in question thirty-seven is particularly informed by questions twenty-seven and twenty-eight on processions and relations, respectively ("The Holy Spirit Proceeding as Mutual Love: An Interpretation of Aquinas' *Summa Theologiae*, I.37," *Angelicum* 77 [2000]: 533–57).

25. The Latin *intelligere* can also be translated "to know," as in T. C. O'Brien, trans., *Summa Theologiae* (London: Blackfriars, 1976), vol. 7: Father, Son and Holy Ghost (1a. 33–43), 81.

26. *ST*, I, q. 37, a. 1c.

it is to approach the more difficult and less apparent of these processions, the procession of the will, in light of the procession of the intellect that is more readily apparent to the human mind. To move with Aquinas toward that end, it is necessary to be clear, first, about how he understands the idea of procession in God and, second, about how he refers to the Son's procession in order to make sense of the Spirit's.

In question twenty-seven, Aquinas distinguishes between an outward procession and an inward procession and affirms only the latter with respect to God. He observes that in relation to God Scripture uses names that signify procession, as in John 8:42.[27] Aquinas then explains that procession in God has been understood differently by different thinkers. In two main positions it has been taken to mean an outward act, namely, an act that produces an effect or result outside the agent. The first position is represented by Arius, who understood procession in God in the sense of an exterior effect proceeding from its cause (*effectus procedit a causa*).[28] According to this opinion, the Son proceeds from the Father as the first of his creatures and the Holy Spirit proceeds as the creature of both Father and Son. If that were true, however, neither the Son nor the Holy Spirit would be true God, which runs counter to the teaching of Scripture that attests to their divinity.[29] Representing the second view is Sabellius, who took this procession to mean the cause proceeding to the exterior effect (*causa dicitur procedere in effectum*), in the sense of moving it or impressing its own likeness on it.[30] Thus Sabellius claimed that God the Father is called the Son in assuming human flesh, and that the Father is called the Holy Spirit in sanctifying the rational creature and moving it to life. Whereas Arius, understanding the Son and the Holy Spirit as cre-

27. "Jesus said to [the Jews], 'If God were your Father, you would love me, for I came from God and now I am here. I did not come on my own, but he sent me.'"

28. *ST*, I, q. 27, a. 1c.

29. The two passages that Aquinas cites here as a basis for the divinity of the Son and the Spirit are 1 Jn 5:20 and 1 Cor 6:19, respectively. He refers to many other passages in his more extended discussion of the matter in *ScG*, IV, chaps. 3–9 (on the Son) and 15–17 (on the Holy Spirit).

30. *ST*, I, q. 27, a. 1c.

ated effects proceeding from their cause, denied their essential divinity, Sabellius understood procession as the cause moving the effect externally and did not distinguish among the divine persons. Both of these views take procession in God as an outward act as opposed to an inward one. For this reason neither one of them affirms procession as existing in the Godhead.[31]

According to Aquinas, considering procession in God in an interior sense serves as a necessary corrective to these opinions: "since procession [that is, a coming forth] always supposes action, and as there is an outward procession corresponding to the act tending to external matter, so there must be an inward procession corresponding to the act remaining within the agent."[32] There are only two examples of such a phenomenon: the intellect and will of a rational being. Both will be considered in more detail below, but for now the first is especially instructive. Whenever human beings understand, by the very fact of understanding there proceeds something within them, namely a conception of the object understood, a conception that issues from their intellectual power and proceeds from their knowledge of that object. Signified by the interior or "mental" word, this conception is an intellectual action that remains in the intelligent agent. It is best understood as "an intelligible emanation" (*emanationem intelligibilem*), that is, as an intelligible word that proceeds from the speaker while remaining in that person.[33] This is the kind of procession that exists in God. The procession of a divine person does not take place outwardly, in the sense of an action tending to external matter or to an exterior effect, but inwardly, as corresponding to the act remaining within God. Therefore, to use the easier of the two processions, the Son's procession from the Father does not involve the production of a creature or the movement of a cause moving an effect externally, because this procession is an inward procession by which the Father generates a word—indeed

31. Ibid.

32. Ibid.

33. Ibid.

the Word—proceeding from the Father in an interior sense and thus remaining in the Father precisely as distinct from the Father who is the principle of this Word.[34]

Later in the same question Aquinas refers to the procession by way of the intellect in order to understand the other procession in God, the one that is more difficult to grasp. Scripture attests to the procession of the Holy Spirit in, for example, John 15:26, when Jesus states that "the Spirit of truth … comes from the Father." This same Spirit, sent by the Son from the Father (cf. Jn 15:26a), is distinct from the Son and is in fact another advocate as also indicated by the words of Christ: "I will ask the Father, and he will give you another Advocate, to be with you forever" (Jn 14:15). With regard to the second procession in God, the procession of the Holy Spirit, Aquinas builds on two principles that he established earlier.

First, the very idea of procession in God has a precise meaning, that is, procession exists in God in an inward or immanent manner as opposed to an outward or external manner. Aquinas has already explained that in God the act of procession does not tend toward anything external, whether external matter or an exterior effect. Rather such procession is inward, remaining entirely within God.[35] The specific nature of procession in God serves as one basis on which Aquinas constructs his account of the procession of the Holy Spirit.

The second basis, of course, is Aquinas's exposition of the procession of the Word. Aquinas points out that in a rational agent an action that remains in the agent itself occurs by way of either the intellect or the will. The procession of the Word is that intelligible emanation within God's own life by which the Father, as principle, generates the Son, who proceeds as subsisting in the same nature through the Father's inner act of understanding himself.[36] The Word's pro-

34. Ibid. On the Father as the principle of the Son (and the Holy Spirit), see *ST*, I, q. 33, a. 1.

35. Ibid., I, q. 27, a. 1c, ad 1.

36. Ibid., I, q. 27, a. 2c, ad 1.

cession by way of the intellect is in a certain sense like the Spirit's procession by way of the will. They are similar in so far as they are both processions within God, the former providing a basis for understanding the latter. As the Word proceeds by way of the intellect in God, similarly there is in God a procession by way of the will, the procession of love. The one proceeding as love, the Holy Spirit, is in both the lover and the beloved, as by the Father's generation of the Word the Son is in the Father.

In question thirty-seven, Aquinas makes much of this similarity by moving as he often does from rational creatures to God:

> For as when a thing is understood by anyone, there results in the one who understands a conception of the object understood, and we call this conception a word, so when anyone loves an object a certain impression results, so to speak, of the object loved in the affection of the lover. By reason of this impression the object loved is said to be in the lover, as also the object understood is in the one who understands, so that when anyone understands and loves himself he is in himself, not only by real identity, but also as the object understood is in the one who understands and as the object loved is in the lover.[37]

Through one's love of an object, there comes about in the will of the lover an impression or imprint of the object loved. The object loved is said to be in the lover in this specific sense, as the object understood is in the knower. Therefore, as Aquinas explains, through self-knowledge and self-love someone is present to himself or herself as the object known is in the knower and the object loved is in the lover—a point that leads conveniently to the application of this line of thinking to human understanding of God. For in God three distinct persons indwell one another in an infinitely deeper and more perfect way than anything that is possible by the power of a rational creature alone. The mutual indwelling among Father, Son, and Holy Spirit is consubstantial and eternal on the basis of the immanent processions of the Word and of love.

37. Ibid., I, q. 37, a. 1c.

While the divine processions are similar in some respects, a grasp of their differences helps to clarify the distinctiveness of the procession of the Spirit in God. Due to the nature and limitations of human language, the procession of the Word is more conducive to precise description than is the procession of love. Even when they differ, an exposition of the former provides a certain conceptual clarity with regard to the latter. One such difference concerns the naming of the processions. Whereas in God the procession by way of the intellect is called generation, the procession by way of the will is not. In fact, strictly speaking, this procession lacks a special name. Although they are of an apophatic nature, these two observations about the naming of the Spirit's procession contribute to a fuller understanding of what makes this procession unique.

Regarding the first observation, that the procession by way of the will is not generation, Aquinas distinguishes between the intellect and the will with respect to how each procession is made actual. For the intellect, it is a matter of similitude whereby the object understood resides according to its own likeness in the intellect. The procession of the Word in God is called generation, not in the sense of proceeding from potential to actual life, but rather in so far as it signifies the Word's origin from the Father, as subsisting in the same nature and by way of similitude.[38] The procession by way of the will, however, does not occur by any similitude of the object willed within it, but by its having a certain inclination (*quondam inclinationem*) to the object willed. Therefore, Aquinas perceives, the procession of the intellect occurs by way of similitude and is called generation, since "every generator begets its own like," as in the case of the Father begetting the Son who is the express image of God (cf. Col 1:15).[39] By contrast, the procession of the will is not by way of similitude but rather of "impulse and movement towards an object."[40] Since the very name "spirit" expresses a certain vital movement or

38. Ibid., I, q. 27, a. 2c, ad 2.

39. Ibid., I, q. 27, a. 4c.

40. Ibid.

impulse, it is most appropriate that what proceeds in God by way of love does not proceed as begotten, or as the Son, but proceeds rather as spirit, namely the Holy Spirit.[41] Aquinas clarifies in *Summa contra Gentiles* IV that the third person of the Trinity cannot be called Son but is properly called Spirit, which is in keeping with the manner in which this person proceeds:

> because the beloved in the will exists as inclining, and somehow inwardly impelling the lover toward the very thing loved, and an impulse of a living thing from within pertains to a spirit, it is fitting that God proceeding by way of love be called his "spirit," as it were a kind of existing spiration.[42]

41. Thomas mentions that the name "spirit" denotes a vital movement or impulse in various writings. As noted above in the body of the text, he makes this connection in *ScG*, IV when accounting for the procession of the Holy Spirit by way of love. In addition, commenting on Jn 14, Thomas gives several reasons that Holy Spirit is called "Spirit"; one of them is to indicate the power of the Spirit, who "moves us to act and work well. For the word 'spirit' indicates a certain impulse, and that is why the word *spiritus* can also mean the wind" (*Super Evangelium Sancti Ioannis Lectura*, 5th edition, ed. Raphaelis Cai [Rome: Marietti, 1952], par. 1916; ET: *Commentary on the Gospel of St. John*, trans. Fabian R. Larcher, OP [Albany: Magi Books, 1998]; hereafter *Ioan.*). A lesser known example is found in *Emitte Spiritum*, Aquinas's sermon and collation for the feast of Pentecost, where he observes that impulse of motion is one of the four things that the name "spirit" seems to convey (*Emitte Spiritum*, 1.1). (The other three are subtlety [*subtilitas*] of substance, perfection of life, and hidden origin.) Aquinas goes on to explain this impulse primarily in terms of the created world, that is, *ad extra* (1.3), but in his exposition of the Spirit's subtlety of substance Aquinas considers God's life *ad intra* by describing the Holy Spirit as the love "by which God loves God and by which the Father loves the Son" (1.4). Throughout the sermon Aquinas emphasizes the sending of the Holy Spirit and the effects of this sending, as is fitting given the occasion (the feast of Pentecost). Even though the subject of God's inner life is not the primary concern, this relatively unknown work provides insight into Aquinas's trinitarian theology as well as his pneumatologically rich soteriology, which will be described in more detail in chapter 5. Peter Kwasniewski and Jeremy Holmes have produced a translation of this sermon based on the provisional critical edition of the Leonine Commission, and their translation appears in *Faith and Reason* along with an introductory essay by Kwasniewski, "Aquinas's Sermon for the Feast of Pentecost: A Rare Glimpse of Thomas the Preaching Friar" (*Faith and Reason* 30, nos. 1–2 [2005]: 99–139).

42. *ScG*, IV, cap. 19, n. 10.

The Holy Spirit is not said to be generated any more than the Spirit is said to be born, both of which are proper to the Son, who was generated eternally by the Father and, in the fullness of time, was sent by the Father and born of the Virgin Mary for our adoption as God's children (cf. Gal 4:5). Even though the Holy Spirit is not generated, the Spirit proceeds within God in a distinctive manner (and to anticipate a later topic, the Spirit's temporal mission is also in some sense unique). As love proceeding, the Spirit is the bond of unity between Father and Son, and receives the divine nature.[43] That divine nature is communicated by each of the two inward processions in God.[44] The procession of love in God is not generation, but it is still a genuine procession and thus a communication of the divine nature.

The second statement about the Spirit's procession is also one of negation: the procession of love in God has no proper name of its own. This procession, which is not generation, has remained without a proper name; as Aquinas reiterates, we can only name God from creatures.[45] Aquinas explains: "As in creatures generation is the only principle of communication of nature, procession in God has no proper or special name except that of generation."[46] The procession in God that is not generation therefore lacks a special name. Earlier Aquinas maintained that while the Spirit's procession is not generation it is nonetheless a genuine procession, by which the divine nature is communicated.[47] Here again Aquinas moves from a negative statement to a positive assertion. The procession of love in God has no special name, strictly speaking, but as the procession of the Spirit it can be called spiration.[48]

43. *ST*, I, q. 27, a. 4 ad 1.
44. Ibid., I, q. 27, a. 3 ad 2.
45. Ibid., I, q. 13, a. 1c.
46. Ibid., I, q. 27, a. 4 ad 3.
47. Ibid., I, q. 27, a. 4c, ad 1.

48. Ibid., I, q. 27, a. 4 ad 3. Stanley M. Burgess defines spiration as "the act of breathing as a creative or life-giving act of God" (*The Holy Spirit: Medieval Roman Catholic and Reformation Traditions* [Peabody, Mass.: Hendrickson, 1997], 85 fn. 5). While Aquinas notes that we call breath by the term "spirit" (*ST*, I, q. 36, a. 1c), he

The Divine Relations and the Holy Spirit

Aquinas returns to the idea of spiration in his discussion of a second topic that is foundational for understanding the Holy Spirit as love, the doctrine of the divine relations. Fundamental to Aquinas's trinitarian theology is the understanding that the divine persons are distinguished by their relations, which are based on the processions.[49] So an account of the Holy Spirit as person must take into consideration what Aquinas says about the divine relations, as well as the processions, in order to distinguish the Spirit personally from the Father and the Son without in any way obscuring their common divine essence. Aquinas is clear, first of all, that there are genuine relations in God because God is genuinely triune. Against the Sabellian denial of God's triunity, Thomas maintains that God is Father, Son, and Holy Spirit not simply in a human manner of understanding, but in the very depths of God's own being. That is because, second, the relations in God are founded on the processions in God: "since the divine processions are in the identity of the same nature, as explained above [q. 27, aa. 2, 4], these relations, according to the divine processions, are necessarily real relations."[50] As Aquinas later states, relations in God can be understood only in regard to the processions.[51]

The divine relations make it possible to distinguish the persons from one another while affirming the substantial unity of the Trinity. The trinitarian persons cannot be distinguished by any kind of diversity belying the unity of the one divine essence, nor by a sort

also emphasizes impulse and motion in describing the connection between the Holy Spirit and love. Hence his claim that "it is a property of love to move and impel the will of the lover towards the object loved" (ibid.; cf. I, q. 27, a. 4c). This idea that love moves the lover's will to perform an action evokes a concept that is central to Aquinas's exposition (as explored in more detail later): the imprint of love residing in the will of the lover.

49. Emery, *Trinity in Aquinas*, 137.

50. *ST*, I, q. 28, a. 1c.

51. Ibid., I, q. 28, a. 4c.

of privation, as if to suggest that one of the persons somehow lacks the fullness of divinity *in se*. On the contrary, Father, Son, and Holy Spirit can only be distinguished by a relation of origin that derives from the two processions described above. There are four such relations in God: paternity (the relation of the Father to the Son), filiation (the relation of the Son to the Father), "active" spiration (the relation of the Father and the Son to the Spirit) and "passive" spiration or procession (the relation of the Spirit to the Father and the Son). Of these relations, three constitute the persons themselves: paternity (the Father, in relation to the Son), filiation (the Son, in relation to the Father), and "passive" spiration or procession (the Spirit, in relation to the Father and the Son). The relation of "active" spiration (the Father and the Son in relation to the Spirit) is not a personal property since it is common to both the Father and the Son, who are not constituted by the spiration of the Spirit but by their paternity and filiation, respectively.[52]

Aquinas identifies the Holy Spirit as a relation subsisting in God on the basis of the Spirit's immanent procession as love. Again, following from the two processions in God are the relations of origin. Of those four relations in God—paternity, filiation, spiration ("active" spiration), and procession (or "passive" spiration)—it is procession in particular that distinguishes the Spirit from the Father and the Son. In this case, of course, procession has a quite specific meaning, denoting the Spirit's origin in, and thus relation to, the Father and the Son from whom the Spirit proceeds. The Spirit's procession as love distinguishes the Spirit by a relation of origin with respect to the Father and the Son, who together are one principle of the Holy

52. Ibid. Emery refers to "active" spiration and "passive" spiration or procession ("The Doctrine of the Trinity in St Thomas Aquinas," in Thomas Weinandy, Daniel Keating, and John Yocum, eds., *Aquinas on Doctrine: A Critical Introduction* [London: T&T Clark, 2004], 45–65, in particular 53; cf. *The Trinitarian Theology of Saint Thomas Aquinas*, 236). Heribert Mühlen also speaks of "active" spiration in his exploration of the axiom "duo spirantes, sed unus spirator" (*Der Heilige Geist als Person: In der Trinität, bei der Inkarnation und im Gnadenbund: Ich-Du-Wir* [Münster: Aschendorff, 1988], 143–56).

Spirit.[53] Because the procession on which this relation is founded is precisely an immanent procession, the relation itself can be seen to subsist in God. In so far as the procession is internal and not external, the relation in God of procession or "passive" spiration is literally a relation *in God*, that is to say, it is a subsisting relation within God's own life on the basis of the immanent procession that derives from the action of the will, the procession of love. This is one way in which the doctrine of relations, grounded in the processions, contributes to Aquinas's exposition of the Holy Spirit as love.[54]

Another pertinent connection, and perhaps a more basic one, is also found in question twenty-eight. While in article one Aquinas accounts for the real relations in God, relations that he specifically names in article four, in the second article he considers whether relation in God is the same as the divine essence. In his affirmative response, Aquinas explains that relation can be considered in two modes. The first is what he calls "assistant" relations, which signify a thing in respect to something else outside of or apart from that thing. Such relations are affixed externally but not in the thing itself. By contrast, the second approach considers relation as an accident. In this sense, a relation inheres in a subject and has an accidental existence in it. Obviously relation in God cannot be understood in the first sense because the divine relations are entirely internal, as are the inward processions on which they are founded. Yet relation in the second sense does not apply directly to God either. Moving from creatures to God, Aquinas modifies this version of relation to make a crucial point. Whereas it is possible for something to have an accidental existence in creatures, the same is not true in the case of God, in whom there are no accidents. Transferred to God, the idea of accidental existence in creatures reaches another level entirely—that of substantial existence—because everything in God is his essence. In this way, then, relation in God has the existence of

53. *ST*, I, q. 36, a. 4.

54. Ibid., I, q. 28, a. 4c.

the divine essence, which is to say that relation in God is the same as his essence.[55]

In view of this idea, one of the issues addressed by the guiding questions raised earlier comes more clearly into focus. Precisely how can love, an essential name, be used in a personal sense to denote the Holy Spirit per se? How can love by accommodation signify both the essence or an essential property (in this case, the mutual indwelling among Father, Son, and Holy Spirit in their single unity of substance) and a person (the Holy Spirit)? Aquinas's point here, that relation and essence are the same in God, helps clarify the manner in which love denotes relation. That the essential term of love signifies relation in God is in keeping with the principle that relation and essence do not differ from each other in God, but are "one and the same."[56] When love is spoken essentially of God, in reference to the divine essence that God is, Aquinas's association of relation and essence in God enables one to see the deep interconnectedness of the various components of his doctrine of God, for relation in God has the existence of precisely that divine essence. On this basis, love can be said to assume relation in God. This association between relation and essence may shed some light on the questions posed above, but what needs to be addressed in a more detailed manner is the personal import of these questions.

The Holy Spirit as Person

Building on the doctrine of relations, the quest for a deeper appreciation of the sense in which the Spirit can be called personal love leads to a third pillar of Aquinas's trinitarian theology in general and his pneumatology in particular, the doctrine of the divine persons.[57] The importance of this doctrine is indicated by the fact that in addition to what Aquinas has said about the divine persons so far, the subject as a whole represents the major heading in the

55. Ibid., I, q. 28, a. 2c.

56. Ibid.

57. Ibid. Cf. Emery, "The Doctrine of the Trinity," 53.

remainder of his treatise on God (qq. 29–43). Within this rather lengthy section of the *prima pars*, Aquinas's account can be divided into three subsections. First, he discusses the divine persons according to what is common to them (qq. 29–32). Second, he then considers what is proper to each person (qq. 33–38). Third and finally, he proceeds to treat the three persons according to their relationships (qq. 39–43).[58] These sections present some of the central themes that will be pursued later in this study.[59]

Aquinas begins his general consideration of the divine persons with a definition. Following Boethius, Aquinas defines a person as "an individual substance of a rational nature" (*persona est rationalis naturae individua substantia*).[60] A person is characterized by three marks. The first is individuality, according to which a person is distinct from other things. The second mark of a person is substance, so that a person is rightly understood as an existing subject in the genus of substance. Third, a person possesses intellect and will, which means that a person is capable of freely thinking and acting. While it can be said of creatures who are individual substances of a rational nature, the term "person" is applied to God "in a more excellent way" because God is the supreme self-subsisting being and the most perfectly intelligent being.[61] In reference to God, this term signifies both relation and the divine essence. To be precise, a divine person signifies "a relation as subsisting" (*relationem ut subsistentem*) or "the relation through the mode of substance, which is a hypostasis."[62] Again, in God relation is identical with the divine essence itself.[63] Because of this, Aquinas's conception of a divine person as subsisting relation affirms the essential unity of the triune

58. This schematization is based on the work of Emery (*Trinity in Aquinas*, 136).

59. For example, the notion of the Spirit as the mutual love of the Father and the Son (q. 37, a. 2) will serve as the focus of chapter 4. Also, the mission of the divine persons (q. 43) will figure prominently in chapter 5, which explores some of the soteriological implications of the Holy Spirit as love.

60. *ST*, I, q. 29, prologue to a. 1; cf. Boethius, *De duabus naturis*, ch. 3.

61. *ST*, I, q. 29, a. 3 ad 1.

62. Ibid., I, q. 29, a. 4c.

63. Ibid., I, q. 28, a. 2c.

God. The three persons of the Trinity, who are distinguished by way of relation, subsist as one in the unity of the divine essence.[64]

Aquinas's teaching that a divine person signifies a subsisting relation has important implications for conceiving the Holy Spirit as love. As the third person of the Trinity, the Holy Spirit signifies a relation that subsists in God. This relation is specifically one of love, following from the procession of love by way of the will. Therefore the relation that results from this particular procession can actually be said to constitute the person of the Holy Spirit in so far as it is precisely the Spirit who proceeds by way of the will as love. Or in other words, the Holy Spirit, who is love proceeding, is *in se* a relation subsisting in God.

In all these ways, by positing love as a name proper to the Holy Spirit Aquinas draws from the doctrines of processions, relations, and persons that he had set forth earlier in the *Summa* and elsewhere. Essential to this first phase of his *amor*-centered pneumatology is the claim that an understanding of the Spirit's procession enables one to conceive a relation that subsists in God, the very relation that the Holy Spirit, as personal love, is. Emery helpfully identifies this initial move that Aquinas makes in his teaching on the Spirit as love.[65] Now that the doctrines of processions, relations, and persons have been introduced, we are ready to expand and deepen the analysis. Tracing Aquinas's argument in greater detail will make it possible not only to elaborate on Emery's observation but also, and thereby, to investigate in a more comprehensive way Aquinas's account of the Holy Spirit as personal love, with particular attention to the idea of immanent procession in God.

The Person of the Holy Spirit: Love Proceeding

Aquinas seeks to penetrate the mystery of the Spirit's procession and personal property as love by both drawing from his doctrine of

64. Ibid. Cf. Emery, "The Doctrine of the Trinity," 55.

65. Emery, *The Trinitarian Theology of Saint Thomas Aquinas*, 236.

the Word and the Son's procession, in one sense, and carefully distinguishing that doctrine from his doctrine of love and the Spirit's procession in another sense. Building on the doctrines of divine processions, relations, and persons that serve as the basis of Aquinas's trinitarian theology as a whole, additional attentiveness to the nuances of this approach elicits key aspects of the doctrine of love and the corresponding procession. The name "Word" (*verbum*) can be said of God personally (though not essentially) because it signifies an emanation of the intellect. Since the person who proceeds in God by way of emanation is the Son, the title "Word" is attributed specifically to the Son, of whom it designates a personal property. In this procession his personal distinction from the Father, and from the Holy Spirit, is made known.[66]

What is crucial for the purpose at hand is that Aquinas uses the concept of love (*amor*) in an analogous way to explain how the procession and personal property of the Spirit should be conceived. The word "*amor*" in God has two meanings: the essential love common among the three persons and the personal love identified specifically with the Holy Spirit.[67] Taken essentially, *amor* denotes the single divine love shared essentially by the Father, the Son, and the Holy Spirit. Taken personally, *amor* is the proper name of the Holy Spirit.

Yet the question arises again as to exactly how love, an essential term, can be applied to the Spirit personally in a distinctive manner. For Aquinas, the answer is found through a critical analysis of what he has said about the Son. The Spirit's personal name of love is conceived of in a way comparable to the Son's name of Word. As through the act of understanding there results in the one who understands a conception of the object understood (a conception called a word), so when anyone loves an object a certain impression (*impressio*) results of the thing loved in the affection of the lover.[68] On account of this *impressio*, the object loved is in the lover, as the

66. *ST*, I, q. 34, a. 2 c, ad 3.
67. Ibid., I, q. 37, a. 1c, ad 4.
68. Ibid., I, q. 37, a. 1c.

thing understood is in the one who understands. Aquinas describes such an impression as an affection for (*affectio*), an impulse toward (*impulsio*), and an attraction (*attractio*) to the beloved.[69]

An understanding of this impression, affection, or impulse of love sheds light on the personal property of the Holy Spirit because the Holy Spirit is love proceeding from the Father and the Son. In Emery's felicitous phrase, the relative property of the Spirit as this impression or affection of love "verifies the presence of a 'God beloved in God who loves' and it is this which creates a window through which to glimpse the Holy Spirit."[70] That is, the doctrine of love teaches that God is in himself as the beloved is in the lover, just as the doctrine of the Word teaches that God is in himself as the object known is in the knower. In the *Compendium theologiae* Aquinas's explanation of this notion of indwelling, specifically concerning love as a *proprium* of the Holy Spirit, is instructive: "The lover is, in some way, moved by the beloved with a certain inward movement. Therefore, since a mover is in contact with the object moved, the beloved must be intrinsic to the lover."[71] The act of loving, Aquinas goes on to say, takes place "according to a certain movement produced in the lover by the beloved" by which the lover is drawn to the beloved (*amatum enim trahit ad seipsum amantem*).[72] Elsewhere Aquinas has established that the way in which God is in himself, as the object known is in the one who knows, is expressed by the person of the Son, who is the Word of God. Similarly, and directly to the point here, the way in which God is in himself, as the beloved is in the lover, is brought about by acknowledging in God a spirit, indeed the Holy Spirit. That same Spirit, as the love of God proceeding, subsists in the divine essence just as the Father and the Son do.[73] The procession by way of the will thus serves to

69. Ibid.

70. Emery, "The Doctrine of the Trinity," 58.

71. *Compendium theologiae*, cap. 45, in vol. 42, *Opera omnia*, Leonine edition, Cura et studio fratrum praedicatorum (Rome and Paris: 1882–present).

72. Ibid., cap. 46.

73. Ibid.; cf. cap. 48 on love in God being substantial and not accidental.

demonstrate the personal relative property of the Holy Spirit while also affirming the unity of the divine essence that is the basis of this procession, and the procession by way of the intellect, in God.

The imprint of love as Aquinas understands it is related to how he describes the concept of love in general and the object of love in particular. Concerning the concept of love in general, there appears to be some development over time in how Aquinas conceives of love with regard to the person of the Holy Spirit. H. F. Dondaine identifies two ways of presenting the Holy Spirit in Aquinas. One is as the friendship or mutual love of the Father and the Son, and the other is as the love that God has for God's divine goodness. According to Dondaine, in accounting for the procession of the Holy Spirit Aquinas moves throughout the course of his writings away from the first to the second, so that he ultimately identifies God's essential love for God's own goodness, instead of the mutual love of the Father and the Son, as the principle of the Spirit's procession. Avoiding the danger of anthropomorphism, Aquinas prefers to introduce the procession of the third person by using the second of these approaches rather than the first.[74] Similarly, based on a close comparison of his treatment of the Holy Spirit's procession in the *Scriptum* with the subsequent account in the *Summa*, Albertus Krapiec detects a change in Aquinas's concept of love. He points out that in the *Scriptum* Aquinas conceives of love mostly in terms of the lover and the beloved, as in the *sed contra* to the question of whether the Holy Spirit is the love that the Father has toward the Son:[75] "All love proceeds from the lover into the beloved. But the Holy Spirit is love, as was said above [a. 1 ad 4]. Therefore, it seems that, since the Father loves the Son and the converse, the Holy Spir-

74. Dondaine, "Saint Thomas et la Procession du Saint-Esprit," in *Saint Thomas D'Aquin, Somme Théologique, La Trinité*, I (Paris: Desclée & Cie, 1950), 387–409, in particular 398–400. Yves Congar endorses Dondaine's findings (*I Believe in the Holy Spirit*, vol. 1, trans. David Smith [New York: The Seabury Press, 1983], 90; 91, fns. 14 and 15).

75. Or "into" (*utrum Spiritus Sanctus sit amor quem habet Pater in Filium* [*In I Sent.*, d. 10, q. 1, a. 2 sc]).

it is the love of the Father into the Son and the converse."[76] In the *Summa*, however, while the language of beloved and lover is not absent, Aquinas typically discusses love in relation to the will's desire for the good.[77] According to Krapiec, this change helps to explain the nuanced explanations of the procession of the Holy Spirit that are found in these two works. Whereas in the *Scriptum* Aquinas generally describes the Holy Spirit's procession as the mutual love of the Father and the Son, in the *Summa* there is more emphasis on the Holy Spirit's procession as a procession from the Father's will for or love of the divine goodness.[78] With this subtle shift, Aquinas develops a theme that has a crucial bearing on his understanding of the object of love, particularly as he describes it in the *Summa*.

Prima facie, however, such a move might seem to belie the implicit order in Aquinas's account of the Holy Spirit as love that Torrell and Emery have detected: the procession of the imprint of love that comes about in the will of the lover (phase one) and the Holy Spirit as the mutual love of the Father and the Son (phase two).[79] Since the works of Torrell and Emery on this point have helped to determine the order of the themes addressed in the present inquiry, the question must be taken seriously as to whether the order should

76. Ibid. In the *corpus* of the same article, Aquinas speaks again of the beloved and the lover, the former as "that in which love has its term" (*amatum ... sit id in quod terminator amor*) and the latter as "that from which love goes out" (*amans a quo exit amor*). Aquinas concludes that "because the Father loves the Son, the Holy Spirit can be called the love of the Father into the Son, and because the Son loves the Father, he can be called the love of the Son into the Father" (ibid., c.). Cf. d. 32, q. 1, a. 1 where Aquinas explains the sense in which it is correct to say that the Father loves the Son by the Holy Spirit, and vice versa, namely in so far as the Holy Spirit proceeds from the Father and the Son as love. In passages like these, Aquinas sets forth his understanding of love primarily in terms of the lover and the beloved.

77. Pertinent passages such as q. 20 (God's love) and q. 6 (the goodness of God) will be explored below.

78. Albertus Krapiec, "Inquisitio circa Divi Thomae doctrinam de Spiritu Sancto prout Amore," *Divus Thomas* 27 (1950): 474–95.

79. Torrell, *Saint Thomas Aquinas*, vol. 2: *Spiritual Master*, 184ff.; cf. Emery, *The Trinitarian Theology of Saint Thomas Aquinas*, 236–37.

be reversed. If Aquinas begins his own reflection on the Holy Spirit as love by characterizing the Spirit mostly in terms of mutual love proceeding, as in the *Scriptum*, and later describes the procession of the Spirit based on the Father's love of the divine goodness, as in the *Summa*, then do Torrell and Emery (and does this account) have it backwards? Should not the first phase in Aquinas's exposition of the Holy Spirit as love be identified as the problem of mutual love and the second phase as that of love's specific object and its corresponding imprint in the will of the lover? In a strict chronological sense it would perhaps seem so, as that is the order in which Aquinas treats matters, beginning with his earlier account in the *Scriptum* (where the entry point to the discussion is the concept of mutual love) and then leading to his later work in the *Summa* (where the initial focus is on love's object and imprint).

Yet Aquinas does not present two partial accounts in these sources, as if the *Scriptum* somehow contained the only first phase, the *Summa* contained only the second, and the two needed to be combined in order to make an integrated whole. Rather these are two accounts of the same specific issue, and while each can complement the other, each stands on its own as a separate text. Thus it is quite illuminating to trace the development in Aquinas's thinking along the lines proposed by Dondaine, Krapiec, and others. Moreover, recognizing the unique character of the *Summa*—Aquinas's *magnum opus*—allows one to discern the place of particular prominence that it occupies in his entire corpus. There Aquinas puts forward his mature treatment of the issue at hand, and however compressed it may be, his account in the *Summa* deserves a kind of interpretive priority vis-à-vis the *Scriptum* in so far as the *Summa* contains his most developed thought. On that basis, the order of themes set forth by Torrell and Emery, and followed here, can be justified. By beginning question thirty-seven of the *prima pars* with particular attention to the imprint of love that arises in the lover's will, Aquinas clarifies the order of themes that he addresses in his mature thought on the person of the Holy Spirit as love. A discussion of the imprint of love lays the foundation for an account of the Holy Spirit as the mutual love of the Father and the Son. While that point will be developed in chapter 4, what remains to be explored in more detail now is the notion of love's imprint on the will of the lover and its relation to the object of love.

In thinking about the procession of the Holy Spirit, Aquinas observes that the act of loving brings about an imprint of the object loved in the will of the lover. Therefore when anyone loves an object "a certain impression results, so to speak, of the object loved in the affection of the lover."[80] On the basis of the impression produced by God's love for the divine goodness—the Father's love for the Son being rooted in his love for his own goodness—the beloved (the Son) is said to abide in the lover (the Father) in a similar way as the object understood is in the one who understands. This point was introduced earlier in the initial reflection on the nature of the Spirit's procession, and the observation was made that Aquinas seeks to understand this procession by appealing to his prior account regarding the procession of the Son. Now the idea of love's imprint finds deeper resonance in light of the insights gleaned from the doctrines of divine processions, relations, and persons. Distinction among the three trinitarian persons in God is possible only by relation of origin as made manifest in the two divine processions, that of the Son from the Father by way of the intellect and that of the Spirit from the Father and the Son by way of the will. The person of the Holy Spirit proceeding as love assumes the idea of relation in a twofold sense. First, it assumes the relation of the lover to the object loved. This relation is expressed by two terms for loving, *diligere* and *amare*. Second, the Spirit's procession as love also presupposes the relation of the impression or affection of the object loved on the principle of that impression and vice versa. Such an impression or impulse of love is produced in the lover by the fact that he or she loves, as Aquinas indicates in his earlier point about indwelling: the

80. *ST*, I, q. 37, a. 1c.

act of loving gives rise to a certain impression of the beloved in the lover's affection, on account of which the beloved is actually said to be in the lover.

Here again, however, the limitations of human language create a problem that Aquinas must address. Whereas the terms *diligere* and *amare* denote the relationship of the lover to the object loved, there simply are no words devised to express the corelationship between the impression or affection of the object loved and the principle of that impression. Aquinas's solution is to use the closest available terms, love (*amor*) and dilection (*dilectio*), to indicate those relationships that in a sense have no proper names due to the poverty of human vocabulary. Yet that same vocabulary, impoverished as it is, can still serve a vital theological purpose. In and by God's own Word, our feeble words become capable of penetrating the mystery of God's being. This extension of language's reach in Christ is one implication of Aquinas's appeal to the doctrine of the Word to understand the doctrine of love. Regarding the latter of these doctrines, as Aquinas points out, a distinction needs to be made between the two kinds of relations that the concept of love can be used to signify and the corresponding sense of love that is implied. First, in reference to the relation of the lover to the object loved, "love" and "to love" are said of the essence, which is to say that love is used essentially. Theologically speaking, in this sense love denotes the divine essence common to the Father, the Son, and the Holy Spirit. Second, Aquinas also uses these words to express the corelationship between the impression of the object loved and its principle; in that sense love is the name of the person of the Holy Spirit, who is love proceeding, and "to love" is understood notionally, as denoting the spiration of the love proceeding. The theological meaning of love understood in this way is deeply pneumatological, signifying in particular the person of the Holy Spirit who proceeds as love. The ideas of essential love and love as a notional term are integrally related to the imprint of love in Aquinas's exposition of the procession of the Holy Spirit, and they are also important for understanding the nuances of Aquinas's discussion of the object of love.[81]

Love in the first of these two senses, essential love, emerges in the *Summa* as a particularly prominent theme in Aquinas's thought. After taking as his point of departure the notion of love's imprint that comes about in the will of the lover, Aquinas proceeds in question thirty-seven to apply this principle to his understanding of God. When he does make this theological application, he shows that the imprint of love deals fundamentally with God's love for the divine goodness. That is because in God the imprint of love arises precisely from God's love for himself, which makes the divine goodness, in some sense, both the principle and the object of love in God. In asserting that to be the case, Aquinas integrates into his trinitarian theology the conclusions reached in two earlier questions in the *prima pars*, question twenty on God's love and question six on God's goodness.

With question twenty, Thomas begins his consideration of those things pertaining to the will of God by focusing on the topic of God's love. Aquinas locates love in the will and further states that to love anything is to will good to that thing. Since will is in God, it follows that love must be attributed to God as well.[82] The operative definition of love as a verb—to will good to someone or something—leads Aquinas to address the good that God wills for himself and the good that God wills for rational creatures. Each point is predicated on a certain association between God and goodness.

Aquinas establishes this connection earlier in question six on the goodness of God, where he shows that God is in his very essence the greatest good. Good is rightly attributed to God in so far as God is the first cause from whom all life, and every desired perfection, flows.[83] God's essential love for himself is based on God's essential

81. *ST*, I, q. 37, a. 1c.

82. Ibid., I, q. 20, a. 1c. Aquinas points out that there is will in God as there is intellect in ibid., I, q. 19, a. 1c.

83. Ibid., I, q. 6, a. 1c, ad 2.

goodness, a goodness that Aquinas describes in terms of perfection. In the strict sense, perfection by one's own essence belongs only to God, for in God alone is essence also existence, in God alone there are no accidents, and God alone is not directed to anything else as an end but is himself the last end of all things. Since only God has every kind of perfection by God's own essence, God alone is good essentially.[84]

In question twenty, Aquinas applies this insight about God's essential goodness to his discussion of God's love. The good that God wills for himself is none other than God's own being, as God is essentially good.[85] It is in loving himself that God wills for himself the greatest good, which is the divine essence that God *in se* is. Thus God is perfectly happy in himself as God, his essential goodness loved as the good of all goods. God's love for Christ illustrates the irreducibly theological nature of goodness and love. As Aquinas makes explicit, God loves Christ more than God loves not only the human race but also the entire world. It is therefore fitting that God would will for Christ a great good in giving him the name that is in keeping with his true divinity, a name that is indeed above every name (cf. Phil 2:9–11).[86] While the Father and the Son are distinct persons, they are united, with the Holy Spirit, through their one essence; and according to this unity, God's life is marked by essential love among Father, Son, and Holy Spirit.[87] Most of all God loves himself, as God is supremely good and thus the greatest good that God could ever will for himself or for anyone or anything else.

Aquinas states further that God also loves rational creatures, and even all existing things, in so far as they exist, since God has made them and sustains them in existence. Rational creatures are capable of a higher good than other existing things can attain, and they can

84. Ibid., I, q. 6, a. 3c.

85. Ibid., I, q. 20, a. 1 ad 3; cf. I, q. 6, a. 3c.

86. Aquinas uses God's love for Christ as an example of how God always loves the better things more (ibid., I, q. 20, a. 4 ad 1).

87. Cf. *In I Sent.*, d. 10, q. 1, a. 5 ad 1.

find their fulfillment and perfection in God through a participation, in a way that is suited to their created nature, in the creator God's own life and love. Aquinas attributes the cause of goodness in things to God, and specifically to God's love or God's will.[88] The good that God wills for rational creatures is not the divine essence per se.[89] Nevertheless, it is a genuine good that makes possible the ultimate perfection of those creatures in God. Indeed the good willed by God for rational creatures must be understood in light of God's love for the divine goodness, which is to say God's love for himself. That is because Aquinas's explanation of the love of God *ad extra* is rooted in the deep *ad intra* association between God and goodness established already.[90] Therefore, whether love is considered as God's love for himself or as God's love for others, in each case there is a clear connection between God and goodness. From God's perspective, it seems, what makes something lovable is its likeness to God, for God alone is *in se* the supreme good whose love infuses and creates goodness in creatures.[91]

While love in an essential sense denotes the divine essence that is God's goodness and thus the object of God's own love, love understood as a notional term signifies the spiration of the love proceeding.[92] In this way, the verb "to love" is like "to speak" or "to beget." Precision about such matters is rather difficult but essential, and Aquinas provides a characteristically lucid and concise explanation in question thirty-seven. It belongs to the Son neither to produce a word nor to beget, though as the Word proceeding he understands and is himself begotten; similarly, although the Holy Spirit loves in an essential sense, it does not belong to the Spirit to spirate

88. *ST*, I, q. 20, a. 2c and q. 20, a. 4 ad 5, respectively.

89. Ibid., I, q. 20, a. 3 ad 2.

90. Ibid., I, q. 20, a. 4c.

91. Ibid., I, q. 20, a. 2c.

92. This brief initial consideration of love as a notional term, which serves to prefigure the more detailed discussion in chapter 4 (on the Holy Spirit as the mutual love of the Father and the Son), is pertinent now because it helps explain the idea of love in a personal sense, which has been the orienting concern of the present chapter.

love, which is to take love as a notional term. In other words, the Spirit loves essentially as love proceeding but not notionally as the one from whom love proceeds.[93] The idea of love as a notional term poses a challenge for Aquinas, who must make sense of how the act of love within God's own life takes place by virtue of what the act produces. While a fuller account of this challenge and his response will be presented in the following chapter, by way of summary Aquinas thinks that he has found a suitable illustration from creatures in the production of a flower. As a tree is said to flower by the very flowers it produces, so the Father and Son are said to love each other by the Holy Spirit who is love proceeding.[94] In addition to anticipating the next stage of his exposition of the Holy Spirit as love—the theme of mutual love—Aquinas's creaturely analogy points to the connection between love as a notional term and the inward procession of the Holy Spirit. One reason for the importance of that connection is the way in which it serves to illumine love as a *proprium* of the Holy Spirit, who is love in person. Since love taken notionally in God means to spirate love, as to flower is to produce flowers, to love denotes the production of a divine person—the Holy Spirit. It also signifies the person produced by way of love and the relation between love and the object loved.[95]

Each of these two ways in which "to love" can be understood in God, essentially and notionally, contains a certain nuance that helps elucidate the sense in which the Holy Spirit is love in person. In the Holy Spirit's immanent procession as love, the Spirit proceeds precisely as the love of God's own goodness by which God loves himself and all that is.[96] This assertion reflects the idea of essential love in God, according to which the trinitarian persons love one another by their common, singular, divine goodness that is their common, singular, divine essence; and they love creatures in as much as those

93. *ST*, I, q. 37, a. 1 ad 4.

94. Ibid., I, q. 37, a. 2c.

95. Ibid., I, q. 37, a. 2 ad 3; cf. I, q. 37, a. 1 ad 2.

96. Cf. ibid., I, q. 37, a. 2 ad 3.

creatures exist and are thus called good from the divine goodness, and from the similitude of the divine goodness belonging to them.[97] Moreover, as shown particularly by love when it is taken notionally, the Holy Spirit is love "spirated" or breathed forth by the Father and the Son from whom the Spirit proceeds within God's own being as their common love for one another. God's goodness serves as the principle of God's love for himself (essential love in God), which gives rise to the imprint of love in God's will and the corresponding immanent procession of the Holy Spirit whom the Father and the Son breathe forth (notional love in God) as love in person.

What is not yet clear, however, is how an imprint in the lover can be the sort of thing that comes forth from the lover and is irreducibly distinct from the lover, especially in God. Here again, an important concept is easier to grasp in the case of the Son's procession than in the case of the Spirit's spiration. Whereas the idea of a mental word proceeding by way of the intellect within God can, without too much difficulty, be distinguished from God the Father as precisely the person of the Son, the matter is not quite as straightforward with regard to the imprint of love and the Spirit's procession as love by way of the will. On this precise point, though, Aquinas's concept of the Spirit as love in person or personal love provides some clarity when it is considered both alongside and as distinct from his related ideas of essential love and notional love. Essential love denotes God's love for the divine essence—that is, God's love for himself—and is common to all three persons of the Trinity while appropriated to the Holy Spirit. Love understood in this sense secures the idea of the imprint in the will of the lover coming forth from the lover, since the principle of the imprint of love in the will of God is God's own essence. Meanwhile, notional love accounts for the sense in which the Holy Spirit is the common spiration of the Father and the Son, and thus, specifically with regard to the Spirit, allows for distinction by way of relations of origin, with the Spirit being substantially one with but

97. Ibid., I, q. 6, a. 4c.

somehow other than the Father and the Son from whom this third person of the Trinity proceeds. In this way, notional love provides the conceptual clarity necessary for affirming that the Holy Spirit is irreducibly distinct from the Father and the Son.

What remains is to integrate these two insights concerning the imprint's coming forth and its distinctiveness in a manner as coherent as human language, with its inherent limitations, allows; and a sufficient (even if far from absolute) measure of coherence can be inferred from the notion of personal love. Aquinas's identification of the Holy Spirit as love in person assumes both the imprint's procession and its distinctiveness, thereby meeting the two conditions required for the imprint of love. To say that the Holy Spirit proceeds as love in person implies, first of all, that the procession of the imprint of love comes about in the will of the lover in the act of loving, for which reason the Spirit's procession is a procession from the Father's will for, or love of, God's essential goodness (essential love). Second, an understanding of personal love highlights the distinction that can be accounted for by notional love: love is a *proprium* of the Holy Spirit in particular, and not of the Father or the Son, because it is the Holy Spirit who proceeds as love, and the Spirit does so precisely from the Father and the Son in their spiration of love for one another (notional love).

Finally, it is possible to bring together, in a succinct statement, the three ways in which love in God can be understood. The imprint on God's will created by God's love for his own goodness (essential love) is a term of procession in the act of loving; as such, it leads to the immanent procession of love that is the common spiration of the Father and the Son (notional love), namely, the very person of the Holy Spirit whose *proprium* is love (personal love).[98]

98. In the *Scriptum*, Aquinas identifies three ways in which love in God can be understood (essentially, personally, and notionally) and describes the distinctiveness of each as well as the interrelation among the three as follows: "secundum ergo quod est essentiale, est commune tribus, sed appropriator spiritui sancto; ut cum dicitur, deus caritas est, 1 joan. 4, 16; secundum autem quod est personale, est proprium

CONCLUSION

This chapter has focused on the first phase of Aquinas's account of the Holy Spirit as love, the theme of the Holy Spirit as love in person. Situating his pnuematology in its proper trinitarian context, Thomas shows in question thirty-seven of the *prima pars*, as well as elsewhere in the *Summa* and in some of his other writings, that grasping the Spirit's immanent procession makes it possible to conceive of a relationship subsisting within the triune God. That relationship is none other than the person of the Holy Spirit, who proceeds by way of the will within God and whose being is substantially the same as that of the principle of the procession. The Holy Spirit is love in person or personal love precisely as divine love proceeding. In this way, the Spirit is *in se* a subsistent relation that is produced by an immanent procession and characterized by love—indeed, the very love with which the Father and the Son love one another, which is the second major theme in Aquinas's *amor*-centered pneumatology.

---

spiritus sancti; et dicitur, quod spiritus sanctus procedit ut amor; secundum autem quod est notionale, est quaedam relation vel notion communis patri et filio, quae etiam dicitur communis spiratio; et hoc modo significatur amor in hoc verbo diligunt: cum dicitur, pater et filius diligunt se spiritu sancto" (*In I Sent.*, d. 10, q. 1, a. 1 ad 4).

Four

AQUINAS ON THE HOLY SPIRIT AS MUTUAL LOVE

As shown in the previous chapter, Aquinas's account of the Holy Spirit as personal love touches at various points upon the doctrine of mutual love, that is, the love by which the Father and Son love one another. Mutual love is a theme that holds significance not only for the task of tracing the subtleties of Aquinas's technical pneumatology but also for the larger scope of this project on the Christian life in Aquinas and Wesley. What is at stake here in regard to the former is the notion of personal communion within God and a deeper understanding of love as a *proprium* of the Spirit, since the same person who proceeds as love in God and who is indeed love in person by relation of origin to the Father and the Son is also their mutual love.

In regard to the overall shape of this study, what is at stake is the affirmation of both personal communion within God and the human person's communion with God by grace in the life of faith. The latter in particular is crucial for an analysis of the Holy Spirit and the Christian life that is in keeping with the insights of Aquinas and Wesley, for whom in distinctive and yet basically complementary ways the idea of our genuine sharing in God's life through the Spirit is central. Aquinas's understanding of the Holy Spirit as mutual love prepares the way for a full affirmation of this point in so far as it implies in secondary fashion God's relation to human persons, whom God loves with the same love with which the Father loves himself and the Son.[1] Aquinas's inquiry into the Spirit as mutual love thus further solidifies the trinitarian foundation of his reflections on the person and work of the Spirit. It is this foundation that the *doctor communis* goes on to use as a basis for his account of the Christian life, an account that has noteworthy implications not only for a greater appreciation of the Spirit as love in Aquinas's thought but also, it will be argued, for Methodists in their quest for a more theological understanding of sanctification.[2]

In a way that makes clear the relevance for a study such as this, Torrell offers a concise explanation of the significance of the Holy Spirit as the bond of love, given the connection between this pneumatological affirmation and the doctrine of processions in Aquinas's speculative theology: "If we suppress in our minds this communion of the Father and the Son, we also suppress the procession of the Holy Spirit, for these two realities are interdependent. We can, then, neither think of the distinction of the Third Person, nor take into account the work that he achieves in ecclesial communion."[3] Part of that work relates to the Spirit's role as the source of holiness and unity for the members of Christ's body, which is a topic of mutual interest to Aquinas and Wesley as we will see. Because of the wider implications of this issue, to return to the subtleties of the argument advanced by Aquinas on the Spirit as love is not to delay needlessly a more direct pairing of Aquinas and Wesley (and their theologi-

1. "The Father loves not only the Son, but also himself and us by the Holy Spirit" (*ST*, I, q. 37, a. 2 ad 3).

2. This argument will be advanced in chapter 6 below.

3. Jean-Pierre Torrell, OP, *Saint Thomas Aquinas*, vol. 2: *Spiritual Master*, trans. Robert Royal (Washington, D.C.: The Catholic University of America Press, 2003), 187–88.

cal heirs), but rather a way of laying the groundwork for what is to come.

After a consideration of the Holy Spirit as personal love, the love proceeding from the will through which God loves himself, the Holy Spirit as the mutual love of the Father and the Son becomes the focal point of the next stage of Aquinas's inquiry into the personal property of the Holy Spirit. That Aquinas sees a certain relation between personal love and mutual love is suggested by the two articles in question thirty-seven of the *prima pars* of the *Summa.* In question thirty-seven Aquinas considers the name of the Holy Spirit as love understood personally.[4] He then investigates whether the Father and Son love one other by the Holy Spirit.[5] The idea of mutual love thus comes in the second stage of Aquinas's pneumatology. Building on his identification of the Spirit as love proceeding and the prior discussion of the Spirit's *proprium* as love in person, Aquinas goes on to explore the sense in which the Father loves the Son, and vice versa, by the Holy Spirit.

When it comes to Aquinas's teaching on mutual love, even relative consensus among his interpreters has proven quite elusive. In fact, scholars have offered vastly differing interpretations of his writing on the Spirit as the love by whom the Father and the Son love one another. The two main approaches, as we will see, call for a reappraisal of Aquinas on this topic, one that is informed by a close reading of his mature discussion in question thirty-seven of the *Summa.*

THE SPIRIT AS MUTUAL LOVE IN AQUINAS: TWO INTERPRETATIONS

Although Aquinas addresses the idea of mutual love at several points in the pneumatological questions in the *Summa*, scholars are far from unanimous in how they understand the place of this con-

4. *ST*, I, q. 37, a. 1.
5. Ibid., I, q. 37, a. 2.

cept in his thinking as a whole. The question of how best to interpret Aquinas on the Holy Spirit as mutual love has been addressed in two very different ways. Each of these two interpretations raises some compelling points, but in the end a balanced perspective is needed in order to discern the significance and promise of Aquinas's systematic and nuanced approach to this topic, which is critical to how he relates love and the Holy Spirit.

Mutual Love as Minor and Ultimately Unnecessary

One interpretation posits that the theme of mutual love in Aquinas is minor at best, being basically subsidiary to the notion of essential love. Moreover, because of its apparently diminishing importance in the development of Aquinas's work, the argument is advanced that mutual love is ultimately unnecessary in his scheme of thought. Representative of this approach is the work of Maurílio T.-L. Penido.

Penido presents his views on the subject in two articles published in the late 1930s. The first article is "Gloses sur la procession d'amour dans la Trinité."[6] The second article is "A propos de la procession d'amour en Dieu."[7] Penido notes an evolution in Aquinas's thought through a comparison of various texts spanning Aquinas's literary career, including the *Scriptum*,[8] *De potentia*,[9] and the *Summa*.[10] Specifically, Penido detects a shift in the language that Aquinas uses to describe God's inner love, a shift away from the social analogy of Richard of St. Victor and toward the psychological analogy of Augustine and Anselm. Penido argues that the conception of mutual love set forth by Richard of St. Victor is flawed by an overly anthropomorphic tendency that reduces the trinitarian mystery to interpersonal love. Aquinas, however, is able to avoid this tendency, according to Penido, by relegating mutual love to a less prominent

6. *Ephemerides theologicae lovanienses* 14 (1937): 33–68.
7. *Ephemerides theologicae lovanienses* 15 (1938): 338–44.
8. Especially, *In I Sent.*, d. 10, a. 1 ad 4 and a. 5 ad 1.
9. *De potentia*, qq. 9–10.
10. *ST*, I, q. 37.

position and adopting certain features of Anselm's essentialist perspective instead.

As Penido observes, the Holy Spirit as the mutual love of the Father and the Son is a recurring theme in the *Scriptum*. Yet Aquinas does not use the language of mutual love nearly as much in his subsequent writings, which shift the focus to God's essential love for the divine goodness. After a total absence in the *Summa contra Gentiles*, the concept of mutual love reappears in the *Summa*, but only in a subsidiary fashion, now that Aquinas has established that the love between the Father and the Son is simply their own divine essence as love.[11] While Aquinas does not abandon the terminology of mutual love, he downgrades its role considerably in favor of a critical adaptation of an essentialist orientation as found in Anselm.[12] Having been supplanted by the theme of God's essential love for the divine goodness, mutual love is now revealed for what Aquinas has discerned it to be, a secondary and basically inconsequential metaphor that is devoid of any theological substance or meaning.

Penido spells out the implications of his conclusion, both negative and positive, in unambiguous terms. Negatively, he calls for the rejection of any attempt at identifying mutual love as the *ratio* or underlying reason of the spiration of the Holy Spirit. This argument is not without controversy.[13] Positively, he says that the necessary response to his findings is the "transfert, avec saint Thomas, de cette réciprocité sur le plan essentiel, où elle joue un rôle secondaire, dans la procession d'amour en Dieu."[14] The idea of the reciprocal or mutual love between Father and Son must not be made to appear more important than it actually is. Instead, it should be viewed against

11. Maurílio T.-L. Penido, "A propos de la procession d'amour en Dieu," *Ephemerides theologicae lovanienses* 15 (1938): 340–44.

12. E.g., *Monologion*, 50.

13. With this and other contested assertions, Penido has been criticized for undervaluing the theme of mutual love in Aquinas. The criticism of Penido on this point forms the basis of a second interpretation that is described below.

14. Maurílio T.-L. Penido, "Gloses sur la procession d'amour dans la Trinité," *Ephemerides theologicae lovanienses* 14 (1937): 67–68.

the backdrop of essential love, which constitutes Aquinas's preferred theme and provides the driving force behind his argument. The upshot is that mutual love has been eclipsed by essential love and therefore has no work left to do.

This line of reasoning has a certain compelling quality to it, as mutual love generally seems less prominent in Aquinas's later writings than in his earlier ones. The claim that its leading position in the *Scriptum* gradually gives way to a more essentialist orientation, quite possibly under the influence of Anselm, is a plausible explanation. Yet the question of Aquinas's use of sources, which Penido rather suggestively pursues, exceeds the scope of the present inquiry.[15] Here the concern is not so much the sources that Thomas uses, nor how he uses them, but rather the precise conclusions that he reaches specifically in his understanding of mutual love. As explained later, an assessment of Penido yields mixed results, for despite the merits of Penido's historical study a more balanced presentation of Aquinas makes Penido's reading appear somewhat strained. What is particularly noteworthy at this stage is that Penido's characterization of mutual love as a theme of tapering import throughout the course of Aquinas's writings—a theme that figures prominently in the *Scriptum* but is later superseded to the point of uselessness—has exerted such influence that it now constitutes one primary school of interpretation.

Penido represents a position that has itself come under careful

15. Penido notes, for example, the change in Aquinas's use of Richard of St. Victor and Augustine as authorities, on the basis of which he detects a shift in influence and emphasis in Aquinas. Whereas Richard's notion of reciprocal love—labeled a social analogy by others—informs Aquinas's argument in the *corpus* of the articles in the *Scriptum* (e.g., bk. 1, d. 10), with the psychological analogy of Augustine playing only a minor role, Penido finds that in later works the uses of these sources have been inverted. For example, in *De potentia*, q. 9, a. 10, Augustine's psychological analogy comes to the forefront while Richard of St. Victor's influence has diminished somewhat, appearing only in the *sed contra*. Eventually, in the *Summa*, Richard is relegated to the objections (Penido, "Gloses sur la procession d'amour dans la Trinité," 48–68).

scrutiny. By extending the scholarly conversation in rather provocative fashion, it has helped engender another main school of interpretation on the subject of mutual love in Aquinas.

Mutual Love as Central and Singularly Decisive

Whereas the first approach deems mutual love minor and ultimately unnecessary, a second interpretation stresses the significance of the theme in Aquinas's reflections on the Holy Spirit and maintains that it is in fact central to his thought. From such a perspective, the designation of the Holy Spirit as the love between Father and Son, far from being an essentially meaningless vestige of a tradition gone awry, is actually quite important to Aquinas, even seemingly his primary pneumatological concern, and as such singularly decisive—not just in his early writings but in his later thought as well. A major proponent of this position is François Bourassa.

Bourassa has written extensively on the doctrine of the Spirit as mutual love of the Father and the Son.[16] Acknowledging the differences between Anselm and Richard of St. Victor, Bourassa associates Anselm with one strand of Augustine's trinitarian theology, the psychological theory, and Richard with another, the identification of the Holy Spirit as mutual love.[17] Unlike in the first school of

16. As in "Le Saint-Esprit unité d'amour du Père et du Fils," *Sciences ecclésiastiques* 14 (1962): 375–415 (reprinted in *Questions de théologie trinitaire* [Rome: Presses de l'Université Grégorienne, 1970], 59–123); *Questions de théologie trinitaire*, 229–38; "Sur la propriété de l'Esprit, Questions disputées (I)," *Science et Esprit* 28 (1976): 243–64; "Sur la propriété de l'Esprit, Questions disputées (II)," *Science et Esprit* 29 (1977): 23–43; "L'Esprit Saint, 'Communion' du Père et du Fils (I)," *Science et Esprit* 29 (1977): 251–81; "L'Esprit Saint, 'Communion' du Père et du Fils (II)," *Science et Esprit* 30 (1978): 5–37; "Dans la communion de l'Esprit Saint: Étude théologique I," *Science et Esprit* 34 (1982): 31–56; "Dans la communion de l'Esprit Saint: Étude théologique II," *Science et Esprit* 34 (1982): 135–49; and "Dans la communion de l'Esprit Saint: Étude théologique III," *Science et Esprit* 34 (1982): 239–68.

17. After citing Penido, Bourassa contrasts Anselm and Richard in the following way: "En fondant sa théologie trinitaire sur la théorie psychologique, saint Anselme prolonge la théologie augustinienne. Il s'en écarte dans la mesure où il réduit toute la théologie trinitaire à la théorie psychologique, à la différence de Richard,

thought, however, here the avenues of analysis created by Anselm and Richard, while differing in emphasis, are not placed in opposition to one another. In fact, Bourassa views the idea of mutual love from another perspective entirely. His primary concern is twofold, touching on, first, the influence of Augustine on Aquinas and, second, the place of mutual love in Aquinas's own reflection on the person of the Holy Spirit.

Bourassa discerns the imprint of Augustine at various points throughout Aquinas's account. Bourassa's concern to stress the theological continuity between Augustine and Aquinas is reflected in the structure of his own work, for Bourassa uses Augustine as an entry point into the topic of *amor mutuus* and then, from Augustine, moves to the principal texts of Aquinas. At a basic level, such a move can certainly be justified given the undeniable importance of Augustine's writings in the development of Aquinas's doctrine of the Holy Spirit, as well as his trinitarian doctrine as a whole, and Bourassa is by no means unique in beginning a study of Aquinas with reference to Augustine. What is noteworthy about Bourassa's approach, however, is not simply the fact that he cites Augustine in studies that go on to deal chiefly with Aquinas but, rather, the precise manner in which he does so.

Not content with merely a passing reference to Augustine, Bourassa illustrates in a clear and rigorous way the connection between Augustine and Aquinas on the subject of the Holy Spirit as mutual love. Bourassa later shows that Aquinas does more than replicate Augustine's work as Aquinas builds on the insights of Augustine; but in his numerous studies of pneumatology and love, Bourassa's conventional procedure is to provide an extended quotation, or quotations, from Augustine in order to lay the foundation for what follows in Aquinas. For example, he begins what is essentially a four-part study on

qui reprend la thèse augustinienne de l'amour mutual … en ce qu'il y ramène toute la théologie trinitaire a l'exclusion de la théorie psychologique … [et] en assignant comme propriété de l'Esprit le rôle d'ami commun" ("Le Saint-Esprit unité d'amour du Père et du Fils," 378, fn. 11).

the property of the Holy Spirit—that is, what makes the Holy Spirit unique and distinguishes this person of the Trinity from the other two—by quoting, in the first paragraph alone, some twenty-one lines of *De Trinitate* on the doctrine of the Spirit as mutual love of Father and Son and its repercussions for the church.[18] After alluding to diverse developments of this doctrine in medieval theology, Bourassa proceeds to cite Aquinas as one who stands out because of the way in which he constructively synthesizes and advances the Latin tradition as developed and passed on by Augustine.

While Bourassa readily admits that Aquinas's account has been subject to various interpretations among his commentators, he offers a distinctive reading of Aquinas that both illumines his Augustinian roots and addresses, in systematic fashion throughout a series of articles, three central issues pertaining to the association between the Holy Spirit and love: the Holy Spirit as (1) *amor procedens*, as (2) the mutual love of Father and Son, and as (3) a link to their mutual intimacy or as their communion.[19] Bourassa's reflections on these issues are characterized to a considerable degree by the way in which he locates Aquinas squarely within the Augustinian tradition. On that basis, both of the analogies employed by Augustine to consider the person of the Holy Spirit—the psychological analogy of the mind, the word, and love, and the interpersonal analogy likening the Holy Spirit to the communion or *nexus* between Father and Son—can be legitimately utilized in subsequent reflection on the person of the Holy Spirit that is in the spirit of Augustine.[20] The

18. "Sur la propriété de l'Esprit" (I), 243, 244. The quotations come from *De Trinitate*, VI, 7 and XV, 37, respectively.

19. "Sur la propriété de l'Esprit" (I), 252. The four-part series of articles cited above consists of the following studies: "Sur la propriété de l'Esprit: Questions disputées (I)," "Sur la propriété de l'Esprit: Questions disputées (II)," "L'Esprit Saint, 'Communion' du Père et du Fils (I)," and "L'Esprit Saint, 'Communion' du Père et du Fils (II)." Bourassa later adds three more articles, further illustrating the emphasis that he places on the notion of communion: "Dans la communion de l'Esprit Saint: Étude théologique I–III."

20. Augustine uses these approaches, for example, in *De Trinitate*, XIV, 11 (on

interpersonal analogy, which accentuates the themes of communion and reciprocity, lends itself especially well to the kind of study of the Holy Spirit as mutual love that both Augustine and Aquinas conduct. From Bourassa's perspective, while Aquinas does more than repeat Augustine's findings, he does not represent a departure from Augustine but is best understood in keeping with the tradition that he received, a tradition profoundly shaped by the thought of the Bishop of Hippo.

Bourassa not only finds the influence of Augustine on Aquinas to be considerable but also regards Aquinas's work as an extension of the line of inquiry set forth centuries earlier by Augustine. As Bourassa points out, there are numerous texts in Aquinas, whether one consults the *Scriptum,* or later works such as the *Summa,* or his commentary on John, that suggest a kind of Augustinian elaboration, to the effect that the Holy Spirit is properly mutual love because the love that is a *proprium* of the Spirit implies a certain relation of the Father to the Son. This relation is characterized by love, namely, the love that the Father and the Son mutually have for one another.[21]

Along with the difficulty of accounting for love as the very essence and life of the Trinity while also identifying love as a property of the Spirit in particular, Aquinas also inherits from Augustine the proposed solution that, as Bourassa puts it, "les trois Personnes sont amour car l'amour est la substance même de Dieu, mais l'Esprit est proprement l'amour mutuel du Père et du Fils, de même que le Père est amour paternal, et le Fils amour filial."[22] Aquinas sheds

---

the mind remembering, understanding, and loving itself) and VI, 7 (on the Spirit as communion or mutual love of Father and Son).

21. E.g., "The Holy Spirit is said to be the bond (*nexus*) of the Father and Son, in as much as he is Love (*Amor*). Because, since the Father loves himself and the Son with one love, and the Son loves the Father with one love, there is expressed in the Holy Spirit (*importatur in Spiritu Sancto*), as Love, the relation of the Father to the Son, and of the Son to the Father, as that of the lover to the beloved (*ut amantis ad amatum*). But from the fact that the Father and Son mutually love one another, it is proper that this mutual love, the Holy Spirit, proceeds from both" (*ST*, I, q. 37, a. 1 ad 3). This is a passage that will come under closer scrutiny later.

22. "Sur la propriété de l'Esprit" (II), 37. Cf. *De Trinitate*, XV, 37: "Si charitas,

additional light on the solution to this difficulty through his elucidation of the principles of trinitarian theology, to which Bourassa appeals in his exploration of love as the Spirit's personal property. Bourassa repeats the axiom, which is clarified by Aquinas, that the distinctions within God are made according to the relations of origin. Since the Holy Spirit is love proceeding from the Father and the Son, the Spirit's *proprium* of love can be considered, with respect to the Father and the Son, as love for the divine goodness but precisely in terms of an "encounter" (*rencontre*) of paternal love and filial love, so that the Holy Spirit is the mutual love of the Father and the Son as proceeding from both.[23] As a result, Bourassa is able to view the biblical assertion that God is love (1 Jn 4:8, 16) from the perspective of communion, in so far as the Holy Spirit, with regard to the relation of the Father to the Son and vice versa, is their mutual love or the communion of love uniting Father and Son.[24]

In a manner of speaking, then, the seed of mutual love sowed by Augustine bears additional fruit with Aquinas's careful nurture. While the claim that Aquinas's *amor*-based theology of the Holy Spirit builds on Augustine is in itself in no way original to Bourassa, such a claim figures with particular prominence in the work of Bourassa and in the position that he has come to represent. Aquinas is here presented as a skilled interpreter of Augustine, who advances some of Augustine's deepest insights on the Holy Spirit as the bond of love between Father and Son, in his own constructive synthesis.

In addition, from this perspective mutual love is viewed as not merely peripheral but in fact fundamental to Aquinas's concerns. Bourassa makes mutual love the main focus of his scholarship, both historical and constructive, on the Spirit as communion. That

qua Pater diligit Filium, et Patrem diligit Filius, ineffabiliter cummunionem demonstrat amborum, quid convenientius quam ut ille dicatur charitas proprie, qui Spiritus est communis ambobus?" Cf. Ibid., VI, 7, where Augustine, while affirming that the Spirit has the same unity and equality of substance as the Father and the Son, describes the Holy Spirit as the very communion of the Father and the Son.

23. "Sur la propriété de l'Esprit" (II), 37.

24. Ibid.

mutual love in Aquinas's pneumatology is a fruitful area of study is suggested by the extended inquiry conducted by Bourassa. With no less than six substantive articles exploring a pneumatology of communion, each of which draws heavily from Aquinas, Bourassa finds the notion of mutual love in Aquinas to be a fertile theme worthy of careful consideration. Using it as his point of entry into Aquinas, he takes it to be central to Aquinas's pneumatology:

> non seulement la théologie constante et définitive de saint Thomas reconnaît comme étant la propriété personnelle de l'Esprit-Saint d'être le lien d'unité du Père et du Fils, comme leur mutual Amour, mais le progrès même de cette théologie tend plutôt vers une mise en valeur de ce caractère personnel et interpersonnel de l'Amour qui est l'Esprit.[25]

Bourassa presents a strong case that contrary to the claims of Penido and others, this image is more than a theologically vacuous metaphor, but actually contributes to a deeper understanding of the Spirit's person and work. As Bourassa shows, it is quite capable of sustaining further study, and opens up promising avenues for additional research in terms of both love in the Trinity, concerning the personal and interpersonal nature of the love that the Holy Spirit is, and the Trinity's love in the world, as in the grounds for human union with God through the Spirit.[26]

While a more detailed analysis of this second interpretation will come in the following section, in the context of a fresh assessment of mutual love in Aquinas, already it is possible to outline the main contours of a critical response. The position represented by Bourassa has certain merits but, like the first interpretation, does not adequately account for the nuanced richness of Aquinas's thought. Positively, this second interpretation highlights the textual support from some of Aquinas's later works as to the place of mutual love in Aquinas's mature thought, Augustine's influence and the way in

25. "Le Saint-Esprit unité d'amour du Père et du Fils," 382.

26. On the former, see "Le Saint-Esprit unité d'amour du Père et du Fils." On the latter, see "Dans la communion de l'Esprit Saint: Étude théologique III."

which Aquinas builds on Augustine in his own constructive theology of the Holy Spirit, and the connection between love as personal relation and the Holy Spirit as mutual love. These three points lend credibility to Baroussa's claim that mutual love plays an important role in Aquinas. Ultimately, however, the defense of mutual love in Aquinas seems to have become such a driving concern that the fact can sometimes be obscured that this theme is not treated in isolation in his work but, especially in the *Summa*, comes in a sequence of topics addressing a larger issue (i.e., the immanent procession of the Spirit as love, as discussed below). For this reason, the second approach to Aquinas is not quite sufficient either.

MUTUAL LOVE IN THE *SUMMA*

These two schools of interpretation invite a reappraisal of Aquinas on mutual love, a reading that carves out space between the radically divergent positions described above. The first interpretation posits that the theme of mutual love is effectively unnecessary, and the second attempts to reclaim its perceived centrality and even singular importance in Aquinas's thought. There is ample room, however, for a third alternative, one that affirms the true significance of the theme of mutual love for Aquinas (over against the first interpretation) while also clearly putting it in its proper place (over against the second) in the second phase of Aquinas's pneumatology and as part of a sequence of topics aiming at the greater purpose of disclosing the nature of the Spirit's immanent procession as love. At the same time, of course, the legitimate points made by the main interpretive traditions of Aquinas on this issue should also be taken into consideration. Torrell and Emery have pointed out the need for a more balanced approach, and each has outlined key aspects of such an approach.[27] Following their gestures, the reading that

27. Torrell, *Saint Thomas Aquinas*, vol. 2: *Spiritual Master*, 183–88; Gilles Emery, OP, *The Trinitarian Theology of Saint Thomas Aquinas*, trans. Francesca Aran Murphy (Oxford: Oxford University Press, 2007), 233–45.

will be provided here seeks to call renewed attention to the theme of mutual love with specific reference to its location and function in the *Summa*.

A close reading of Aquinas on mutual love, presented in conversation with these two main perspectives, can be both instructive and constructive in so far as it suggests that this idea represents neither a minor and ultimately disposable metaphor nor the seemingly all-encompassing elucidation of the view that Aquinas inherited from Augustine, but rather a noteworthy supplement to what is in the *Summa* (that is, in Aquinas's mature reflections) the chronologically prior and, especially, theologically decisive exposition of personal love. To substantiate this claim, attention to the nuances of Aquinas on the Holy Spirit as love, and in particular mutual love, is necessary. For that reason, before a deeper engagement with the two main alternatives, we will turn directly to Aquinas's own work, for it is there that the basis for a more balanced view can be discovered and its authenticity confirmed.

An account of mutual love in the *Summa* reveals an implicit logic in Aquinas's presentation of the material. It also serves to identify some of the points of controversy among Aquinas's interpreters. Since the questions on pneumatology in the *Summa* represent Aquinas's mature reflection on the person of the Holy Spirit, we will turn our attention to these questions.

Amor mutuus serves as the focus of question thirty-seven article two, but Aquinas does not hesitate to bring up the subject before then. His prior references to it, such as those in article one, anticipate and help prepare for the subsequent analysis. While article one is mostly devoted to the notion of personal love as covered in chapter 3 above, in this first article of question thirty-seven Aquinas also provides glimpses of an issue that will later occupy him more directly, the related description of the Holy Spirit as the mutual love of the Father and the Son.

Aquinas introduces this topic in the third objection when, commenting on Pseudo-Dionysius, he refers to the unitive force of love, that is, to the sense in which love is the bond between lovers.[28] By definition, however, a bond is not something that proceeds but something that unites; it is a medium between what it joins together (*medium inter ea quae connectit*).[29] Aquinas has already asserted that the Holy Spirit proceeds from the Father and the Son.[30] Now this claim, at least *prima facie*, seems to render problematic the naming of the Spirit as mutual love. It seems unintelligible that the bond of love between the Father and the Son, which is to say their mutual love, could also proceed from them as a result of their love. How can the Spirit be the love of the Father and the Son in the sense of bond if the Spirit proceeds from both?[31]

Aquinas's answer hinges on a distinction between considering the Holy Spirit from the perspective of origin on the one hand and the perspective of relation on the other. The Holy Spirit is called the bond between the Father and the Son in so far as the Spirit is love.[32] As Aquinas has also pointed out earlier, the Spirit is love precisely as the love proceeding.[33] Yet from the perspective of origin the Holy Spirit is not the medium or bond between Father and Son, but the third person of the Trinity who proceeds as love by way of the will in God. This same Spirit, of course, is love in person, which means that the one love with which the Father loves himself and the Son, and with which the Son loves the Father, can be identified in a special way with the person of the Holy Spirit. With love being a *proprium* of the Spirit it is possible to describe the relation between Father and Son as a relation between lover and beloved.[34]

28. Cf. Pseudo-Dionysius, *De divinis nominibus* 4, 15.

29. *ST*, I, q. 37, a. 1 obj. 3.

30. Ibid., I, q. 36, a. 2.

31. Ibid., I, q. 37, a. 1 obj. 3.

32. "The Holy Spirit is said to be the bond of the Father and Son in as much as he is love" (ibid., I, q. 37, a. 1 ad 3).

33. Again, Aquinas explains in the *corpus* that when taken personally love is a name proper to the Holy Spirit: "by 'love' is understood the love proceeding … in that sense 'love' is the name of the person" (ibid., I, q. 37, a. 1c).

34. "since the Father loves himself and the Son with one love, and the Son loves

From the perspective of relation, however, the Holy Spirit is the bond between the two persons, and is this bond precisely as the one proceeding from both.[35] The basis for the Spirit's procession from the Father and the Son is found in the mutual love between the two, and in the specific sense in which the Spirit is this mutual love.

Therefore, Aquinas reasons, the one love with which the Father loves himself and the Father and the Son love one another is the Holy Spirit, who is love in person by relation of origin to the Father and the Son as eternally proceeding from both. In other words, the love uniting the Father and the Son denotes relation—the relation of the Father and the Son as that of the lover and the beloved—while the Spirit as personal love implies procession, specifically the Spirit's own procession as love. The Holy Spirit does not originate as bond but as person, and yet as person the Spirit is called love and thus serves as the bond between the Father and the Son, from whom the Spirit proceeds. In the sense of origin the Spirit is love in person but not love as medium or bond, whereas in the sense of relation the Spirit, as mutual love, is the medium uniting Father and Son in their perfect and eternal communion of love.[36]

This line of reasoning may satisfy the objection as Aquinas sees it, but its meaning has not been so readily apparent to all of his interpreters. Catherine Osborne, for example, asserts that Aquinas's statements point to a seemingly contradictory conclusion: "the Spirit is a *nexus* and not a *nexus*."[37] Can Aquinas have it both ways?

Aquinas's response is sufficiently nuanced that, despite the criti-

---

the Father with one love, there is expressed in the Holy Spirit, as love, the relation of the Father to the Son, and the relation of the Son to the Father, as that of the lover to the beloved" (ibid., I, q. 37, a. 1 ad 3).

35. "in regard to the aforementioned relation [that is, the relation of the Father to the Son and vice versa], the Spirit is the bond between the two persons, as proceeding from both" (ibid.).

36. Ibid.

37. Catherine Osborne, "The *nexus amoris* in Augustine's Trinity," *Studia Patristica* 22 (1987): 309–14, in particular 310. Here Osborne refers to Aquinas's exposition of Augustine and in particular to the reply to objection three in question thirty-seven, article one of the *prima pars*.

cism to the contrary, it appears as though he can. That is because of the distinction between understanding the Holy Spirit in regard to origin and understanding the Spirit in regard to relation that he makes and is able to sustain. Thus Osborne is actually on the right track with her formulation, "the Spirit is a *nexus* and not a *nexus*."[38] Still, some qualification is obviously required. The matter can be resolved through a deeper reading of Aquinas, for the origin-relation juxtaposition that is at the heart of Aquinas's argument here provides the terms necessary for such a qualification. Again, as Aquinas states, concerning origin the Holy Spirit is not the "medium" in and through which the Father and the Son are united but the third person of the Trinity, although concerning relation the Spirit is the bond between the Father and the Son as proceeding from both.[39] Osborne observes that there seems to be an implicit privileging of procession in Aquinas's analysis of love in the Trinity.[40] Other sections of the trinitarian treatise, however, indicate that relation is by no means a neglected theme in Aquinas, but a topic that has a significant connection to that of procession. In question twenty eight, for example, Aquinas clarifies that relations in God can be understood only in regard to the eternal processions in God.[41] For this reason, his later argument in question forty, that persons are distinguished by their relations, also points back to the processions.[42] Moreover, Aquinas takes procession as foundational, as reflected in the order of topics in his treatise on the Trinity, which begins not inconsequentially with question twenty-seven on procession.[43] Aqui-

38. Ibid.

39. "In regard to origin … the Holy Spirit is not the medium, but the third person in the Trinity; whereas in regard to the aforementioned relation [that is, the relation between the Father and the Son] he is the bond between two persons, proceeding from both" (*ST*, I, q. 37, a. 2 ad 3).

40. Osborne, "The *nexus amoris* in Augustine's Trinity," 314.

41. "relations in God can be understood only in regard to those actions according to which there are internal, not external, processions in God" (*ST*, I, q. 28, a. 4c).

42. Ibid., I, q. 40, a. 2; cf. a. 1 on relation as being the same as person.

43. Here Aquinas expounds the two processions in God, that of the Word by way of the intellect and of love by way of the will (ibid., I, q. 27, esp. aa. 3 and 5).

nas thus appears quite consistent in factoring that principle into his account of mutual love in the way that he does. Rather than as a bond uniting Father and Son, the Spirit is distinguished from the other trinitarian persons by relation and by origin in as much as the Spirit proceeds as love. Therefore, in one sense the Spirit is a *nexus* between the Father and the Son, as love proceeding, and in another sense the Spirit is not a *nexus* but rather the third person of the Trinity, love in person.[44]

Already one can begin to see how Aquinas relates three important principles in accounting for love as a *proprium* of the Spirit: the Spirit as (1) love proceeding, as (2) personal love or love in person, and as (3) mutual love. The interconnections among these themes in Aquinas's thought become more explicit in the next article, article two of question thirty-seven.

In this article Aquinas investigates the topic of mutual love in a deeper way by considering first whether, and then precisely how, the Father and the Son love each other by the Holy Spirit. The original sequence of Aquinas's work suggests that he organizes the material in this way for a reason, which a close review brings to light. Aquinas acknowledges from the start that a problem is introduced by the presence of the ablative clause. Grammatically, the ablative case often indicates a cause. If taken that way in this instance, it seems to mean that the Holy Spirit is the principle—the cause—of love to the Father and the Son (*principium diligendi et Patri et Filio*).[45] Yet the Holy Spirit cannot properly be termed a principle of the inner trinitarian love, for if the Spirit were the cause of the Father's love for the Son then the basis of this love would be found in a person other than the Father and the Father would therefore not be its true source.[46] The difficulty raised by the ablative clause has given rise to various positions, and Aquinas briefly outlines five approaches before clarifying his own.[47]

44. Ibid., I, q. 37, a. 1 ad 3.

45. Ibid., I, q. 37, a. 2c.

46. Cf. *In I Sent.*, d. 32, q. 1, aa. 1-2.

47. Aquinas distinguishes among close shades of meaning in the *corpus* of this

The first response cited by Aquinas posits a negative answer to the question, concluding that the Father and the Son do not love one another by the Holy Spirit. Some advocates of this view contend that when Augustine posits that the Father is not wise by the wisdom begotten,[48] he implicitly rules out the principle of mutual love vis-à-vis the Holy Spirit.[49] A second approach is to deem the proposition that the Father and the Son love each other by the Holy Spirit as inaccurate, requiring the qualification that essential love, not the Holy Spirit as mutual love, is really the operative force here. Hence, according to this line of reasoning, in loving the Son by the Holy Spirit the Father loves the Son by an essential love (*amore essentiali*) that is appropriated to the Holy Spirit, not by the Holy Spirit per se.[50] Third, others interpret the ablative as importing a sign so that the Holy Spirit is understood as a sign that the Father loves the Son, in that the Spirit proceeds from them both as love.[51] The fourth position limned by Aquinas assumes that the ablative construction indicates a formal cause. This claim is based on the identification of the Holy Spirit as the love with which the Father and the Son love one another formally, which is to say that the Holy Spirit is like a form or "resource for action" of the mutual love of the Father and the Son, a principle of something in the Father that causes the Father's love for the Son.[52] Fifth, yet another response is that the ablative should be construed as signifying a formal effect instead of a

question, and it is crucial to note the subtle differences between each of these approaches and his own. Therefore each position that he cites will be mentioned in the above text, as a way of leading into the explanation that he goes on to give. The purpose here is not merely to summarize Aquinas, but to trace his logic through a careful account so the precise meaning that he finds in the idea of mutual love can be identified and its importance constructively assessed.

48. See *De Trinitate*, VII, 1–3; *Retractiones*, I, 29.

49. One proponent of this position is Peter of Poitiers, *I Sent.*, 21.

50. E.g., Pseudo-Alexander of Hales, *Summa theologica*, II, 460.

51. E.g., Simon of Tournai, *I Sent.*, n. 45.

52. E.g., William of Auxerre, *Summa aurea*, I, 8, 7. T. C. O'Brien defines a form as "a resource for action" (*Summa Theologiae*, vol. 7: Father, Son and Holy Ghost [1a. 33–43], trans. T. C. O'Brien [London: Blackfriars, 1976] 86, n. e.).

formal cause. With this response, the principle that the Father and the Son love one another by the Holy Spirit does not suggest that the Holy Spirit causes their mutual love, but rather names the Holy Spirit as the formal effect of their love.[53] Aquinas observes that this position comes closer to the truth than any of the others. Even so, when he maintains that the ablative clause in this case imports the relation of formal effect as opposed to these other alternatives, exactly what is he saying?[54]

Aquinas's explanation relies on two crucial distinctions. The first distinction is between understanding the ablative as importing a formal cause, which Aquinas rejects, and understanding it as denoting a formal effect, which he accepts. The second distinction, concerning essential love and notional love, comes into play a bit later. Aquinas must first distinguish between formal cause and formal effect. To do so, he explains that a thing is usually named from its form. The examples that he provides are straightforward: something white is named from the category of whiteness, and a man is named from the category of humanity. Thus, the basis for naming a thing is found in its form. The ablative can be construed in relation to the formal cause of a thing, as in the phrase "this man is clothed with a garment." Strictly speaking the garment is not a form, because the garment is not within the subject but contacting the subject.[55] Nevertheless, the ablative stands in this case for a formal cause, in so far as the man is clothed by the garment that he wears. What makes the man clothed is the fact that he is wearing the garment. In this sense, the ablative clause denotes a formal cause.[56]

53. E.g., Bonaventure, *I Sent.*, d. 32, q. 1, a. 2.

54. *ST*, I, q. 37, a. 2c.

55. Here Aquinas alludes to Aristotelian categories, one of which is "having" (as in being dressed), which does not signify something within a subject but rather something that contacts a subject. See Aristotle, *Categories*, 4 and 15. That the garment is not a form in that sense seems to have no bearing on the point of the illustration, which is to give an example of the ablative as having a relation to the formal cause.

56. *ST*, I, q. 37, a. 2c.

While the ablative can be used to signify a cause, it is not necessarily limited to that usage. This point, however, seems to have been overlooked by advocates of the first position that Aquinas describes, who erroneously conclude that the Father and the Son do not love one another by the Holy Spirit. The ablative in question does not have to be construed causally since it can also denote an action's effect. As Aquinas makes explicit, a thing can be named by what proceeds from it "not only as an agent is from its action but also as from the term itself of the action, which is the effect, when the effect itself is included in the idea of the action" (*non solum sicut agens actione, sed etiam sicut ipso termino actionis, qui est effectus, quando ipse effectus in intellectu actionis includitur*). Of the two creaturely examples provided by Aquinas—fire warming by heating and a tree flowering with the flower—the illustration that he finds particularly useful is the flowering of a tree. Although the flowers are not the form of the tree, but the effects coming forth from it, the analogy can be drawn because in this case the flowers themselves (the effects of the action) are part of the tree's act of flowering (the action). According to Aquinas, the solution to the question follows from such usage of the ablative clause, signifying formal effect over against formal cause.[57]

In teasing out the implications of this insight, Aquinas goes on to differentiate between essential love and notional love, which is his second key distinction here. As a verb, love has two basic meanings in reference to the inner divine life. The first use of the term refers to the sense in which the Father and the Son love one another by their essence. While the Holy Spirit is still love in another sense, Aquinas calls this meaning essential love because the basis for such love is not in the person of the Holy Spirit but in the common divine essence uniting the persons of the Godhead. From this understanding the first four opinions cited above proceed logically, for it is true, to take the second opinion as an example, that the Father loves the Son

57. Ibid.

by their essence, and thus by the essential love appropriated to the Holy Spirit.[58]

The second verbal use of love in God is notional love, which denotes the act of spirating love as in the particular procession of the Spirit by way of the will in God. This procession is fittingly called "spiration" because the Spirit's very name implies "a certain vital movement and impulse, as anyone is described as moved or impelled by love to perform an action."[59] Just as to speak is to produce a word and to flower is to produce flowers, to love in this sense means to produce love. That is, as the act of flowering occurs by virtue of the flowers that it produces, similarly the act of loving occurs by virtue of the love that is produced in that act; in both cases the effect is included in the idea of the action. In reference to God, love in a notional sense means to spirate love, such that God's act of love for his own goodness produces a certain effect that is included in the idea of the action.

The pneumatological import of Aquinas's logic finally becomes clear because now he is able to explain that the Holy Spirit is the term or effect produced by this act. The Spirit proceeds as the love of God's own goodness whereby the Father loves himself and the Son, and the Son loves the Father. As precisely this love, the Spirit, in person, is the bond uniting the Father and the Son: "The Holy Spirit is said to be the bond of the Father and Son, in so far as he is Love; because, since the Father loves himself and the Son with one love, and vice versa, there is expressed in the Holy Spirit, as Love, the relation of the Father to the Son, and vice versa, as that of the lover to the beloved."[60] This, of course, is a principle that Aquinas laid down earlier in article one as a way of explaining personal love by an appeal to mutual love. With the subsequent elaboration of mutual love in article two Aquinas is now able to deepen the inquiry, specifically

58. Ibid.

59. The procession in God that is not generation has no special name but can be called spiration because it is the procession of the Spirit (*ST*, I, q. 27, a. 4 ad 3), which is by way of impulse and movement toward an object (ibid., I, q. 27, a. 4c).

60. Ibid., I, q. 38, a. 1 ad 3.

with the elucidation of the meaning of notional love as importing an effect when the effect itself is included in the idea of the action.[61]

In a notional sense, God's love for himself takes place by virtue of what the act produces—the person of the Holy Spirit, proceeding as love, who is thus *in se* the mutual love of the Father and the Son. To spirate love is to produce love, as to speak is to produce a word and to flower is to produce flowers. Moving once more from creatures to God, Aquinas relates the acts of flowering, speaking, and spirating in the order of human knowledge: as a tree flowers by its flowers, so by his Word or Son the Father speaks himself and his creatures (*Pater dicens Verbo vel Filio se et creaturam*), and likewise by the Holy Spirit or by love proceeding the Father and the Son love each another and us (*Pater et Filius dicuntur diligentes Spiritu Sancto vel Amore procedente et se et nos*).[62] So Aquinas's solution to the problem of mutual love lies in the distinction between essential and notional love and the discerning use and recognition of love in a notional sense in particular.

Aquinas's account of mutual love quite naturally leads him to address the Father's love for himself and for the Son as well as, of course, the Son's love for the Father. Aquinas goes on, however, to mention that the Father loves not only himself and the Son but also us by the Holy Spirit, which is puzzling because there does not appear to be anything inherent in God's love *ad extra* for its inclusion in a discussion of God's inner trinitarian love. Certainly, the potential risk is significant—confusion of the love that is constitutive of God's own life, a perfect and infinite and eternal love, with the notion of participation in this love that is made possible by grace for finite and created beings. Given the enormity of this problem the stakes are high here, and one must proceed carefully. In the third

61. "Now it may happen that something be denominated from that which proceeds from it, not only as an agent is from its action, but also as from the term itself of the action, which is the effect, when the effect itself is included in the idea of the action" (Ibid., I, q. 37, a. 2c).

62. Ibid.

objection, Thomas elaborates on a theme that he mentions in passing in the context of the *corpus*, the claim that "the Father and the Son love each other *and us* by the Holy Spirit, or by Love proceeding."[63] That is, he extends the discussion by referring not only to God's inner love but also to God's love for all creatures, the latter of which he addresses in a deeper way than before. Even though the subject of God's love for creatures certainly is not essential to an investigation into the Spirit as mutual love, Aquinas explores it here nonetheless. How can this move be explained, and is it justifiable?

Obviously, at a very basic level Aquinas refers to God's love for creatures in an objection to the claim that the Father loves the Son by the Holy Spirit. Since this claim is, after all, the principle in question, Aquinas seems justified in referring to those outside of God in so far as the love of God for created beings helps to elucidate the sense in which the Spirit is mutual love. Beyond this self-evident explanation, however, a closer reading of Aquinas suggests that he may intend something more at this stage. To be precise, his reference to God's love *ad extra* prefigures a crucial connection that he later establishes more explicitly, the connection between his dogmatic theology and his soteriology. Even in the midst of a detailed investigation of the Trinity's inner life, it seems that the soteriological implications of God's love are not out of mind for Aquinas. Those implications, which we will reflect on more fully in the next chapter, have a deeply trinitarian and indeed pneumatological thrust as indicated by the content of Aquinas's discussion, specifically his expansion of the scope of inquiry to include rational creatures in this account of the Holy Spirit as love, and as intimated by its location in the pneumatological questions of the *Summa*, which are part of his treatise on the Trinity. In this way, through an investigation of God's love *ad intra*, Thomas does not fail to point out the sense in which rational creatures can be rightly named and God's relation to us implied, in a kind of secondary fashion, based on the Holy Spirit

63. Ibid., I, q. 37, a. 2c, emphasis added.

proceeding as precisely the love of God's own goodness, whereby the Father loves himself and every creature.[64]

The claim that God loves created beings with the same love with which the Father loves himself and the Son may at first raise questions about Aquinas's association of the Holy Spirit and love, but in fact they can serve to illustrate the interior logic of this association. Based in part on the order of his presentation, Aquinas actually preserves the distinction between the Creator and the creature while also accounting for the depth and intimacy of participation in God's life and love that is possible for human persons by grace. When love is taken in an essential sense, it is true to say that the Father and the Son love one another based on their divine essence.[65] In this sense love in God is unique to God, for human beings cannot "possess" the divine essence in the same way that the three persons of the Trinity do, which is by nature. Yet God has graciously opened up his divine life in Jesus Christ, who is the way for human beings to attain God as their true end. By way of participation, the faithful come to share in God's life and love and, in a certain sense, to "possess" God through their union with Christ and through the indwelling of the Holy Spirit. That this is a point that Aquinas goes on to address in detail in the next question of the *Summa*, question thirty-eight, indicates the integrative depth and systematic presentation of his writing in this work.[66]

Aquinas's teaching about notional love gives words to describe the mystery of human participation by grace in the life of God, which later serves as an orienting concern not only in question thirty-eight but also, and perhaps especially, in his discussion of the *missiones* (q. 43) toward which this allusion points. Already he has begun to gesture toward that theme based on both the structure and content of article two of question thirty-seven, as this article begins

64. Ibid., I, q. 37, a. 2 ad 3.

65. Love in God, when understood essentially, "means that the Father and the Son love each other not by the Holy Spirit but by their essence" (ibid., I, q. 37, a. 2c).

66. Ibid., I, q. 38, a. 1c.

with a clarification of notional love.[67] The article then explores the implications of notional love for understanding God's inner life and love.[68] Finally, it ends with a discussion of God's love for creatures.[69] The discussion of God's love for creatures leads fluidly to the subsequent exploration of the Holy Spirit as gift (q. 38). On account of the participation in God's life that is possible for rational creatures, Aquinas deduces that in this sense God loves his people with the same love with which the Father and the Son love another—the person of the Holy Spirit. God's love for the faithful is therefore the very love that the Father has for the Son, so that we are drawn into God's own life through the temporal missions of the Son and the Spirit who proceed eternally as Word and Love, respectively. Such is the intimacy of the life of faith, an intimacy that Aquinas's account of mutual love prepares him to plumb more deeply later in the *Summa* and elsewhere.

To anticipate, one implication of God loving us with the same love with which the Father loves the Son is that it is thereby possible for us to become like Christ. Through our adoption as children of God, as daughters and sons in the Son, we are conformed to Christ's image, with Christ living in us. As God's beloved, loved by the Father through the Son and in the Holy Spirit, we thus come to share in God's own life and love.[70] The basis for our participation is precisely the divine love poured into our hearts by the Holy Spirit. In his commentary on Romans 5:5, Aquinas draws a clear connection between the love that the Spirit is and the love that the Spirit gives us: "The Holy Spirit, who is the love of the Father and the Son, is given to us in order to bring us to participate in the love who is the Holy Spirit. By this participation we are made lovers of God."[71]

67. Ibid, I, q. 37, a. 2 obj. 1 and ad 1.

68. Ibid., I, q. 37, a. 2 obj. 2 and ad 2.

69. Ibid., I, q. 37, a. 2 obj. 3 and ad 3.

70. For more on the interrelated themes of adoption and conformation to the image of Christ, see, e.g., Aquinas's discussion of adoption as befitting to Christ (ibid., III, q. 23).

71. *In Epistolam ad Romanos*, 5, lect. 1, n. 392; henceforth referred to as *Ad Rom.*

As Aquinas suggests, the soteriological ramifications of the Spirit as love are profound. While a fuller exploration of this dimension of Aquinas's pneumatology will come in the next chapter, it bears noting that the deep interrelatedness of Aquinas's dogmatic theology and his moral theology allows him, and his readers, to move quite easily from an exploration of the Trinity *in se* to a richly theological account of the Christian life and vice versa.

So after beginning his investigation in the *Summa* of the Holy Spirit as love, with an account of the Spirit as personal love, Aquinas then moves, in the second phase of his *amor*-based pneumatology, to a consideration of the Spirit as mutual love that demonstrates his penchant for theological rigor and coherence. Attention to the content and the interior logic of the pneumatological questions in the *Summa* brings to light both the contributions and limitations of the first and second interpretations mentioned earlier, and paves the way for the articulation of a balanced perspective that can more effectively identify and tease out the subtleties implicit in Aquinas's mature reflections on the Holy Spirit.

The first interpretation has certain merits, but in taking mutual love as minor and ultimately unnecessary it proves misleading. Penido and others rightly assert that the Holy Spirit as the love uniting Father and Son is not the leading theme in Aquinas's mature thought on the Spirit as love, coming as it does in the second part of his pneumatology from midcareer onwards. Aquinas had earlier given it a prominent place in his writing on the Spirit, as in his commentary on the *Sentences*.[72] His views developed over time, how-

72. E.g., *In I Sent.*, d. 10, q. 1, a. 3, where Aquinas associates the Spirit with an act of subsisting love: "it should be said that love always supposes a good pleasure (*complacentiam*) of the lover with the beloved. But whenever someone takes pleasure in someone, he transports himself into that other and joins himself to it as much as he can, so that the other might become his own; and it is for this reason that love has the sense (*rationem*) of uniting the lover and the beloved. And because the Holy Spirit proceeds as love, he has from this mode of procession that he is the union of the Father and the Son. For the Father and the Son can be considered either in so far as they come together in essence, and thus they are united in essence, or in so far

ever, and gradually he would bring to the fore another explanation by which to introduce the mystery of the Holy Spirit: the love with which God loves his own goodness.

According to this way of thinking, mutual love no longer comes at the beginning of Aquinas's inquiry because he now assumes another starting point that has the added benefit of allowing him to account more adequately for the person of the Spirit. The idea of mutual love cannot penetrate to the level of the Spirit's actual personhood, namely, to the personal love that the Spirit *in se* is, but places its primary stress on the notional act of love, the spiration of the Holy Spirit by the Father and the Son. A more promising alternative, however, is to begin with the acknowledgement that love in God can be taken either essentially or personally, and to move from there into an exposition of the Holy Spirit as love in person, which is precisely what Aquinas does in the *Summa*.[73] For the Holy Spirit is not simply an act of subsisting love, the act through which the Father and the Son reciprocally love one another, but the very person who proceeds as the love of the divine goodness and who is therefore love in person. That is, more than merely an act or a thing—an "it"—the Spirit is above all a person, and to be precise, the person who is love proceeding in God.

The Spirit's genuine personhood, of course, is a basic principle

as they are distinguished in person, and thus they are united by the consonance of love (*per consonantium amoris*): for if it were supposed by an impossibility that they were not one through essence, it would be necessary for their perfect joy to admit between them a union of love." This description of the Spirit as love, however, is relatively insufficient because the juxtaposition of the act of notional love with that of personal love partially obscures the latter and prevents it from being probed in a deeper way. A fuller understanding of the person of the Spirit can be obtained by more direct consideration of the act of personal love as found in the *Summa*, where mutual love comes in the second phase rather than in the first and yet still makes a valuable contribution to the overall inquiry into love as a *proprium* of the Spirit.

73. Cf. the *corpus* of *ST*, I, q. 37, a. 1, which Aquinas begins by stating that "the name Love in God can be taken essentially and personally. If taken personally it is a proper name of the Holy Spirit (*est proprium nomen Spiritus Sancti*), as Word is a proper name of the Son."

that Aquinas long affirmed, so it is not at all the case that between the writing of the *Scriptum* and the writing of the *Summa* he had changed his mind on the matter. Rather, there seems to be a clarification in his thought in so far as the idea of mutual love, in the words of Torrell, "has the disadvantage of superimposing the 'notional' act of love, which is to say the spiration of the Spirit by the Father and the Son, upon the 'personal' act of love, which the Holy Spirit in Himself is, the mutual love of the two first Persons."[74] Torrell goes on explain that this representation of the Spirit as the bond uniting Father and Son "raises a difficulty for its origin, since it is through its relation of origin that it is convenient to grasp the Divine Person who proceeds."[75] Aquinas elucidates the nature of this procession with particular clarity in the *Summa.* Just as God, in knowing himself, produces his Word, so in loving himself, God produces his Spirit.[76] Furthermore, by God's act of loving his own divine essence, and so of loving himself as God, Aquinas perceives the presence of a loving "impression" or "affection" in God through which the beloved is found in the lover.[77] While God's inner life remains, to a certain extent, shrouded in mystery because of the limitations of human understanding and the poverty of human vocabulary, Aquinas

74. Torrell, *Saint Thomas Aquinas*, vol. 2: *Spiritual Master*, 184.

75. Ibid., 185.

76. This is the theological application of the principle stated in *ST*, I, q. 37, a. 1c: "For as when a thing is understood by anyone, there results in the one who understands a conception of the object understood, which is called a word, so a when anyone loves an object, a certain impression results, so to speak, of the thing loved in the affection of the lover, by reason of which the object loved is said to be in the lover, as the object understood is in the one who understands. Thus, when anyone understands and loves himself he is in himself, not only by real identity, but also as the object understood is in the one who understands, and the object loved is in the lover."

77. Again, "when anyone loves an object, a certain impression results (*provenit quaedam impressio*), so to speak, of the thing loved in the affection of the lover, by reason of which the object loved is said to be in the lover (ibid.). Cf. "procession exists in God only according to an action that does not tend to anything external, but remains in the agent itself.... The operation of the will within ourselves involves also another procession, that of love, whereby the object loved is in the lover" (ibid., I, q. 27, a. 3c.).

proceeds to couch the procession of the Holy Spirit in terms of this inward term produced in God by the act of God's love for the divine essence, a production that is analogous to a tree flowering by its flower.[78] An explanation of the Spirit's immanent procession is what Aquinas is aiming for, and ultimately is able to grasp, in his mature reflection on the Spirit as love.

In addition to the specific content of the pneumatological questions in the *Summa*, and especially of question thirty-seven, the order of the articles reflects a certain interior logic that further indicates the place of mutual love in Aquinas's exposition. Again, Aquinas devotes the first article to the question of love as a name proper to the Spirit, a question that takes him to the heart of the Spirit's person as love. While in his response to the third objection in article one Aquinas uses mutual love to explain a particular nuance pertaining to the problem of personal love, it is not until the second article that he investigates in earnest whether the Father and the Son love each other by the Holy Spirit. In the *Summa*, the Holy Spirit as mutual love is integrated more explicitly than before into a larger explanation that has as its starting point for introducing the mystery of the third person the love with which God loves his own goodness, which is the very love that the Spirit proceeds as and so in person is. For this reason, the first school of interpretation, as represented by Penido, does well to highlight the development in Aquinas's thought from the *Scriptum* to the *Summa*, and properly concludes that the Holy Spirit as the love uniting Father and Son does not serve as the point of departure in Aquinas's mature pneumatology.

This interpretation is somewhat misleading, however, when it comes to the function of mutual love. By pitting Anselm and Richard of St. Victor against one another and stressing so heavily the essentialist orientation, which he attributes to Anselm, Penido opens the door to the possibility of undervaluing the theme of mutual love in Aquinas, given the way he associates it with Richard, whom he is

78. Ibid., I, q. 37, a. 2c.

keen to critique. It appears as though over time Aquinas does become increasingly concerned with God's own love for the divine essence and its implications for exploring the Spirit as love. While not included in the *Summa contra Gentiles*, the language of mutual love does not drop out of Aquinas's vocabulary altogether; it emerges once more in the *Summa* but now occupies a different position in Aquinas's thought. These observations, which are sometimes considered to fan the proverbial flames of the kind of argument presented by Penido, are indisputably true. Yet the assumption that mutual love has become for Aquinas essentially nothing more than a meaningless remnant of a misguided tradition, faultily propagated by Richard of St. Victor, can be questioned on several grounds.

First, its absence in the *Summa contra Gentiles* is not necessarily a telltale sign that Aquinas basically finds no more use for the designation of the Holy Spirit as the bond of love uniting Father and Son. As Emery points out, Aquinas's silence can be explained by the genre of the work, a much more concise study than the *Summa*, as well as the particular structure of its treatise on the Trinity. Besides, Aquinas only minimally discusses the notion of the Holy Spirit as gift in the *Summa contra Gentiles*, without even defining the meaning of the term "gift," but that notion is quite clearly operative in the *Summa*, where he devotes an entire question to it.[79] Just because Aquinas says little, if anything, about a certain concept in the *Summa contra Gentiles* does not by necessity mean that he no longer finds it worthy of discussion or that it no longer has a bearing on the argument that he presents elsewhere.[80]

Second, and more importantly, the claim that mutual love has been eclipsed in Aquinas's thought and has no more work to do must be tested based on Aquinas's own words. The account of mutual love in the *Summa* provided earlier in this chapter has shown that the idea plays an important, if not exclusive, role in Aquinas's

79. Ibid., I, q. 38.
80. Emery, *The Trinitarian Theology of Saint Thomas Aquinas*, 235.

exposition of the Spirit as love. In considering first whether, and then precisely how, it is true that the Father and the Son love each other by the Holy Spirit (q. 37, a. 2), Aquinas indicates the location and function of mutual love in his reflection on the doctrine of the Holy Spirit as well as its implications for understanding the love of God *ad extra*. Two concepts underscore the significance of mutual love even in Aquinas's mature or developed pneumatology: the notional sense of love in God and the concept of relation.

While each has been explored in some detail already, these two concepts can now be brought into closer proximity in order to show that Aquinas's identification of the Holy Spirit as mutual love does in fact contribute to his exposition, contrary to what this first school of interpretation characteristically suggests. First, in view of the association between the Spirit and love, the Spirit being the divine person who proceeds within God as the love of God's own goodness, Aquinas explains that the verbal use of love in God can be taken not simply essentially but also notionally. This observation allows Aquinas to reflect on the notional sense of "to love" when applied to God, which leads to his fruitful tree metaphor likening the production of a flower—"a tree flowers by its flowers"—to the production of love in God that is the spiration of the Holy Spirit by the Father and Son in their love for each other.[81]

Second, because the Holy Spirit is love, in the Spirit is expressed the relation of the Father to the Son, and vice versa, a relation of love between the lover and the beloved. In this sense the Spirit is the bond between the two persons, proceeding from both.[82] Moreover, when "to love" is understood notionally it imports (*importat*) not only the production of a divine person, the spiration of the Holy Spirit, but also the person produced by way of love, the Spirit *in se*,

81. *ST*, I, q. 37, a. 2c. Aquinas elaborates on this pneumatological principle in the second objection and reply.

82. In regard to the reciprocal relation between the Father and the Son, which is a relation of lover to beloved, the Holy Spirit "is the bond between the two persons, as proceeding from both" (ibid., I, q. 37, a. 1 ad 3).

in whose production and actual being relation to the object loved is implied.[83] It is in God's act of love for himself that the Holy Spirit is produced. This act implies a certain relation because the Father loves the Son by the Holy Spirit, as by the person proceeding, and by love itself when understood notionally.[84] Aquinas advances the discussion with his point about love taken in a notional sense, also implying the person produced by way of love, and the corresponding relation that this person has to the object loved. This comment may seem self-evident, but it adds to the previous remark about the spiration of the Spirit because of the two ways in which such relation can be understood. First, it can denote relation in God, according to which the Holy Spirit, as love proceeding, is the *nexus* between the Father and the Son, the mutual love by which they mutually love one another. In a secondary way this notion can also mean God's relation to creatures, for God loves himself and every creature by the same love, that is, by the Holy Spirit. In particular, it is the idea of relation in God that Aquinas's account of mutual love brings more clearly into focus. His exploration of the notional sense of love in God serves to illumine the way in which the Father and the Son relate to one another.

The result is a deeper insight into the reality of the Spirit as love than anything that has been achieved up to that point in Aquinas's thought. As instructive as essential love, personal love, and notional love can be, and their importance should certainly not be downplayed, if mutual love were omitted, Aquinas's discussion of the Holy Spirit as love, along with his trinitarian treatise as a whole, would not be as theologically substantial or suggestive. While essen-

83. "The Father loves not only the Son, but also himself and us by the Holy Spirit. Because, as explained above [i.e., in I, q. 37, a. 1c], 'to love' (*diligere*), understood notionally, not only imports the production of a divine person, but also the person produced by way of love, who has relation to the object loved" (ibid., I, q. 37, a. 2 ad 3).

84. "'[T]o love' (*diligere*), taken in a notional sense, means to produce love. And thus it can be said that the Father loves the Son by the Holy Spirit, as by the person proceeding, and by love itself as a notional act" (ibid., I, q. 37, a. 2 ad 2).

tial love highlights the single, divine essence that is at the heart of God's life, personal love names the Holy Spirit as love, and notional love denotes the production of a divine person and the person produced by way of love, it is possible to probe even more deeply the question of relation in God. With the concept of mutual love, Aquinas profitably extends his trinitarian treatise along those lines. He does so by considering, in particular, how the Father and the Son relate to one another. As Aquinas is able to show, the relation of the Father to the Son, and vice versa, is like unto that between a lover and the beloved. This relation is expressed in the Holy Spirit, who is the love by whom the Father and the Son love one another, thus signifying something of the reciprocity, depth of intimacy, and personal indwelling that characterize God's own life and love. In evoking the perfectly loving relation of the Father and the Son, the Holy Spirit can rightly be called their mutual love, a designation that further penetrates the mystery of God's triune life. That is, the identification of the Spirit as mutual love, building on the work done by the related themes of essential love, personal love, and notional love, places the discussion of the Holy Spirit in an explicitly trinitarian context, since mutual love assumes the Father and the Son, as the two who love each other mutually, and explores in a more extended way precisely how the Father and the Son relate to one another, namely, in their reciprocal communion of love by the Spirit.

Therefore the theme of mutual love is more than the theologically empty metaphor that Penido and others posit. It actually does something to advance Aquinas's inquiry in the *Summa*, extending the discussion of relation in God through a consideration of the Holy Spirit as the love by which the Father and the Son love one another. The identification of the Spirit as *amor mutuus* is not ultimately meaningless or unnecessary, but rather makes a notable contribution to Aquinas's account. In this way, then, the first interpretation can be corrected, and its excess avoided, through a more evenhanded reappraisal of Aquinas on the Spirit in the *Summa*.

Likewise the second interpretation, in attempting to reassert the significance of mutual love in Aquinas, picks up on an element found in his thought but ultimately reflects a certain one-sidedness that makes it no more sufficient than the first. This one-sidedness, to be sure, points in the opposite direction than does the first interpretation, for in this case mutual love is brought to the center of discussion rather than being pushed to the periphery. The problem is that mutual love arguably becomes so much of a focal point that Aquinas's overall aim—to account for the immanent procession of the Spirit as love—can be overlooked.

Representative of this approach, Bourassa has no problem identifying texts that indicate that mutual love occupies a meaningful place in Aquinas's mature reflections on the Holy Spirit, that suggest the influence of Augustine and Aquinas's extension of Augustine's line of inquiry vis-à-vis the Spirit as love, or that underscore the connection between love as personal relation and the Holy Spirit as the bond of love uniting Father and Son. While Bourassa does well to note such texts in Aquinas, and while he correctly asserts that mutual love is an idea of some import to Aquinas, given Bourassa's focused concern to defend this theme what tends to be slightly underemphasized is Aquinas's larger purpose in his exposition of the Spirit as love in the *Summa*.

That larger purpose is specifically to disclose, by way of a creaturely analogy, an immanent procession of love. Yet interpersonal love, as known and experienced by human beings, simply cannot provide an adequate example of an immanent procession. The reason is that love between two human persons is not really one in a sufficiently internal sense. It flows from two different people, two beings who are essentially distinct. Granted, these people come to share a certain connection by the love that is in each, but the love between them consists in a double external procession—first, a procession from the first person, outward, to the second; second, a procession from the second person, outward, to the first. In the case of the Holy Spirit, however, there is an essential unity in the immanent procession as love. The Spirit proceeds from the Father and the Son, as Aquinas maintains, and does so precisely in a procession that is inward or internal to God's own life such that the Spirit is consubstantial with the Father and the Son.[85] In the first article of his treatise on the Trinity, Aquinas establishes that procession in God is entirely inward, not outward, and this is an orienting principle directing his subsequent reflections throughout this treatise.[86] If one uses mutual love as the immediate entrance into the study of the Holy Spirit as love, it becomes difficult to come to terms with the unity of the Spirit's immanent procession.

Whereas mutual love proves relatively insufficient in this sense, a better starting point is the procession of the imprint of love that comes about in the will of the lover. Significantly, that is the specific point of departure chosen by Aquinas in his mature reflection on the matter in the *Summa*. To explain the manner in which the Holy Spirit is the mutual love of the Father and the Son, Aquinas first seeks to understand the Spirit's immanent procession, which as he discerns is a matter of an imprint of love in the will of the lover: "when anyone loves an object, a certain impression results, so to speak, of the thing loved in the affection of the lover, by reason of which the object loved is said to be in the lover."[87] Viewing the Spirit's procession in terms of the analogy of the imprint of love in the loving will makes it possible to conceive of a relation subsisting within God. The imprint of love arising from God's love for himself, in the words of Emery, "can be understood as a subsistent relation, the very person the Holy Spirit is."[88] The Spirit is this relation because it is the Spirit who proceeds

85. As Aquinas points out, the Spirit's procession is in the identity of the divine nature, the Spirit being consubstantial with the Father and the Son (*ST*, I, q. 27, a. 4c).

86. Ibid., I, q. 27, a. 1. The idea of immanent procession also comes into play, for example, in Aquinas's discussion of the divine relations (ibid., I, q. 28) and the divine persons, both as a group and when each of the three is considered in turn (ibid., I, qq. 29, 33, 34–35, 36–38, respectively).

87. Ibid., I, q. 37, a. 1c.

88. Emery, *The Trinitarian Theology of Saint Thomas Aquinas*, 236.

by way of the will in God, and whose being is substantially the same as that of the principle of the procession. In this sense, the Spirit is *in se* a subsistent relation that is produced by an immanent procession and characterized by love, even the love with which the Father and the Son love one another.

As a result, the imprint of love in the will of the lover allows one to grasp the unity of the immanent procession of the Holy Spirit more easily than does the analogy of human interpersonal love. It is therefore fitting that Aquinas discloses the property of the Spirit as love by exploring the topic of love in God as understood personally, denoting the particular person of the Holy Spirit who proceeds as the love of God's own goodness (q. 37, a. 1), and then by taking up the question of whether the Father and the Son love one another by the Spirit, which is the question of the Holy Spirit as their mutual love (q. 37, a. 2).

Again, however, beyond simply the sequence of articles, the content of Aquinas's discussion shows that mutual love is not understood in isolation from personal love, but as part of the same question concerning love as a *proprium* of the Spirit. Even when he explicates the sense in which the Holy Spirit is mutual love, Aquinas never loses sight of the fact that the Spirit is not a thing but a genuine person, the person proceeding as love.[89]

More precisely, helping to clarify the role of mutual love with respect to the second interpretation are two concepts identified earlier: love in God understood notionally and the twofold sense of relation as applied to God. First, Aquinas's observation that "to love" in God can be understood notionally as well as essentially takes him to the heart of his exploration of the Spirit as the love uniting Father and Son. The Spirit is not simply love in person but also the love whereby the Father and the Son love one another. If the Spirit as personal love is not sufficiently accounted for then the notional act

89. E.g., "to love, taken in a notional sense, means to produce love, and thus it can be said that the Father loves the Son by the Holy Spirit, as by the person proceeding, and by love itself as a notional act" (*ST*, I, q. 37, a. 2 ad 2).

of love, that is, the spiration of the Holy Spirit by the Father and the Son, can be superimposed upon the personal love that the Spirit is *in se*.[90] A close reading of Aquinas obviates this problem: he first names the Spirit as love in person, love proceeding from the Father and the Son.[91] Then, having discerned the person of the Spirit as this very love, he further identifies the Spirit as the one by whom the Father and the Son love each other in a notional sense.[92] As a result, Aquinas can now probe the mystery of mutual love while affirming, rather than in any way obscuring, the personal identity of the Spirit.

In keeping with Aquinas's analogy, just as to speak is to produce a word, and to flower is to produce flowers, so to love is to produce love, for which reason Aquinas concludes that the Father and the Son love one another by the Holy Spirit, as by the person proceeding, and by love itself as a notional act.[93] With this analogy, Aquinas solves the problem introduced earlier about how the Spirit can at the same time (1) be the mutual love of Father and Son and (2) proceed from both.[94] In the case of a tree flowering by its flower, the action is named after what proceeds from its act, flowers. Similarly, the act of the Father and Son loving one another is named by what that act produces, the Holy Spirit. The Spirit is the imprint of love within God that blossoms from the unity of Father and Son. Aquinas addresses an objection that "to love" cannot be taken notionally in God (a. 2 obj. 2) by appealing again to this tree analogy, and one upshot of the discussion is an indication that the notional sense of love in God in no way belies the personal love that the Spirit is, but rather serves to illumine the Spirit's personal property as love. Since "to love" in a notional sense means to produce love, and imports a person proceeding as love, it is true that the Father loves the Son by the Holy Spirit, who is this person proceeding, and by love as a notional act.[95]

90. Cf. Torrell, *Saint Thomas Aquinas*, vol. 2: *Spiritual Master*, 184.

91. *ST*, I, q. 37, a. 1c.

92. Ibid., I, q. 37, a. 2c.

93. Ibid., I, q. 37, a. 2c and ad 2.

94. See ibid., I, q. 37, a. 3 ad 3.

95. The tree analogy comes into play here to distinguish between (1) the idea of

From Aquinas's explanation of the proper sense of the notional act of love in God, a second point follows: because the Holy Spirit is love, in the Spirit is expressed both relation within God and God's relation to creatures. This principle also serves to disclose the true function of mutual love in Aquinas's mature pneumatology, in contrast to the slightly exaggerated understanding presented in the second interpretation discussed earlier. As Aquinas clarifies, in the person of the Holy Spirit there is expressed relation both *ad intra* and *ad extra* with respect to God, not because the Spirit is the medium uniting the Father and the Son, but because the Spirit is love in person and, to be precise, the one proceeding as the love of the primal goodness by which the Father loves himself and every creature.[96] That is, Aquinas's account of relation in God and, consequently, of God's relation to creatures—both of which relations are characterized by love—is predicated not on the basis of mutual love *per se* (though this idea does later come into play), but fundamentally on the basis of the love with which God loves his own goodness.

By the end of Aquinas's consideration of the Spirit as love in question thirty-seven, it has now become clear that such love, which is none other than the love that God has for his own goodness, serves as the foundation of the association that Aquinas discerns between the Holy Spirit and love. Appropriately, this is an association that he articulates by first establishing that the Spirit is love in person, the

an action including a determined effect (in which case the principle of the action may be denominated both from the action and from the effect) and (2) the idea of an action that does not include a determined effect (in which case the principle of the action cannot be determined from the effect). As Aquinas observes, we can say that a tree flowers by its flowering and by its flower. We do not say, however, that the tree produces the flower by the flower, but by the production of the flower. Similarly, because "spirates" denotes a notional act, we cannot say that the Father spirates by the Holy Spirit, but by the production of the Spirit (i.e., spiration). Again, though, "to love" understood notionally means to produce love and imports a person proceeding, the Holy Spirit, so it can be said that the Father loves the Son by the Holy Spirit, who is this person proceeding as love, and by love itself as a notional act (ibid., I, q. 37, a. 2 ad 2).

96. Ibid., I, q. 37, a. 2 ad 3.

love proceeding in God on the basis of God's single and unique affection for himself, and then addressing the problem of mutual love, in so far as the Holy Spirit, as love, implies that reciprocal connection between the lover and beloved as proceeding from both.

CONCLUSION

For these reasons, then, over against the limitations of each of the two main interpretations, a more balanced perspective affirms that mutual love is significant and by no means unnecessary (contra the first interpretation), and important but not quite singularly decisive or central in and of itself (contra the second) because it is part of a sequence of themes aimed at a larger issue, namely, how to account for the immanent procession of the Holy Spirit as love. Aquinas does precisely that by relating the Spirit as love proceeding, personal love, and mutual love in a certain manner. The Spirit is properly mutual love because the very love that the Spirit *in se* is, love in person who proceeds from the Father and the Son as the love of God's own goodness, constitutes the Spirit's relation to the Father and the Son, a relation rooted in love. So the Spirit, as personal love inwardly proceeding in God, is also mutual love, the love that the Father and the Son have for one another, which turns out to be the same love with which God loves us.

Coming in the second phase of Aquinas's mature reflections on the Holy Spirit as love, mutual love is not the initial point of departure—that role is reserved for the procession of the imprint of love that comes about in the will of the lover, which, in the case of God, arises from God's love for himself and can be understood as a subsistent relation, the person of the Holy Spirit as love. The idea of mutual love, however, still performs a key role in Aquinas's account, deepening the inquiry with regard to the theme of relation in God and the corresponding topic of God's relation to creatures. It is that latter topic, the soteriological implications of which are immense, that now takes center stage in this study of Aquinas's pneumatology.

Five

GIFT OF THE SPIRIT

The Holy Spirit, Love, and the Christian Life in Aquinas

THE PREVIOUS two chapters have examined the link that Aquinas perceived between love and the person of the Holy Spirit. Two orienting concerns have emerged thus far in Aquinas's pneumatology: first, the Spirit as personal love or love in person, and second, the Spirit as the mutual love of the Father and the Son. Proceeding from the Father and the Son as love in person, the Spirit is also their mutual love, in whom is expressed their relation as that of the lover to the beloved.[1] While it is chiefly concerned with the inner life of God as Trinity, this pneumatological affirmation implies, in a secondary way, God's relation to rational creatures, and in doing so it anticipates the soteriological ramifications of the Holy Spirit as love that Aquinas goes on to explore in what might be called a third phase of his pneumatology.

As Aquinas points out in the prologue to the next question of the *Summa*, after a consideration of the sense in which the Holy Spirit can rightly be called love (q. 37), the topic of gift logically fol-

1. *ST*, I, q. 37, a. 1 ad 3.

lows (q. 38). Under this heading, and in view of the related concepts of mission (q. 43) and the theological virtue of *caritas* (II–II, qq. 23–46), he is able to deepen his pneumatological inquiry in a way that not only further clarifies the personal identity of the Holy Spirit but also helps solidify the connection between dogmatic theology and moral theology that is central to his work. In other words, Aquinas constructs his account of the Christian life on the foundation that he has laid in his trinitarian theology and in his pneumatology in particular. The multivalent phrase "gift of the Spirit" conveys something of the theological depth and breadth achieved by Aquinas's inquiry, as this phrase can be used to signify in one sense the Holy Spirit as the gift of the Father and the Son, in another the Spirit's greatest gift of love in the economy of salvation, and in another still the Christian life itself as gift under the Spirit's agency, all of which are fruitfully interrelated in Aquinas's pneumatology.

THE HOLY SPIRIT, GIFT OF THE FATHER AND THE SON

Aquinas considers gift as a name of the Holy Spirit by asking first whether it is a personal name of the Spirit (q. 38, a. 1) and then whether it is a name proper to the Spirit (a. 2). Under both of these headings, Aquinas affirms the Spirit's identity as the gift of the Father and the Son in the mystery of God's triune life, and indeed as the very gift poured out upon the world at Pentecost in the economy of salvation. Regarding the first, Aquinas explains what the idea of gift implies in order to clarify the sense in which gift is a personal name of the Spirit. A gift, he observes, imports a capacity for being given, such that what is given, first of all, can be given, which means that it belongs to the one who is to give it. In addition to a relation to the giver, who must first possess what is to be given, a gift also assumes a relation to the recipient, to whom the gift comes to belong. Having pointed out that the notion of gift implies an aptitude for being given and a relation between the gift and the giver, on the one hand, and between the gift and the recipient, on the other, Aquinas begins to contemplate the theological application of this notion, and particularly its pneumatological meaning. A divine person can belong to another in one of two ways, either by origin or as possessed by another. In the first sense the Son is said to belong to the Father, and the Spirit to the Father and the Son, on the basis of procession. Understood in this way, gift signifies possession by the giver, such that the gift belongs to the giver specifically because the gift originates in the giver. Or to be precise, in the case of the Spirit as gift, gift signifies possession by the givers, for the Spirit is the gift of the Father and the Son as proceeding from both. Yet the signification of possession by the giver still allows the gift to be personally distinguished from the giver. The aptness of the Spirit's personal name as gift thus becomes clear, since this name suggests that the Holy Spirit, who proceeds from the Father and the Son as love, belongs to them by origin and can be personally distinguished from them as the gift of the Father and the Son within God's own life.[2]

Aquinas notes that the other way in which a divine person can belong to another is by possession, though not as in possession from origin, but possession following from reception. In this sense, the rational creature can be said to possess God precisely through the creature's union with God that is made possible by the gift of God's own self in the economy of salvation. That is, the rational creature is united to God by having been made a partaker of the Trinity's life, a participant of "the divine Word and of the Love proceeding, so as freely to know God truly and to love God rightly."[3] Aquinas makes explicit that such participation in God's own life, the *telos* of human existence, is not possible by human power but must come from above.[4] While a divine person is said to be given, and hence is called a gift, the initiative for this gift always lies entirely with the giver, that is, with God. The person of the Holy Spirit is rightly called gift

2. Ibid., I, q. 38, a. 1c, ad 1.

3. Ibid., I, q. 38, a. 1c.

4. Ibid.

because, while given in time as the promised advocate of God (cf. Jn 14:16), the Spirit has an eternal aptitude to be given, an aptitude that is *in se*—personal to the one proceeding as love—not something evoked by the recipients of this gift.[5]

The fact that the Spirit is gift not from being actually given but from having an eternal aptitude to being given is noteworthy for two reasons. First, it allows Aquinas to explain the specific nature of the Spirit's title as gift. Second, it helps to resolve an apparent difficulty arising from an insufficiently clear understanding of this title. To take the latter point first, if calling the Spirit "gift" implies a relation to creatures, then it seems as though there must be creatures for the Spirit to be given to, if "gift" is an appropriate title for the Spirit. One might even assume that the existence of creatures is somehow constitutive of the person of the Spirit. Of course, Aquinas could not abide either of these conclusions. One way that he is able to avoid them is by clarifying that this pneumatological title implies a relation to creatures only in a certain sense, not in a strictly determinative one, in keeping with the nature of the Spirit's title as gift. The personal name of gift as applied to the Spirit is in no way necessitated by creatures. That is because the basis for this name is found in something deeper than the fact that the Spirit has been given in time; it is found in the Spirit's aptitude for being given as the one who proceeds eternally in God as love. In other words, the Spirit can be—and is—gift *in se* without having anyone *in se* to whom to be given simply because of who the Spirit is, independent of any created reality. As Thomas explains, although given in time, the Spirit is "called gift from eternity," and relation to the creature, while implied in the name "gift," is implied in only a secondary and nondeterminative way.[6]

As to the second question, whether gift is a *proprium* of the Spirit, Aquinas defines the concept of gift and explores its implications

5. Ibid., I, q. 38, a. 1c, ad 4.

6. Ibid.

vis-à-vis an understanding of the Spirit in order to support his affirmative answer. Following Aristotle, Aquinas defines gift as a giving that can have no return (*donum proprie est datio irreddibilis*), or, in other words, "a thing that is not given with the intention of a return," but given simply out of good will.[7] For this reason, a gift contains the idea of a gratuitous donation. Aquinas specifies that the *ratio* for such gracious giving is love, which has the nature of a first gift, for it is through love that all free gifts are given. The pneumatological import of this observation is significant, and promptly pointed out by Aquinas:

> Now the reason of the donation being gratuitous is love, since we give something to anyone gratuitously in as much as we wish him well. So what we first give him is the love whereby we wish him well. Thus it is manifest that love has the nature of a first gift, through which all free gifts are given. So because the Holy Spirit proceeds as love, as stated above [q. 27 a. 4; q. 37 a. 1], he proceeds as the first gift.[8]

This passage helps clarify the significant relation of love and gift in Aquinas's thought, a relation that allows him to extend his inquiry into the person and work of the Holy Spirit by tying together these crucial themes. Not only is love the basis of a gift's gratuitous character but the Holy Spirit, who proceeds as love, is the first gift and as such the *ratio* of all actual gifts to creatures, so that all such gifts are rightly viewed in relation to the Spirit. To explain, Aquinas returns to the principle of procession and draws an analogy with the person of Christ: just as the Son is fittingly called image because of his procession by way of the intellect, so the Holy Spirit, in proceeding as love, is fittingly called gift. Aquinas pinpoints a distinctively pneumatological meaning in this title even though the Spirit is not the only divine person said to be given. While the Son is also given, he is given precisely from the Father's love (cf. Jn 3:16), which serves to illustrate that the basis of God's gratuitous giving to the world is

7. Ibid., I, q. 38, a. 2c. Cf. Aristotle, *Topica*, bk. iv, part 4.
8. *ST*, I, q. 38, a. 2c.

love.[9] Moreover, seeing that a *proprium* signifies a certain property, Aquinas returns to the earlier point about origin in the Godhead as an explanation for one divine person belonging to another. Because a gift involves the idea of the gift belonging to the giver through origin, the property that it entails is precisely that of the Spirit's origin, which is to say the procession of the Holy Spirit as love.[10] The affirmation that gift is a name proper to the Holy Spirit calls attention to the Spirit's procession, which denotes the nature of the Spirit as the first gift, the gift who proceeds eternally as love in God and has been gratuitously given in time.

Aquinas's discussion of the Holy Spirit as gift therefore has two interrelated dimensions, each of which is decisive to a proper understanding of the issues at stake. The first aspect denotes God's inner life, as the Holy Spirit is the gift of God *ad intra*, the gift belonging to, and proceeding from, the Father and the Son by origin. The second implies the economy of salvation, as the Spirit is the gift poured out upon the earth through God's self-donating love. The Holy Spirit, then, is both the gift of the Father and the Son in God's own life, and the same gift promised by Christ to his disciples and bestowed upon the church at Pentecost. For Aquinas, the personal name of gift designates the Spirit whose *proprium* it is, the same Spirit who is the common gift of Father and Son *ad intra* and is also freely sent by God to the world in time. With this association between the idea of gift and the person of the Spirit, Aquinas is able to perceive that it is through the Spirit, who as love proceeding is the gift of the Father and the Son, that the gifts of God *ad extra* are given.

THE SPIRIT'S GIFT OF LOVE

In his pneumatology Aquinas also deals with the Spirit's gift of love, which is to say, the created gift of charity that makes us God's friends, a gift that depends upon the donation of the Spirit who is

9. Ibid., I, q. 38, a. 2 ad 1.
10. Ibid., I, q. 38, a. 2 ad 2.

uncreated love. Thomas does not formally number love among the gifts of the Spirit but affirms the traditional understanding of seven gifts based on Isaiah 11:2–3.[11] Nevertheless, clearly there is a relationship in his thought among the idea of gift, the role of the Holy Spirit in the economy of salvation, and the theological virtue of love.[12] Love might also be considered a gift of the Holy Spirit, with gift understood in a broader sense, in so far as it is through the Holy Spirit who has been given to us that the love of God has been shed abroad in our hearts (Rom 5:5). Love or charity, friendship, and the doctrine of the Holy Spirit, as well as trinitarian doctrine as a whole, share a vital connection in Aquinas's work.

Caritas: Friendship with God

For our purposes here, three features of charity stand out: first, what might be called its essence, or what it is; second, its effect; and third, its object. As a discussion of each one will show, these features are crucial for investigating the subject of the Spirit's gift of love in the economy of salvation.

First, Aquinas defines *caritas* in terms of friendship. It is, he says, a certain friendship (*amicitia*) between the human person and God.[13] Although this is a friendship among unequals, it is nothing less than true friendship, established by God. Friendship requires a mutual love uniting friends that is founded upon some kind of communication between them.[14] Hence the love of *caritas*, as friendship, presupposes

11. Ibid., I–II, q. 68.

12. For a detailed inquiry into the seven gifts of the Holy Spirit in Aquinas, see John of St. Thomas, *Cursus theologicus*, vol. 5 (Paris: Desclée et Sociorum, 1931). A translation of part of this volume has been provided by Dominic Hughes, OP, with a foreword by Walter Farrell, OP, *Gifts of the Holy Ghost* (London: Sheed & Ward, 1951). John explains that the seven gifts "presuppose all three of the theological virtues as their root and foundation, since it is through them that the soul is united to God and able to be moved by His Spirit," 239.

13. *ST*, II–II, q. 23, a. 1c.

14. Ibid.: "Talis autem mutua benevolentia fundatur super aliqua communicatione." Recalling the controversies among Aquinas's interpreters, Eberhard Schock-

communication between God and human beings, a communication of God's happiness to us (in the sense of sharing). The Father communicates this happiness to us by calling us into the fellowship of his Son, through the power of the Holy Spirit (cf. 1 Cor 1:9). In this way, God gives freely of his own beatitude and invites us to participate in the fullness of his triune life, graciously opened up to human beings in supernatural friendship.[15]

While the notion of friendship had been richly developed in philosophy, especially Aristotelian philosophy, it also has a scriptural basis upon which Aquinas builds. In the Gospel of John, for instance, Christ says to his disciples, "I do not call you servants any longer ... but I have called you friends" (Jn 15:15). Aquinas observes that when Christ says these words he is speaking out of the love of friendship. Excluding what is opposed to friendship, namely, servitude and ignorance, the incarnate Word here "sets down the true sign of friendship" by revealing the secrets of his heart—all that he has heard from the Father—to his friends.[16] Thus, the communica-

---

enhoff mentions the difficulty associated with translating the term *communicatio* in this context. He concludes that it is best interpreted to embrace both "an active, dynamic aspect as well as an intransitive one, which, on account of its substantive character, is gladly understood as a possession of a common essential form." Such an interpretation accounts for the active self-communication of divine love to human beings and the work of God's grace in inwardly transforming the human person in his or her created reality by means of a new quality (*quaedam qualitas*) or a "permanently given form" (*habituale donum*). Aquinas suggests both senses in *ST*, II–II, q. 23, a. 1c: "Cum igitur sit aliqua communicatio hominis ad Deum secundum quod nobis suam beatitudinem communicat, super hac communicatione oportet aliquam amicitiam fundari" (Eberhard Schockenhoff, "The Theological Virtue of Charity [IIa IIae, qq. 23–46]," trans. Grant Kaplan and Frederick G. Lawrence, in *The Ethics of Aquinas*, ed. Stephen J. Pope [Washington, D.C.: Georgetown University Press, 2002], 244–58, in particular 247–48).

15. Here the term "supernatural" is used to denote the uniqueness of this friendship, a friendship that is beyond human nature in the sense that it is made possible by the sheer grace of God that perfects human nature. On God's communication to human beings as a call to for them to share in his triune life, see Schockenhoff, "The Theological Virtue of Charity (IIa IIae, qq. 23–46)," 247.

16. *Ioan.*, par. 2016.

tion (now in the sense of information) between God and human beings that is necessary for *caritas* occurs through God's Word. *Caritas* is the love based on God's communication of his own happiness to us. As such, *caritas* is our friendship with God, which is made possible by the way in which God has chosen to relate to us.[17]

Second, the effect of *caritas* is twofold, for as something created in the soul by God it both unites us to God and attains God. Although human beings, again, are in no way equal to God, we become one with him through *caritas*. While this is the work of the whole Trinity, it can be attributed specifically to the Holy Spirit, who as the love between the Father and the Son moves the human will to the act of love.[18] Yet the movement of *caritas* does not occur through the Holy Spirit as an extrinsic principle alone, because then the act of *caritas* would not be voluntary and meritorious, when in fact it is both.[19] In order for an act to be voluntary, the principle of the act needs to be in the agent of the act.[20] Therefore the will must be the efficient cause of the act of love. *Caritas*, however, is supernatural; as a theological virtue, it is above and beyond human nature in itself. Aquinas now faces a dilemma: How can he affirm both the supernatural character of the act—it must be the work of the Spirit—and the voluntary nature of the act of *caritas* by which we are united to God? His answer is that in order for us to perform the act of *caritas* that ultimately exceeds our natural capacities, there must be in us some habitual form "superadded to the natural power, inclining that power to the act of *caritas*, and causing it to act willingly and delightfully."[21] Or, as he says in *De caritate*, the Spirit moves the human will to the act of love by providing the form and power whereby the will is inclined to that to which the Spirit moves it, so that the will tends to the act of love not in any coerced way but

17. *ST*, II–II, q. 23, a. 1c.

18. On the Spirit as the love between the Father and the Son, see ibid., I, q. 37, a.1 ad 3; I, q. 37, a. 2; and II–II, q. 24, a. 2c, as well as chapters 3 and 4 of the present study.

19. Ibid., II–II, q. 23, a. 2c.

20. Ibid., I–II, q. 6, a. 1.

21. Ibid., II–II, q. 23, a. 2c.

rather on its own free accord.[22] Charity therefore unites us to God by means of the infusion of the Spirit, who makes possible and inclines us toward our voluntary act of love.

What distinguishes *caritas* from the other theological virtues of faith and hope, as well as from all the other virtues, is that *caritas* attains God and enables one to rest in him. Faith and hope can also be said to attain God, but only in so far as we derive from God the knowledge of truth or the acquisition of good. *Caritas* attains God in a deeper way, for it is in this supreme theological virtue—created by the indwelling of the Holy Spirit—that we come to rest finally in God.[23]

Along with what has been said already about friendship, first of all, and union and attainment, secondly, a third key feature of Aquinas's understanding of *caritas* is its object or end. Aquinas identifies the object of *caritas* in terms of the last end of human life, that is, everlasting happiness in God.[24] God is loved by *caritas* for his own sake. To be precise, *caritas* regards principally one aspect of God's lovableness, namely his goodness.[25] Every act of *caritas* is performed therefore in respect to God as the object of *caritas*. In other words, God is the principal object of the love of *caritas*.[26] All who are loved out of *caritas* are loved ultimately in relation to God. The aspect under which we love our neighbors is God, since what we ought to love in our neighbors is that God may be in them.[27] God is to be loved first and best out of *caritas*, since he is loved as the cause of happiness, whereas our neighbor is loved as receiving together

22. *De caritate*, a. 1c.

23. *ST*, II–II, q. 23, a. 6c. Cf. Schockenhoff: Aquinas's treatise on *caritas* "promises that any persons who have entrusted themselves to the path of love and who pursue God's invitation to friendship with Him will be given a definitive coming-to-rest and attaining-the-goal of human life" (256).

24. *ST*, II–II, q. 23, a. 4 ad 2.

25. Ibid., II–II, q. 23, a. 5 ad 2.

26. Ibid., II–II, q. 23, a. 5 ad 1.

27. Ibid., II–II, q. 25, a. 1c. Cf. *De caritate* a.4c: "caritas diligit Deum ratione sui ipsius; et ratione eius diligit omnes alios in quantum ordinantur ad Deum: unde quodam modo Deum diligit in omnibus proximis; sic enim proximus caritate diligitur, quia in eo est Deus, vel ut in eo sit Deus."

with us a share of happiness from God.[28] It is proper for God to be loved above all because the happiness that is integral to friendship with God "is in God as in the common and fountain-like principle of all who are able to participate in that happiness" (*beatitudo est in Deo sicut in communi et fontali omnium principio qui beatitudinem participare possunt*).[29] The friendship of *caritas* extends even to our enemies, for through the Holy Spirit we are able to love them also in relation to God, to whom the friendship of *caritas* is primarily directed.[30] Likewise, in loving ourselves and our own bodies out of *caritas*, we do so precisely with respect to God.[31] Every act of *caritas* is therefore done in regard to God and for the sake of God, who alone is the principal object of *caritas*.

As these three points suggest, Aquinas believes that there is a deep relationship between *caritas* on the one hand and the doctrine of God, specifically the person and work of the Holy Spirit, on the other. *Caritas* is a matter of friendship with God that is established through the Spirit, union with the inimitable object and end of human life. In an important sense, then, Aquinas's account of *caritas* is an outgrowth of trinitarian doctrine and of his doctrine of the Holy Spirit in particular. Through *caritas* we are united in friendship with the triune God who is both the source and end of love, and so united precisely through the Spirit, who proceeds as love in God's own life and is sent forth in mission in and for the sake of the world.

Love in the Spirit: *Caritas* as Trinitarian Theology

The relevance of pneumatology and trinitarian doctrine more broadly speaking for Aquinas's understanding of *caritas* as friendship can be further explored through a consideration of processions, relations, persons, and missions. These pivotal themes in Aquinas's account of the trinitarian mystery indicate with additional clarity the connection between *caritas* and the doctrine of the Holy Spirit

28. *ST*, II–II, q. 26, a. 2c.

29. Ibid., II–II, q. 26, a. 3c.

30. Ibid., II–II, q. 23, a. 1 ad 3.

31. Ibid., II–II, q. 25, a. 12c.

that he is able to discern. That connection, in turn, finds clear expression in Aquinas on the work of the Spirit.

Processions, Relations, Persons, and Missions In addressing the divine processions, relations, and persons, Aquinas presents the core of his trinitarian theology, the doctrines of the Word and of love.[32] As noted earlier, Aquinas's accounts of the Word and of love instruct readers how to think about the procession and property of the Son and those of the Spirit, respectively. The name "Word" (*Verbum*) can be said of God personally, though not essentially, because it signifies an emanation of the intellect, whereas *amor* must be said of God both essentially in one sense and, in another, properly of the Spirit in particular. Since the person who proceeds in God by way of emanation is the Son, the title "Word" is attributed specifically to the Son, of whom it designates the personal property. In this procession his personal distinction from the Father is made known.[33]

Similarly, Aquinas uses the concept of love (*amor*) to explain how the procession and personal property of the Spirit should be perceived. The word "*amor*" in God has two meanings, the essential love common among the three persons and the personal love identified specifically with the Holy Spirit.[34] Taken personally, *Amor* is the proper name of the Holy Spirit. The Spirit proceeds from the Father and the Son in a procession that is called spiration.[35]

The Spirit's personal name of love is conceived of in a comparable way as the Son's name of Word, though accounting for this pneumatological title is more difficult since "word" is not essential when spoken of God but "love" is. Even so, just as through the act of understanding there results in the one who understands a concep-

32. The claim that these doctrines constitute "the heart of Thomas' trinitarian theology" is advanced by no less an authority than Gilles Emery, OP ("The Doctrine of the Trinity in St Thomas Aquinas," in Thomas Weinandy, Daniel Keating, and John Yocum, eds., *Aquinas on Doctrine: A Critical Introduction* [London: T&T Clark, 2004], 57).

33. *ST*, I, q. 34, a. 2c, ad 3.

34. Ibid., I, q. 37, a. 1c, ad 4.

35. Ibid., I, q. 27, a. 4 ad 3.

tion of the object understood (a conception called a word), so when anyone loves an object a certain impression (*impressio*) results of the thing loved in the affection of the lover.[36] By virtue of this *impressio*, the object loved is in the lover just as the thing understood is in the one who understands. Aquinas describes this impression as an affection (*affectio*) for, an impulse (*impulsio*) toward, and an attraction (*attractio*) to the beloved.[37] This impression, affection, or impulse of love illustrates the personal property of the Holy Spirit by allowing the Spirit to be distinguished from the Father and the Son. Emery puts the point well: "This impression of love has a relation of origin with the will from which it proceeds, and with the Word which necessarily comes before that love (the will loves what intelligence has first conceived)."[38] The doctrines of the Word and of the Spirit, then, serve to demonstrate the personal relative properties of the Son and the Holy Spirit, respectively, while also accounting for the unity of the divine essence in which the divine processions occur.

Another reason for the importance of the doctrine of the divine processions is that it provides the necessary grammar for speaking about the sending of the Son and the Spirit in their temporal missions. In his account of the missions (*missiones*) of the Son and the Spirit, Aquinas explains that the union between God and the faithful is accomplished precisely through these missions. In order to see how he reaches this conclusion, it is necessary to trace certain features of his argument. The mission of a divine person includes two elements: first, the eternal procession of this person from another, and second, the gift of a created effect in time, namely, sanctifying grace. Regarding the first element, Aquinas clarifies that mission does not comprise a movement, strictly speaking, because the divine persons are eternal and unchanging. Rather it simply implies relation of origin, as in the Son's relation of origin to the Father and

36. Ibid., I, q. 37, a. 1c.

37. Ibid.

38. Emery, "The Doctrine of the Trinity," 58.

the Spirit's relation of origin to the Father and the Son in the divine eternity. There is neither superiority nor inferiority implied in the Father's sending of the Son and of the Spirit because mission means in this sense the procession of the person sent from the sender.[39] Whereas the procession is eternal, the mission is only temporal. Or, put somewhat differently, mission includes the eternal procession with the addition of a temporal effect.[40]

Regarding the second element, Aquinas points out that the divine person who is sent begins to exist "in a new way" in the saints.[41] The change, however, occurs in the creature and not in the divine person. The missions of the divine persons do not mean that God is sent to a place where he was not before, but that through these missions God is present in a new capacity.[42] This new mode of presence is the effect of grace, by which God dwells in his people. The Father sends the Son and the Spirit, who come to inhabit those who receive God's grace. The Father also inhabits those who receive grace, though the Father is not sent but does the sending. Yet precisely in sending the Son and the Spirit, the Father comes with them. As a result, the whole Trinity inhabits the saints.[43]

Mission is best described not only in terms of sending but also of giving. A divine person is sent and given, in so far as "to send" entails existing in a new capacity and "to be given" implies a certain possession in the human person (in the sense of union, not ownership).[44] The existence of a divine person in a new capacity and the

39. *ST*, I, q. 43, a. 1c.

40. Ibid., I, q. 43, a. 2 ad 3. By making this distinction between mission and procession, Aquinas avoids collapsing the former into the latter, which would suggest that the economy of salvation is constitutive of the divine persons.

41. Ibid., I, q. 43, a. 1c.

42. Ibid., I, q. 43, a. 2 ad 2; I, q. 43, a. 1c.

43. Ibid., I, q. 43, a. 1c, 2c, 8c. Cf. Gilles Emery, OP, *Trinity in Aquinas* (Ann Arbor, Mich.: Sapientia Press, 2003), 160–61.

44. *ST*, I, q. 38, a. 1c: "Habere autem dicimur id quo libere possumus uti vel frui, ut volumus. Et per hunc modum divina Persona non potest haberi nisi a rationali creatura Deo coniuncta."

"possession" of a divine person by the faithful Christian yield the sanctification of the human person.[45]

In order to grasp this idea of dwelling, Aquinas develops two lines of thought. The first can be called "ontological."[46] The Son and the Holy Spirit impress upon the souls of the saints a likeness of the eternal property of each, namely, wisdom and love, respectively. The exemplary cause of this likeness is the eternal property of the Son and the Spirit. In his commentary on the *Sentences* Aquinas employs the concept of a "sealing" or "sigillation" (*sigillatio*) of the Son and the Spirit, who enable human persons to participate in their eternal relation to the Father.[47]

The second explanation of the Trinity's inhabitation of the saints has been termed "objective" or "intentional."[48] This one finds clear articulation in the *Summa*, especially in question forty-three on the missions. By God's gift of grace, the faithful are joined to God in a striking degree of immediacy by knowing him and loving him.[49]

45. Ibid., I, q. 43, a. 3c: "Respondeo dicendum quod divinae Personae convenit mitti, secundum quod novo modo existit in aliquo; dari autem, secundum quod habetur ab aliquo. Neutrum autem horum est nisi secundum gratiam gratum facientem." Cf. Herwi Rikhof, "Trinity," in *The Theology of Thomas Aquinas*, ed. Rik Van Nieuwenhove and Joseph Wawrykow (Notre Dame, Ind.: University of Notre Dame Press, 2005), 36–57, in particular 45.

46. This designation is in keeping with Emery (*Trinity in Aquinas*, 161; "The Doctrine of the Trinity," 61).

47. Aquinas, *In I Sent.*, d. 15, q. 4, a. 1.

48. The naming of this second line of thought also reflects the influence of Emery (*Trinity in Aquinas*, 162; "The Doctrine of the Trinity," 61).

49. Thomas limns the immediacy of this union in *ST*, I, q. 43, a. 3c: "Est enim unus communis modus quo Deus est in omnibus rebus por essentiam, potentiam et praesentiam, sicut causa in effectibus participantibus bonitatem ipsius. Super istum modum autem communem, est unus specialis, qui convenit creaturae rationali, in qua Deus dicitur esse sicut cognitum in cognoscente et amatum in amante. Et quia, cognoscendo et amando, creatura rationalis sua operatione attingit ad ipsum Deum, secundum istum specialem modum Deus non solum dicitur esse in creatura rationali, sed etiam habitare in ea sicut in templo suo." On the relationship between charity and knowledge, see Michael Sherwin, OP, *By Knowledge and By Love: Charity and Knowledge in the Moral Theology of St. Thomas Aquinas* (Washington, D.C.: The Catholic University of America Press, 2005), especially chapters 5 ("Charity's

Those in a state of grace are assimilated to God. Through the mission of the Son, the saints are assimilated to the Son by the illumination of their intellect. Through the mission of the Spirit, they are assimilated to the Spirit by the gift of *caritas*. In each case, as Emery observes, the saints come to participate in the property of the divine person by an effect of grace appropriated to that person.[50] The soul's assimilation to the Trinity yields the intellectual illumination that conveys the knowledge of God, as regards the Son, and an ardor of *caritas*, as regards the Spirit, as both the Son and the Spirit are sent in their temporal missions by the Father.

There is a difference in the effect of the two missions.[51] Nevertheless, Aquinas emphasizes the profound connection between the two. The Son, the Word, is "not just any word, but the Word breathing Love."[52] Therefore the Son is not sent "in accordance with just any kind of intellectual perfection, but according to the intellectual illumination that breaks forth into the affection of love."[53] The Father's sending of the Son in time leads to the human intellect's bursting forth in love precisely because the indwelling Son himself eternally bursts forth in Love—the Holy Spirit. Meanwhile, the Spirit's mission is according to the mode of *caritas*: "because the Holy Spirit is Love (*Amor*), the soul is assimilated to the Holy Spirit by the gift of charity."[54] Sent by the Father, the Holy Spirit takes up residence in the saints and fills them with the love that the Spirit *in se* is. It logically follows that *caritas* is the soul's participation with the Holy Spirit.[55] In the friendship of charity, those in a state of grace become participants through the Holy Spirit in the life of the triune God. They do so precisely because of the indwelling of the Holy Spirit, which Aquinas refers to often—particularly in his biblical commentaries—as the ba-

Relationship to Knowledge in Human Action") and 6 ("Charity's Status as a Virtue"). More will be said about this issue, and this particular study, in chapter 6 below.

50. Emery, *Trinity in Aquinas*, 162.

51. *ST*, I, q. 43, a. 5 ad 3.

52. Ibid., I, q. 43, a. 5 ad 2.

53. Ibid.

54. Ibid.

55. Ibid., II–II, q. 23, a. 3 ad 3.

sis of the Christian life. For example, commenting on Christ's words to the disciples in John 14:17, Aquinas picks up on the reference to the Spirit dwelling with them. He underscores in particular the intimacy indicated here: "You know [the Spirit], because he abides with you, and he will be in you" (Jn 14:17)—that is, Aquinas says, "in the depths of your heart" (cf. Ez 11:19).[56] For Aquinas, the same Spirit who proceeds eternally as the bond of love between the Father and the Son is sent, in temporal mission, to inhabit the hearts of the faithful in the gift of sanctifying grace, to make them like God by grace, and to draw them into the life and love of God.[57]

On this concept of inhabitation, Aquinas specifies that the missions make possible a new, special way in which God is present. It is through the missions that God comes to dwell in the saints "as the object known is in the knower and the beloved in the lover."[58] From this perspective, the human person is not only a rational creature in whom God is present; the person has actually become God's temple, in which God resides and is worshiped.[59] This special mode of presence is realized in the rational creature through the missions of the Son and the Spirit. By these missions the soul is assimilated to God, God dwells intimately therein, and the soul is sanctified by God's grace.

This exploration of Aquinas's account of the missions began by stating his conclusion that union with God is accomplished precisely through these missions. Now that some of the main features of his argument in this question have been outlined, it is possible to see how he reaches this conclusion. Those in a state of grace are assimilated to God by an illumination of their intellect and an enkindling of their affection, that is, by their participation in the temporal mis-

56. *Ioan.*, par. 1920.

57. *ST*, I, q. 43, a. 3c; I, q. 43, a. 5 ad 2.

58. Ibid., I, q. 43, a. 3c.

59. Ibid. Cf. Rikhof, "Trinity," 46; D. Juvenal Merriell, CO, "Trinitarian Anthropology," in *The Theology of Thomas Aquinas*, ed. Rik Van Nieuwenhove and Joseph Wawrykow (Notre Dame, Ind.: University of Notre Dame Press, 2005), 123–42, in particular 136.

sions of the Word and of love. The soul is therefore united to God and attains him. Such language is strikingly similar to the point mentioned earlier about how Aquinas describes the effect of *caritas*, namely, as union with God and the attainment of God. This parallel indicates that Aquinas's trinitarian theology serves as the basis of his moral theology. More precisely, it shows that his account of the theological virtues, and of *caritas* in particular, is grounded in his understanding of the divine processions and missions.[60] Through the temporal missions of the Word and of love, the whole Trinity comes to dwell in the human soul. By grace the saints are assimilated to God and so are enabled to know God truly and love God rightly, as God's own beloved, in the friendship that *caritas* is.[61] Statements like these point to the basic link between *caritas* and the doctrine of the Trinity, and pneumatology in particular. A greater understanding of the trinitarian basis and scope of *caritas* in Aquinas, and especially of its properly pneumatological point of reference, can be gained by noting Aquinas's attention to the Spirit and his designation of the Eucharist as the "sacrament of charity" (*sacramentum caritatis*).[62]

Aquinas on the Work of the Holy Spirit: A Reading of Summa contra Gentiles IV Aquinas provides an especially rich account of the work of the Spirit in *Summa contra Gentiles* IV.[63] After outlining the

60. Emery reaches the same conclusion: "This doctrine of the presence of the known in the knower and of the beloved in the lover, with which St. Thomas expounds the inhabitation of the divine persons, manifestly benefits from his doctrine of the procession of the Word and of Love. Trinitarian doctrine furnishes here the foundation of St. Thomas' theological anthropology (doctrine of the image of God), of his moral theology (doctrine of theological virtues in particular), and of his eschatology (doctrine of the vision and of the fruition of God)" (*Trinity in Aquinas*, 163).

61. Aquinas makes explicit the connection between the missions of the divine persons, on the one hand, and the human acts of knowing and loving, on the other, in his important formulation in *ST*, I.38.1c: enjoyment of God occurs when a rational creature "is made partaker of the divine Word and of the Love proceeding, so as freely to know God truly and to love God rightly."

62. *ST*, III, q. 73, a. 3 ad 3; III, q. 78, a. 3 ad 6.

63. A good English translation of book four of the *ScG* has been produced by Charles J. O'Neil (Notre Dame, Ind.: University of Notre Dame Press, 1975).

effects attributed to the Spirit in Scripture regarding the whole of creation (chapter 20), he devotes the next two chapters to plumbing Scripture's teaching about the work of the Spirit in and for the rational creature. In contemplating various passages pertaining to the work of the Spirit, Aquinas discerns among them a common underlying theme of love. He begins by quoting Paul: "God's love has been poured into our hearts through the Holy Spirit that has been given to us" (Rom 5:5). Elsewhere, in his commentary on Romans, Aquinas remarks that in this verse *caritas Dei* can be interpreted in two ways, either the love with which God loves us or the love with which we love God.[64] In both senses, the love of God is poured into our hearts through the Holy Spirit. For the very love of the Father and of the Son, the Holy Spirit, is given to us in order to bring us up to the participation of love.[65] Although Aquinas does not give such a detailed commentary on Romans 5:5 in the *Summa contra Gentiles*, he deduces from it here that the charity by which we love God is in us by the Holy Spirit. God is the object of the charity shed abroad in our hearts through the gift of the Holy Spirit, as noted in the third aspect of this virtue discussed above.[66] The presence of charity in us is an indication that the Spirit has been given to us and is also present in us (cf. 1 Cor 3:16). Dwelling in us, the Spirit kindles our love for God. The Spirit thus makes us lovers of God. Because of the common operation of the Father, Son, and Holy Spirit, another way of expressing this point is to say that God makes us lovers of himself through the gift of himself in the person of the Holy Spirit.[67]

64. *Ad Rom.*, 5, lect. 1, n. 392. As noted by Rikhof, the double meaning corresponds to the mutual relationship that is characteristic of friendship (Rikhof, "Trinity," 53; cf. *ST*, II–II, q. 23, a. 1).

65. *Ad Rom.* 5, lect. 1, n. 392.

66. I.e., charity's object.

67. Aquinas applies the doctrine of common operations in the following manner: "Since, then, the power of the Father, and of the Son, and of the Holy Spirit is identical just as the essence is, necessarily whatever God effects in us must be, as from an efficient cause, simultaneously from the Father and the Son and the Holy Spirit." He also acknowledges the special role of the Spirit: "the charity which is in us, although it

Moreover, because every beloved is in the lover, for such is the intimacy of love, through the Holy Spirit the Father and the Son dwell in us (Jn 14:23, 1 Jn 3:24), and we in them (1 Jn 4:16, 13). Through the Spirit, therefore, we are drawn into the life of God.[68]

In his contemplation of various biblical passages on the Spirit's work, Aquinas discovers that these passages are best understood in terms of friendship. While he is clearly influenced by Aristotle, his chief interest seems to be in understanding the teaching of Scripture in the deepest possible way. Reading attentively, he learns that the work of the Spirit in the faithful bears many of the distinctive marks of friendship. Just as it is proper to friendship to reveal secrets to one's friend, so Scripture teaches that the Spirit, who searches even the depths of God, reveals God's mysteries to the faithful (1 Cor 2:9–10).[69] Just as a friend is like another self, such that one person's possessions are shared with a friend, so too Scripture testifies that God freely lavishes his gifts, through the Holy Spirit, upon those who share with him in the love of friendship (e.g., 1 Cor 12:8, 11).[70] Like a person adopting a friend as a daughter or son, and thus pledging to this person a share of the inheritance, God adopts the faithful through his Spirit of adoption, leading us to cry "Abba, Father" (Rom 8:15).[71] By the fact that one is established as the friend of another, every offense is removed, since offenses are contrary to friendship. That is why it is by the Holy Spirit, who establishes us as God's friends, that God forgives our sins (cf. Jn 20:22–23).[72] It is proper to friendship that one is present to a friend, enjoys the company of a friend, and finds in this friend safety and refuge in difficult times. Because the Holy

---

is an effect of the Father, the Son, and the Holy Spirit, is nonetheless for a special sort of reason said to be in us through the Holy Spirit" (*ScG*, IV, ch. 21, par. 2). This reason is related to Aquinas's identification of the Spirit as not only efficient cause but also exemplar cause, which makes our love for God "proprium repraesentativum Spiritus Sancti" (ibid.).

68. Ibid., IV, ch. 21, par. 3.

69. Ibid., IV, ch. 21, par. 5

70. Ibid., IV, ch. 21, par. 7.

71. Ibid., IV, ch. 21, par. 9.

72. Ibid., IV, ch. 21, par. 10.

Spirit makes us God's friends and establishes a mutual indwelling between us and God, it follows that through the Holy Spirit we rejoice in God, take delight in his presence, and have security in the midst of trials and adversity. The Spirit is specifically named in Scripture as our source of joy (cf. Rom 14:17) and our comforter (Jn 14:26).[73] Since another property of friendship is to consent to a friend in what she or he desires, it is by the Spirit that we are driven to fulfill, freely and lovingly, what God desires and expects of us (cf. 2 Cor 3:17, Jn 14:15).[74] All this is the work of the Spirit, who in friendship inclines the human will to love the true good, and especially the chief good who is the triune God himself.[75]

By explaining the texts about the Spirit with a hermeneutic of friendship, Aquinas points to the profound relation of *caritas* and the doctrine of God. The Holy Spirit, through whom God's love has been poured into our hearts, establishes us as the friends of God. As a result of the Spirit's temporal mission, we come to love God in the love of friendship. *Caritas* is precisely that love, as is clear from a key principle identified above: for Aquinas, *caritas* is friendship with God. It is friendship with the God who loves us and who has befriended us in his own Word and Love.[76] In the vivid language of Herwi Rikhof, "The relationship with God Father-Son-Spirit breathes the atmosphere of personal warmth, open-heartedness, and generosity."[77] Put simply, this relationship breathes the atmosphere of friendship and love. The work of God that can be attributed specifically to the Holy Spirit brings about such friendship.

While the Spirit figures prominently in regard to friendship and love, by virtue of the standard teaching about unity of operation among the three persons of God, Aquinas is able to affirm the fully trinitarian depth and *telos* of charity. Central to his vision of the Christian life as one of loving union with the Trinity through the

73. Ibid., IV, ch. 22, par. 3.
74. Ibid., IV, ch. 23, pars. 4–6.
75. Ibid., IV, ch. 23, par. 6.
76. Cf. Rikhof, "Trinity," 54.
77. Ibid.

Spirit, Aquinas's conception of charity has a decidedly sacramental thrust. Perhaps the preeminent way in which the Spirit's gift of love is received is through the Eucharist.

Eucharist: The Sacrament of Charity Aquinas's designation of the Eucharist as the *sacramentum caritatis* sheds additional light on the relationship between charity and the doctrine of the Holy Spirit as well as that of the Trinity as a whole. As this title suggests, the friendship that is established by the Holy Spirit is sustained and deepened in a special way in the sacramental bond. Once the Holy Spirit comes upon the eucharistic gifts and makes them holy, Christ's saving presence in the Eucharist effects the union of the soul with the triune God in the friendship of *caritas*.

Charity orients us to God, our last end, and unites us to God, for the effect of charity is union with and the attainment of God. Anything worthy of the title *sacramentum caritatis* must therefore yield such union. Aquinas asserts that the Eucharist is this sacrament. Yet in what sense? As he explains, the Eucharist is called the sacrament of charity because it both commemorates and re-presents the meritorious sacrifice of Christ, such that those who partake of it are united with Christ who willingly suffered out of charity.[78]

Aquinas observes that one reason for Christ's eucharistic presence is friendship. Friends naturally want to be together in person. It is fitting, then, for Christ to desire to be present bodily with his followers, whom he calls his friends (cf. Jn 15:15). He is present where he promises to be, precisely in the bread that is his body and the wine that is his blood (e.g., Mt 26:26–28). By virtue of his bodily presence, he makes possible our communion with him even now. While we await full and eternal fellowship with the triune God, Christ does not deprive us of his bodily presence in our pilgrimage, but unites us with himself in this sacrament through the living real-

78. On the Eucharist as union with Christ, see *ST*, III, q. 73, a. 3 ad 3; on Christ suffering out of charity, see III, q. 48, a. 2c; a. 3 ad 3.

ity of his body and blood. This sacrament "is the sign of supreme charity, and the uplifter of our hope, from such familiar union of Christ with us," for Christ himself says, "Those who eat my flesh and drink my blood abide in me, and I in them" (Jn 6:56).[79] Christ becomes tangibly present to his followers whenever this sacrament is celebrated, as the bond of communion and fellowship between disciples and the risen Lord grows deeper in the Spirit.[80]

By calling the Eucharist the sacrament of charity, Aquinas underscores the centrality of charity in the Eucharist. With respect to charity, the Eucharist is "figurative and effective."[81] Indeed, the supreme virtue is the reality of this sacrament, in regard not only to its habit but also to its act, as charity is kindled through the consumption of Christ's body and blood.[82] One of the effects of the Eucharist is the bestowing of grace and, spiritually, with it the virtue of charity. In this sacrament, God not only conveys the habit of grace and of charity but also arouses it to act. The Eucharist therefore serves both to increase and to stimulate charity.[83] These salubrious effects occur through the recipient's union with Christ, which is itself the effect of charity. Moreover, as Thomas shows, the *res* of the sacrament—its reality—is the love of the members of the church, the mystical body of Christ, for each other.[84] As a result of Christ's suffering out of charity, the faithful are united to him and to one another in and because of him. Aquinas is clear that Christ's main purpose in instituting the Eucharist was, after all, "not for satisfaction, but for nourishing spiritually through union to Christ and to his members, as nourishment is united with the person nourished."[85] As head of his body, Christ nourishes his members through the lavish gift of

79. Ibid., III, q. 75, a. 1c.

80. Joseph Wawrykow, *The Westminster Handbook to Thomas Aquinas* (Louisville, Ky.: Westminster John Knox Press, 2005), s.v. "Real Presence," 126.

81. *ST*, III, q. 78, a. 3 ad 6.

82. Ibid., III, q. 79, a. 4c.

83. Cf. ibid., III, q. 79, a. 6 ad 3.

84. Ibid., III, q. 73, a. 3c; III, q. 73, a. 2 sc.

85. Ibid., III, q. 79, a. 5c.

his own body and blood, a loving self-donation through the Spirit invoked in the eucharistic prayer.

The eucharistic title *sacramentum caritatis* brings together in one concise phrase two important strands in Aquinas's thought, namely, love and the Eucharist, and expresses their integral connection not only to one another but also to the doctrine of God. The union between Christ and the members of his church is established through the charity of friendship. In the Eucharist, God freely and extravagantly shares with us his own life and love through the bodily presence of Christ. Because Christ is truly present in the Eucharist, the love of God the Father is conveyed to us through the power of the Holy Spirit. In this sacrament of charity we are united with Christ, and so with the Blessed Trinity. We thereby come to know God in the deepest possible sense, the experiential knowledge that is properly called wisdom. This is what Aquinas elsewhere refers to as "knowledge by taste" (*sapida scientia*).[86] The spiritual tasting in the Eucharist ensures that the knowledge gained through this sacrament is truly knowledge by taste. In the Eucharist we are "spiritually nourished through the power of this sacrament," as Aquinas rhapsodizes, "spiritually gladdened, and as it were inebriated with the sweetness" of God's goodness and love:[87] "Eat, friends, drink, and be drunk with love."[88] The Eucharist, as the *sacramentum caritatis*, is the supreme meal of love. It is the meal of communion with Christ, and so with the Father and the Spirit, in the charity of friendship that is made possible through the enlivening activity of this same Spirit.

Aquinas's account of *caritas* illustrates the significance of the link between the Holy Spirit and love, since the friendship with God that *caritas* is, is established by the Holy Spirit. It also shows the trinitarian basis for his vision of the Christian life. The divine processions, relations, and persons serve to indicate that God is none other than

86. Ibid., I, q. 43, a. 5 ad 2.

87. Ibid., III, q. 79, a. 1 ad 2.

88. Song of Solomon 5:1, as quoted by Aquinas in ibid.

Father, Son, and Spirit, precisely as God has revealed himself, in the missions of the divine persons, to be. Furthermore, the Father's sending of the Son and of their common Spirit is what makes possible friendship with God, and so charity, the effect of which is union with God and the attainment of God. As friends of the Father through the Son and in the Spirit, the faithful come by grace to love God chiefly, as the principal object of all charity. The final result is the realization of the summit of Christian existence and the last end for which all human beings have been made, happiness in the triune God.[89]

THE CHRISTIAN LIFE AS GIFT

Aquinas's identification of the Holy Spirit as love has meaningful implications for understanding not only the related name of the Spirit as gift of the Father and the Son, and the Spirit's gift of love in the life of grace, but also the Christian life as a whole, which can itself be described as a gift. Aquinas makes clear that human power on its own avails nothing for participation in God, which must be given from above.[90] Such participation is therefore first and foremost a gift, and the virtues and practices in which life in Christ consists are also gifts of the Father through the Holy Spirit. Aquinas expresses the Spirit's ubiquitous effects upon the world, and especially upon the human mind and soul, in a particularly lucid and eloquent way in a sermon for the Feast of Pentecost entitled *Emitte Spiritum*, which comes most likely from his second regency in Paris, between 1268 and 1272.[91]

89. E.g., *ST*, I–II, qq. 1–5.

90. Ibid., I, q. 38, a. 1c.

91. A translation of this previously unpublished sermon, produced by Jeremy Holmes and Peter Kwasniewski, appears in *Faith and Reason* along with an introductory essay by Kwasniewski, "Aquinas' Sermon for the Feast of Pentecost: A Rare Glimpse of Thomas the Preaching Friar" (*Faith and Reason* 30:1–2 [2005], 99–139). It is in the essay that Kwasniewski reports its likely setting during Aquinas's second term in Paris. Meanwhile, as Louis-Jacques Bataillon continues preparing the text of the sermon for the Leonine edition, which he has provided to Jean-Pierre Torrell, OP,

The scriptural text on which Aquinas bases his sermon is Psalm 103:30 (104:30 *iuxta Hebraeum*), "Send forth Thy Spirit and they shall be created, and Thou shalt renew the face of the earth," which appears both in the liturgy of Pentecost and as part of a traditional prayer to the Holy Spirit that begins, "*Veni sancte Spiritus, reple tuorum corda fidelium, et tui amoris in eis ignem accende*," to which this verse from the Psalms is added and read responsively.[92] Aquinas readily admits in humility his dependence upon the subject of this sermon, since it is the Spirit who gives the ability to speak and to speak truthfully. In fact, the preacher's opening words underscore the necessity of the quickening and illuminating activity of the Holy Spirit in such an enterprise:

> We should speak about Him without whom no one can speak rightly, about Him who gives speech and gives the power to speak copiously. And indeed, it is impossible to speak rightly without Him.... Therefore, even though we are mute, we shall ask that He who gives abundant speech shall give me words to speak.

With that disclaimer, Aquinas quotes the first part of the verse in question ("Send forth Thy Spirit and they shall be created") and proceeds to identify the entire verse as a prophecy of Pentecost, when God's Spirit was manifestly poured out upon the apostles (Acts 2).[93]

In celebration of this feast, Aquinas divides the homily into two parts, one given in the morning, the *sermo*, and the other, the *collatio*, given in the evening. While the first part deals with what is proper to the Holy Spirit and with the sending of the Spirit, in the second Aquinas considers the Spirit's effects and the recipient of these effects. More precisely, Aquinas the preacher describes the Holy Spirit,

---

and to Kwasniewski and Holmes, my analysis here represents what is thought to be the most detailed examination of the sermon that has been conducted thus far. All quotations from the sermon come from the translation by Holmes and Kwasniewski.

92. The possible allusion to this prayer is noted by Kwasniewski ("Aquinas' Sermon for the Feast of Pentecost," 127–28, fn. 21). Holmes and Kwasniewski have translated biblical verses exactly as Aquinas quotes them from memory.

93. *Emitte Spiritum*, introduction.

whose personal property is love, as the giver of all life and the source of all being and of all motion, who has been freely sent into the world (part one). With special attention to the Spirit's omnipresence in Christian existence, as pointed out by Torrell, Aquinas further identifies the Spirit as the cause of all holiness, whose effects can be seen in the creation and renewal of the whole world and especially of the human being (part two).[94] These points and what they entail suggest that no less than all of life—in particular the Christian life, marked by signs of the Spirit's work—is aptly named a gift of the Father through the Holy Spirit, a gift that conforms its recipients to the Son.

Perceiving a pneumatological reference in this verse from the Psalms, Aquinas identifies what is proper to the Holy Spirit under the four characteristics that the name *spiritus* seems to convey: "subtleness of substance, perfection of life, impulse of motion, and hidden origin."[95] He then comments on these characteristics in reverse order, beginning with the Spirit as the hidden origin of things. According to Aquinas, everything that exists has a cause. While this cause may be hidden to the naked eye, on the basis of faith and reason it can be perceived. "What is that cause?" Aquinas asks, in the first of many rhetorical questions. His answer, not surprisingly, is that the cause of all that is, is God. Aquinas specifies that as the builder of all things (cf. Heb 3:4), God creates the world in a certain manner—not out of necessity but simply by God's own will, indeed, by God's loving will. Rather than a builder who constructs a house while being "urged on" by a need for profit or for a place to stay, God is like the artisan who builds not because of need or even usefulness but purely out of love for the beauty of the idea conceived

94. Torrell provides a brief but characteristically incisive discussion of this sermon, in which he observes that Aquinas suggests to his hearers "the omnipresence of the Spirit in the Christian life" (*Saint Thomas Aquinas*, vol. 2: *Spiritual Master*, trans. Robert Royal [Washington, D.C.: The Catholic University of America Press, 2003], 174).

95. *Emitte Spiritum*, I.1.

in the mind; what brings this house into being is the artisan's love. Therefore, Aquinas teaches, creation's origin derives from the Holy Spirit, whose property is love.[96]

Second, Aquinas discerns that impulse of motion is also proper to the Holy Spirit. Using an abbreviated version of one of his proofs for God's existence, he reasons that the various motions in the world come from a first mover, that is, from God.[97] Further, God's manner of moving is by will. Aquinas then asks, "But what is the first motion of the will?" and immediately answers, "Surely love." Someone who is moved by love "rejoices by love over the thing loved and sorrows over what is contrary to it." With the power of the Holy Spirit understood as "the inclination of divine love" that is alluded to in Ezekiel 1:12, Aquinas proclaims that this Spirit, then, is the source of all motion who is life and who gives life.[98]

After affirming that all things have their being and their motion from the Holy Spirit, Aquinas makes an apparent deviation from the proposed order.[99] He turns to a third theme, the Spirit's subtleness (*subtilitas*) of substance, in order to describe the very nature of the Spirit as love. In response to his own question as to whose love is under consideration here, Aquinas replies, "That of God and those who love God," a response that indicates the twofold character of the love that the Spirit is. First, with regard to God's own life, the Holy Spirit is love in God: "on the part of the one loved, [the Spirit] is the love by which God loves God and by which the Father loves the Son." Yet in another sense, the Spirit is the bond of love between God and the faithful. Such a love has both a vertical dimension, sig-

96. Ibid., I.2.

97. Cf. *ST*, I, q. 2, a. 3c.

98. *Emitte Spiritum*, I.3.

99. Earlier, Aquinas presented the four topics in the following order: subtleness of substance, perfection of life, impulse of motion, and hidden origin (*Emitte Spiritum*, I.1). He then noted that he would proceed in reverse order (I.2), but he seems to have switched subtleness of substance and perfection of life, since he addresses the former before the latter. In any case, there is obvious overlap among these four points, and the apparent slight inconsistency does nothing to detract from the overall thrust of the sermon.

nifying the joining of the human soul to what is higher, namely, to God, and a horizontal dimension, pertaining to the good of one's neighbors, including their salvation. Indeed, Aquinas observes that "there are some who want to be devoted to God and yet who neglect the salvation of their neighbor," but the Holy Spirit is not like that (*sed non sic Spiritus sanctus est*). Rather, the Spirit comes upon people and makes them genuinely solicitous for their neighbor's standing before God, as was the Apostle Paul, who became all things to all people in view of their salvation (cf. 1 Cor 9:22). While some are "manifold but deceitful," the same is not true for the Spirit, who "is manifold in such a way that He, remaining utterly one, bestows Himself upon diverse things." That is, to anticipate a point on which Aquinas elaborates later in the sermon, in being sent and acting in various ways upon diverse objects, the Spirit nevertheless remains the same. There is surely some change that occurs in this process, although the change is not in the Spirit *per se* but in God's manner of existence with respect to the people upon whom the Spirit acts, in whom God comes to dwell and so to exist in a new way.[100] Thus the change is really in those whom God inhabits in this new way, not in God. It is through the Spirit that those who love God are united to God in love, having been subtly led by the penetrating Spirit to withdraw from inferior things and cling to God.[101]

Fourth, perfection of life is also proper to the Holy Spirit. This Spirit, who is none other than the Holy Spirit, makes people holy, which is to say that the Spirit is in the business of making saints (*immo facit sanctos*). Through sanctifying grace, the Holy Spirit "renders [people] subtle, and contemptuous of temporal things," so that they become holy temples where the living God dwells. It is the Spirit who gives spiritual life by driving human persons forward (cf. Is 59:19) to work well and, in that way, leading them back "to the hidden origin through which we are united to God." Therefore the

100. Cf. *ST*, I, q. 43, a. 1c.
101. *Emitte Spiritum*, I.4.

Spirit is the giver of all life and the source of all being and of all motion, through whom Christ's faithful are made to be like him.[102]

While admitting that the sending of the Spirit is "marvelous and unknown to us" because it takes place eternally in God, Aquinas is nevertheless able to deduce that the Spirit is sent "without needing to be sent, without change of Himself, without subjection, and without separation."[103] First, the sending of the Holy Spirit is not a sending of necessity. The reason for it is not some need on God's part but rather human neediness, which comes "partly from human nature's dignity, and partly from its deficiency." As to dignity, rational creatures are unparalleled among created beings, having been given the potential to attain God as their end. As to deficiency, however, in and of itself human nature cannot reach God. Only by means of a supernatural mover can human beings attain the supernatural end for which they have been made, namely, the supreme good that is nothing other than the triune God. Aquinas then points out that a person is led to an end by knowledge and by love.[104] The knowledge and love in question here, however, transcend human knowledge and desire, respectively, as the preacher infers from Isaiah 64:4 and its basic equivalent, 1 Corinthians 2:9, both of which suggest their inherently supernatural quality. Therefore the knowledge and love of divine things, and indeed of God himself, that are required of us in order for us to reach the enjoyment of God are fundamentally beyond us. They must be revealed to us and enkindled within us: "It was necessary for heavenly secrets to be *made known* to men; it was necessary for the Holy Spirit to be invisibly sent, in order to move man's affections so that he may tend toward that end."[105] In this sense, there is a certain necessity pertaining to the sending of the Holy Spirit, although it is not due to any need of God's but precisely because of our

102. Ibid., I.5.

103. Ibid., II.1.

104. Cf. Sherwin, *By Knowledge and By Love.*

105. Here and elsewhere italics are used to denote emphasis that is original to the sermon. Cf. *ST*, I, q. 1, a. 1.

neediness, and so that we might benefit. The sending of the Spirit is, in other words, pure gift, God's gracious self-donation given freely out of good will for those who would receive it.[106]

Second, the Spirit is sent without any inward or personal change, that is, without change in the Spirit *per se*. A messenger who is sent from place to place experiences a change of location. Yet the Holy Spirit, as true God, is unchangeable and is not sent to a place previously unoccupied, but, again, in being sent comes to exist in a new way in a place where God already was and is, the only change being the precise manner of existence with respect to the person now inhabited by God. The change associated with the sending of the Spirit, therefore, occurs in us, not in God. In response to his own question as to how exactly the Spirit is sent, Aquinas likens the sending of the Spirit to that of the sun: the Spirit "*draws us to Himself*, and in that way He is said to be sent, as the sun is said to be sent to someone when he comes to share in the sun's brightness."[107] Thus, Aquinas proclaims, it is true that the Father has sent the Spirit of his Son into the hearts of God's children, adopted by grace, who can thereby cry "Abba! Father!" (Gal 4:6). There is no change in the gift giver, or in the gift itself (which in this case are one and the same), but for recipients of this gift there is a dramatic change called sanctification.[108]

Third, Aquinas explains that the Spirit is not sent out of subjection either, as though subordinate to the Father, or for that matter, to the Son. Blowing at will (cf. John 3:8), the Spirit makes us free (cf. 2 Cor 3:17) and is therefore no servant, but is said to be sent "only on account of the Father's identity as origin." Somewhat tangential to this discussion is Aquinas's defense of the *filioque*, which he nevertheless offers in abbreviated form here to show that just as subjection is not a feature of the Spirit's procession from the Father and the Son, it is also not a feature of the Spirit's mission. The main

106. *Emitte Spiritum*, II.2.

107. Cf. *ST*, I, q. 9, a. 1 ad 2 and ad 3; I, q. 43, a. 1 ad 3.

108. *Emitte Spiritum*, II.3.

theological point is simply that, as with change *ad intra*, subjection has nothing to do with the sending of the Holy Spirit.[109]

Fourth, nor is separation one such characteristic because, as Aquinas notes, the Holy Spirit is the Spirit of unity (cf. Eph 4:3) in whom no separation is to be found. For the Spirit not only unites persons to the Father but also gathers Christ's faithful together and makes them one as Christ has prayed for them to be (Jn 17:20–23). Aquinas closes this portion of the homily with a prayer of his own—what is perhaps a proto-ecumenical prayer—asking that the Spirit lead him, those with him, and presumably the wider church, deeper into the gift of such unity.[110]

Having considered in the first part of the sermon the morning homily, what is proper to the Holy Spirit, and the sending of the Spirit, Aquinas proceeds in the second part, the evening homily, to address the Spirit's effects and the recipient of these effects. It is in this context that the idea of the Christian life itself as a gift of the Holy Spirit can be grasped particularly well through a consideration of what Aquinas is saying. The words of the Psalmist ("Send forth Thy Spirit and they shall be created, and Thou shalt renew the face of the earth") specify a twofold effect of the Spirit, creation and renewal. In so far as creation designates production into being, it is correct to say that the Holy Spirit has created all that is, in accordance with Judith 16:14.[111] Aquinas, however, prefers to speak of creation in a different sense here, namely, the sense of being pro-

109. Ibid., II.4.

110. Ibid., II.5. While the suggestion that this prayer reflects a kind of proto-ecumenical spirit on the part of Aquinas may sound somewhat simplistic, it is striking to note the connection that Aquinas establishes between Christ's prayer for the unity of his disciples across the ages and an understanding of the work of the Holy Spirit. Later in this study, with Christ's high priestly prayer clearly in view, an attempt will be made to explore the potential for mutual affirmation and amplification between Aquinas and his theological heirs, on the one hand, and Wesley and his theological heirs, on the other, on the basis of pneumatological resonance and compatibility.

111. "Let all your creatures serve you, for you spoke, and they were made. You sent forth your Spirit [less desirably, "spirit" in the NRSV], and it formed them; there is none that can resist your voice."

moted to a higher state, as bishops in the medieval idiom are said to be "created." Understood in this way, the notion of creation relates to the adoption of people as children of God, by which they are "promoted" and can be said to be created anew as a kind of first fruits of God's creatures (cf. Jas 1:18). God has re-created such people in order that they might live a new life in the existence of grace, like the apostles, who were the first fruits of this re-creation that is the effect of the Holy Spirit.[112]

Aquinas then explains that the re-creation of which he is speaking, the renewing of our natures in Christ through the Spirit, consists of various steps. He notes four of them in the sermon. First, it can be viewed with respect to the grace of charity. To consider re-creation in this sense, Aquinas observes that in the natural state of existence the first thing that newly born persons have obtained is life. By analogy, the same is true in the existence of grace, in which one lives principally through charity. While love for our brothers and sisters in Christ confirms that we have passed from death to life, those who do not love, as Scripture teaches, are dead (1 Jn 3:14). In Aquinas's words, charity is "the life of the soul, for just as a body lives through its soul, so the soul lives through God, and God dwells in us through charity" (cf. 1 Jn 4:16). The charity for fulfilling God's commands, which exceeds what is possible by human power alone, comes from the Holy Spirit through whom the love of God is poured into our hearts—the same Spirit who has been given to us (Rom 5:5). Using the sun as an illustration once more, Aquinas says that just as those who have "a share of daylight" have that light "from the sun," so those who have charity have it "from the Spirit." By the gift of love, given through the one who is love, the Spirit re-creates the human soul in the life of grace. It is for this reason that the grace of charity can be associated in a special way with the person of the Holy Spirit, whose effects include our "creation" as beloved, and loving, sons and daughters of God.[113]

112. *Emitte Spiritum*, III.1.

113. Ibid., III.3.

To know God in wisdom is the second step in the Spirit's effect of creation, according to Aquinas, for from sincere love of God there flows a desire to understand and obey the will of God. Aquinas sounds a familiar note on the intimacy of the love of friendship, as he does in the *Summa theologiae* and the *Summa contra Gentiles*, as well as elsewhere in his works.[114] Jesus calls his disciples friends, not servants, because whereas the servant does not know what the master is doing, the Son has made known to his friends all that he has heard from his Father (Jn 15:15). Aquinas expresses the point simply by saying that God reveals his secrets to his friends. The Holy Spirit impresses those secrets upon the hearts and minds of Christ's friends, just as Jesus promised that the Spirit who was to come would teach his disciples all things, call back to mind the words of Christ, and guide them into all truth (Jn 14:26, 16:13). Inclining the heart "to give assent and to carry out what it hears," the Spirit imparts the wisdom of knowledge that contributes to a person's new life in Christ, given from above.[115]

The third step in the re-creation that is from the Spirit concerns the harmony of peace. Hearkening back to the previous point, Aquinas contrasts earthly wisdom with heavenly wisdom in order to identify the source of peace. Earthly wisdom, or wisdom so-called, has been harmfully tainted by the world. It is unchaste and corrupt, and its marks include peevishness and quarrels. For a description of heavenly wisdom, on the contrary, Aquinas turns to James 3:17, which describes the wisdom from above as pure, peaceable, modest, and persuadable. This is the wisdom that draws people to God. Concentrating on the second of those characteristics in particular, Aquinas extends the contrast by stating that whereas earthly wisdom promotes arguments and strife, the wisdom that is from God is peaceable, yielding agreement among those who have received it. The preacher then uses another question rhetorically to drive home

114. E.g., *ST*, II–II, qq. 23–27; *ScG*, IV, chs. 20–24; *In I Sent.*, d. 10, q. 1, a. 4.
115. *Emitte Spiritum*, III.4.

the point: "But who is it that makes the peace? The Holy Spirit" (cf. Eph 4:3), whose peace is twofold, given both in the present, as the battle against vices remains, and in the future, without fighting. Following Augustine, Aquinas mentions the three objects of peace: first, oneself, lest one's intellect, sensitive appetite, or rational appetite be "infected by errors or darkened by passions;" second, one's neighbor, in "the bond of love;" and third, God, in "the fellowship of charity."[116] Surely, then, peace is "utterly necessary" for the life that the Holy Spirit gives.[117]

The fourth step that Aquinas mentions is constancy of firmness. This gift also comes from the Holy Spirit, and it involves the work of strengthening the faithful inwardly so that they remain strong and steadfast in the faith. Hence the Apostle Paul, for example, prays that the Father will strengthen the Ephesians in their inner being with power "through his Spirit," and that Christ may dwell in their hearts as they are being "rooted and grounded in love" (Eph 3:16–17). The creation that is from the Holy Spirit empowers those in Christ to persevere unto the end, even the ultimate end of happiness in God for which God has created them. According to Aquinas, in these four respects—the grace of charity, knowledge of God, harmony of peace, and constancy of firmness—the first effect of the Holy Spirit is the elevation of persons to a higher level of existence, for in this sense the Spirit, poured out at Pentecost, creates anew, and conveys the gift of new life in Christ.[118]

Aquinas states that the second effect is a renewal consisting also of four things, the first of which is cleansing grace. Sin is like an "old age of the soul," whereas grace frees one from this old age through a cleansing from sin. Having been united to Christ, who is risen from the dead, the Christian lives in newness of life that comes from the Holy Spirit (cf. Rom 6:4). Through the laver of regeneration and renewal in the Spirit, one is renewed (cf. Ti 3:5).[119]

116. Cf. Augustine, *Tract. in Ioan.*, 77; *De Verbis Domine*, 57.

117. *Emitte Spiritum*, III.5.

118. Ibid., III.6.

119. Ibid., III.9.

Second, the renewal includes justice that is ever progressing. Just as a diligent worker, exhausted from the labor, rests and is then renewed, so the faithful, by running in the way of God's commandments (cf. Ps 118:32 [119:32 *iuxta Hebraeum*]), experience renewal through the Spirit. The cause of this running, according to Aquinas, is the Holy Spirit, as the preacher shows once more in question and answer form. With God as their end, their bodies and souls are refreshed and they can thus run and not grow weary (Is 40:31) while they continue on the journey toward God.[120]

The third thing in which the renewal of the Holy Spirit consists is what Aquinas calls wisdom that illuminates. By coming to understand divine things more deeply and in new ways than before, the faithful are renewed through the illuminating power of the Holy Spirit. The result is a closer conformity to Christ, whom Aquinas takes as the new man referred to in Ephesians 4:24. Christ is rightly called the new man because everything about him was new—a novel conception, not from human seed but from the Holy Spirit; a novel birth, since his mother remained a virgin after bearing him into the world; a novel suffering, without guilt; a novel rising from the dead, "quick and renewing" (*cita et innouans*); and a novel ascension, by his own power and not by that of another, unlike Enoch and Elijah. Having stripped off the old self with its sinful practices, those in Christ are clothed with the new self, which is being renewed in the knowledge of God (Col 3:9–10). In maintaining that such wisdom comes from the Holy Spirit, Aquinas reinforces the basic point that the Christian life is a gift of God through the Spirit.[121]

The fourth and final characteristic of this renewal is the glory that attains consummation when the saints are bodily renewed, "the oldness of punishment and guilt" having been taken away and replaced with the body of incorruptibility. At this time, Aquinas says, God's promise through the prophet Isaiah to create new heavens

120. Ibid., III.10.
121. Ibid., III.11.

and a new earth (Is 65:17) will be fulfilled. Once again, as he has in nearly every paragraph of the entire sermon, with the rhetorical use of a question Aquinas communicates a vital truth: "And where does this renewal come from? The Holy Spirit." The Spirit, the pledge of the heavenly inheritance for those in Christ, is the giver of life and the cause of all holiness whose effects in creation and renewal bring about the Father's redemptive purposes.[122]

Following his discussion of the effects of the Holy Spirit, Aquinas then closes the discourse with one final heading, concerning the recipient of these effects. In one sense, it is the whole world that receives this renewal, as indicated by the words of the Psalm, "the face of the earth" (Ps 103:30 [104:30]). Aquinas says that the phrase also refers, in another sense, to the human mind, "for just as it is through the face that we see in a bodily manner, so it is through the mind that we see in a spiritual manner." In order for the human mind to receive the renewal of the Holy Spirit, four conditions must be met according to Aquinas. First, the human mind should be clean, as in the psalmist's prayer for a clean heart and a right spirit (Ps 50:10 [51:10]). A mind cleansed from sin is fit to be renewed by the Holy Spirit and, hence, to receive the life that the Spirit gives.[123]

Second, Aquinas points out that the face of the human mind must be uncovered. That is, it should not be covered, whether by the darkness of ignorance or the desire for earthly things, lest the vision of God be needlessly obscured. As the Apostle Paul teaches, once the veil has been removed the faithful will behold the Lord with unveiled faces. Having been created anew, with the image of God cleansed and renewed in them, they are thus transformed into the same image from glory to glory by the Spirit (2 Cor 3:18).[124]

Third, the mind is to be directed in a certain way, which is to say, toward God. By proper intention and by obedience, human beings turn their face toward God, who gives the Holy Spirit to those who

122. Ibid., III.12.

123. Ibid., IV.1–2.

124. Ibid., IV.3.

ask (cf. Lk 11:13) and to those who obey. Aquinas maintains that the faithful should also direct their faces toward our neighbors. From his irreducibly communal reading of Pentecost, according to which the apostles receive the Holy Spirit as a gathered community and not simply as random or isolated individuals, Aquinas infers the relationship between the love and service of God and the love and service of one's neighbor in God. With the latter grounded in the former, the Spirit is given to those who, like the apostles, manifest their love for God through attentiveness to the needs of their fellow Christians and human beings.[125]

A fourth prerequisite of the mind's renewal by the Holy Spirit is firmness. Calling for the perseverance of Anna (1 Sm 1:18) and for that of those who are secure and not afraid (cf. Jb 11:15), Aquinas makes the point that the Spirit empowers persons to endure difficulties in fortitude. The apostles, who waited for the promised Spirit as they had been instructed to do (Acts 1:4, Lk 24:49), model the firm patience necessary for the mind to be renewed by the Holy Spirit. They would not have received the Spirit if they had gone away from Jerusalem. Mindful of the grace of such perseverance, Aquinas closes the sermon by anticipating the prayer for it that he and those listening to him would go on to pray to the Lord.[126]

In his sermon for the feast of Pentecost, Aquinas gives due attention to the person and work of the Holy Spirit. The sermon reflects his richly pneumatological soteriology and thereby invites one to consider the sense in which the Christian life as a whole is itself a gift of the Spirit. As Aquinas the preacher shows, the Spirit is the giver of all life and the source of all motion. Moreover, it is the Spirit who, having been freely sent into the world for its salvation, not only gives all life but also leads persons into a certain kind of life, namely, life in Christ, which is marked by the work of the Spirit and above all by love. Through the Spirit's twofold effects of creation and

125. Ibid., IV.4.
126. Ibid., IV.5.

renewal, the grace of charity is effectively conveyed and the sanctification of the faithful is achieved, unto the end of full salvation in the triune God. In this way, then, the life of grace in its entirety is profitably viewed through a pneumatological lens. The same Spirit who is the gift of the Father and the Son, and who infuses the virtue of love by inhabiting the faithful, is also the source and author of Christian existence, for which reason the Christian life is rightly named a gift of the Spirit, as Aquinas enables his audience to see.

CONCLUSION

The topic of gift, in its theological multivalence, facilitates the move from pneumatology and the doctrine of the Trinity on the one hand to soteriology on the other, and vice versa, that Aquinas so fruitfully makes. The account of the Holy Spirit as love in Aquinas as presented in the last three chapters, is, strictly speaking, an account of the Holy Spirit as love *in Aquinas*. That is to say, it is Aquinas who provides the conceptual tools necessary to construct such an account. Contemplating the revealed truths of *sacra doctrina* and their divine source, Aquinas places his pneumatology in a properly trinitarian context in order to examine the deep connection between the Holy Spirit and love—both in the sense of *Amor*, the love that the Spirit is, and *caritas*, the theological virtue and gift of the Spirit. With a trinitarian foundation as the basis for his conception of the Christian life, Aquinas grounds his moral theology in dogmatic theology, which gives love and holiness their proper depth and *telos* in relation to the doctrine of God and to the doctrine of the Holy Spirit in particular. Furthermore, not simply in his writings but also in his own life and work, St. Thomas Aquinas beautifully exhibits, as do all the saints, the friendship with God that is made possible by grace. Aquinas was a spiritual master.[127] What he discovered through practicing the faith is the fundamental

127. See Torrell, *Saint Thomas Aquinas*, vol. 2: *Spiritual Master*.

intersection of pneumatology, love, friendship, and the doctrine of the Trinity. For truly the one God, Father, Son, and Holy Spirit, is the source and end of all *caritas*, by whose gracious turn toward us in friendship we too come to know, and so to taste, the life-giving love of our gift-giving God.

Six

TOWARD GREATER LOVE

Aquinas, Wesley, and Life in the Spirit

So far this book has included two main sections, an assessment of the problem of sanctification in contemporary Methodist theology and in John Wesley (chapters 1 and 2) and an investigation of Aquinas's *amor*-based pneumatology (chapters 3 through 5). Now the time has come to integrate the findings discovered in the two main sections above. Doing so will reveal that in distinctive and yet largely complementary ways, Aquinas and Wesley provide resources that can be used to reclaim a richer pneumatology, specifically in relation to the theological virtue of love.

AQUINAS AND WESLEY AS SOURCES FOR PNEUMATOLOGICAL RECOVERY

While the thought of each of these figures has nuances of its own, Aquinas and Wesley both discern a connection between the Holy Spirit and love and explore that connection in their theological writings. In order to demonstrate how Methodists might learn from Thomas Aquinas, how Thomists might learn from John Wesley, and how these two traditions might contribute to a pneumatological *ressourcement* for the advancement of ecumenical and constructive theology, this final chapter examines a number of issues pertaining to the compatibility and distinctiveness of Aquinas and Wesley on the Spirit as love, both within God's life and in the lives of believers.

Again, the often considerable differences between these two figures should not be overlooked, lest they be brought into conversation too quickly, even if on an area of common ground. Not only are there differences in the style of theological reflection in which each has characteristically engaged (with Aquinas known for a speculative theology of a high order, and Wesley for his decidedly practical orientation) but also certain conceptual differences must be recognized. Sometimes Aquinas and Wesley do not use exactly the same theological terminology, and at other times they use the same language in what appear to be contradictory ways. Illustrative of the former are the concepts of virtue and the tempers.

Virtue and the Tempers

Aquinas, of course, devoted much attention to reflection on the virtues, and in his preferred definition of virtue he slightly modifies Lombard's *Sentences*: virtue is "a good habit of the mind, by which we live righteously, of which no one can make bad use."[1] Aquinas included in his analysis the cardinal virtues[2] of prudence,[3] justice,[4] fortitude,[5] and temperance[6] as well as, in the more particular Christian sense, the theological virtues of faith,[7] hope,[8] and charity.[9] While an extended analysis of Aquinas's account of the virtues exceeds the scope of this book, it is certainly worth mentioning that crucial to his account is the distinction between virtues that are ac-

1. *ST*, I–II, q. 55, a. 4c.
2. Ibid., I–II, q. 61; and the more detailed account in II–II, qq. 47–169.
3. Ibid., II–II, qq. 47–56.
4. Ibid., II–II, qq. 57–122.
5. Ibid., II–II, qq. 123–40.
6. Ibid., II–II, qq. 141–69.
7. Ibid., II–II, qq. 1–16.
8. Ibid., II–II, qq. 17–22.
9. Ibid., II–II, qq. 23–46.

quired and those that are infused. The acquired virtues perfect the powers of the soul and, through habituation, orient the person to the good that is natural to the person.[10] Meanwhile, the infused virtues, rather than being acquired through the correct use of one's natural powers, are given freely by God for the purpose of raising the human person to an even higher order, the supernatural order, and thus bring the person closer to God as end through the acts of believing, hoping, and loving.[11] In Aquinas's theology the importance of virtues, both the acquired virtues and especially those that are infused by God's grace, is indicated not only by the large number of questions that he devotes to the virtues but also by the location of these questions. In the *Summa*, his account of the virtues comes in the second part, on the movement of the rational creature to God. The virtues in general, and above all the theological virtues, are central to this movement in Aquinas's understanding.[12]

By contrast, Wesley has not provided nearly as orderly or developed an account of the virtues.[13] One related and prominent theme in his moral theology, however, is that of the tempers. For Wesley, tempers are the stable, enduring dispositions of a person—"that fixed posture of [the] soul."[14] As such, tempers are more than simply passive feelings, and more than even motivating dispositions. The lat-

10. Ibid., I–II, q. 63, aa. 2c, 4c.

11. Ibid., I–II, q. 62, a. 2 ad 1; I–II, q. 62, a. 3c.

12. Joseph Wawrykow, *The Westminster Handbook to Aquinas* (Louisville, Ky.: Westminster John Knox Press, 2005, s.v., "virtue," 168.

13. Notable studies on Wesley and the virtues include Richard P. Heitzenrater, "The *Imitatio Christi* and the Great Commandment: Virtue and Obligation in Wesley's Ministry with the Poor," in *The Portion of the Poor: Good News to the Poor in the Wesleyan Tradition*, ed. M. Douglas Meeks (Nashville: Kingswood Books, 1995), 49–63; Lawrence D. Hulley, *To Be and To Do: Exploring Wesley's Thought on Ethical Behaviour* (Pretoria: University of South Africa, 1988); D. Stephen Long, *John Wesley's Moral Theology: The Quest for God and Goodness* (Nashville: Kingswood Books, 2005); and Kevin Twain Lowery, *Salvaging Wesley's Agenda: A New Paradigm for Wesleyan Virtue Ethics* (Eugene, Ore.: Pickwick Publications, Wipf and Stock Publishers, 2008).

14. John Wesley, *Explanatory Notes Upon the New Testament* (London: William Bowyer, 1755; reprint edition, London: Epworth Press, 1954), 1 Thes 2:17.

ter, the motivating dispositions, Wesley commonly terms affections, although his subtle distinction between tempers and affections has not always been traced adequately by his interpreters.[15] According to Wesley, tempers are habituated affections that orient these affections properly toward good choices and actions. Some affections equate with the heart.[16] For those, the tempers are the habits that motivate and direct the affections, thus determining the inclination of the heart. In a more explicitly Christian sense, tempers are a matter of inward holiness that is the basis of, and leads to, outward holiness. In other words, from holy tempers proceed holy actions.[17] Randy Maddox provides a cogent summary that speaks to the implications for Wesley's participatory understanding of sanctification:

> Wesley took for granted a virtue psychology that emphasizes the role of habituated affections in motivating and guiding authentic human actions. Thus for him, love, joy, and peace are not *mere* emotions. They are the holy tempers from which flow holy thoughts, words, and actions. That is why he repeatedly insisted that the essence of sanctification was not mere outward conformity to law, but the renewal of our affections (heart) through participation in the Divine nature.[18]

According to Wesley, it is by sharing in God's own life that our affections are renewed, and the holy tempers that orient those affections properly are freely given to us by God for the corresponding shaping of our thoughts, words, and actions. These are the very tempers in which vital Christianity consists.[19]

15. Cf. Gregory S. Clapper, *John Wesley on Religious Affections: His Views on Experience and Emotion and Their Role in the Christian Life and Theology* (Metuchen, N.J.: Scarecrow Press, 1989), in which the language of tempers tends to be subsumed into that of affections.

16. E.g., *Minutes* (26 June 1744), Q. 4, in Wesley, *Works*, ed. Outler, et al., 10:131.

17. Wesley states that works proceed from tempers in *Explanatory Notes*, 2 Corinthians 9:6.

18. Randy Maddox, *Responsible Grace: John Wesley's Practical Theology* (Nashville: Kingswood Books, 1994), 131.

19. "True religion is right tempers towards God and man. It is, in two words,

Other interpreters of Wesley have perceived the significance of the tempers in his theological anthropology. For example, the findings of Thomas Lessman in his study of the role of the Holy Spirit in Wesley's theology further suggest that Wesley was operating, at least implicitly, from what could be described in contemporary terms as a virtue ethics approach. Lessman makes a case for understanding the fruit of the Spirit as not just the result of sanctification but also as the driving motive for it.[20] Seen in this way, love, joy, peace, and the rest of the virtues associated with life in the Spirit are the divinely infused affections that stimulate ongoing growth in holiness. Geoffrey Wainwright has suggested use of the scholastic notion of *habitus* to help Wesley maintain the constancy of the Holy Spirit's self-gift, ensuring that the works of believers remain the gifts of the Spirit, while affirming the genuine transformation of the believer as the continuing effect of the Holy Spirit on one's personal character.[21] In assessing Wesley on the Beatitudes, Edgardo Colón-Emeric observes that this is precisely the role of the tempers in Wesley's theology.[22]

Common to Aquinas's conception of virtue and Wesley's notion of the tempers is the concern for the exercising of habits in the grace-enabled practice of the faith, even if this concern finds expression in

gratitude and benevolence: gratitude to our Creator and supreme Benefactor, and benevolence to our fellow-creatures. In other words, it is the loving God with all our heart, and our neighbor as ourselves" (Sermon 120, "The Unity of the Divine Being" [1789], §16, in Wesley, *Works*, ed. Outler, et al., 4:66–67). Cf. Journal, 11 December 1785 (Wesley, *Works*, ed. Outler, et al., 23:382); and *A Thought on the Manner of Educating Children* (1783), 5, in Wesley, *Works*, ed. Jackson, 13:475–76.

20. Thomas Lessman, *Rolle und Bedeutung des Heiligen Geistes in der Theologie John Wesleys* (Stuttgart: Christliches Verlagshaus, 1987), 69–72.

21. Geoffrey Wainwright, "Perfect Salvation in the Teaching of Wesley and Calvin," in *Methodists in Dialog* 143–58, in particular 157.

22. Edgardo A. Colón-Emeric, *Wesley, Aquinas, and Christian Perfection: An Ecumenical Dialogue* (Waco, Tex.: Baylor University Press, 2009), 136–37. This assessment comes in the midst of Colón-Emeric's study of Aquinas and Wesley on the Beatitudes. D. Stephen Long also compares the readings of the Sermon on the Mount by these two figures and points out considerable similarities between Aquinas and Wesley in *John Wesley's Moral Theology*, esp. chs. 4 and 5.

distinctive ways in their respective writings. Hence, there are times when Aquinas and Wesley do not use quite the same theological vocabulary, as is true in regard to the virtues and tempers, but their interests in promoting virtuous and godly living are not foreign to one another. More importantly, the difference in vocabulary does not, at least in this case, connote any basic difference in substance or outlook.

In other cases, however, the terminological differences between Aquinas and Wesley are so pronounced that their positions seem outright contradictory. Two examples related to the topic of the Holy Spirit and the Christian life are Wesley's doctrine of assurance and Aquinas's teaching on merit.

Assurance

Wesley's doctrine of assurance, based on his reading of such texts as Romans 8:15–16 and Galatians 4:5–8, concerns the knowledge that one is a child of God, adopted by grace through saving faith in Jesus Christ. According to Wesley, this knowledge is attainable as the common privilege of every Christian through the free and gracious agency of the Holy Spirit, who bears witness with our spirit that we are children of God (cf. Rom 8:16). The doctrine of Christian assurance was the driving force behind Wesley's spiritual pilgrimage, and the shape and particulars of that doctrine changed over time.[23] Nevertheless, central to Wesley's doctrine of assurance is his understanding of the direct witness of the Holy Spirit, which he describes as "an inward impression on the souls of believers, whereby the Spirit of God directly testifies to their spirit that they

23. The nuanced changes in Wesley's understanding of this doctrine, along with the basic theological continuity in the midst of that development, can be seen, for example, in comparing the two sermons called "The Witness of the Spirit," I (1746) and *The Witness of the Spirit*, II (1767). In both discourses, Wesley grounds the doctrine of assurance in the objective witness of the Holy Spirit. The second discourse also reflects his mature emphasis on the Spirit's testimony to Christians through Scripture as confirmed in the cultivation of the fruit of the Spirit in their lives.

are children of God."[24] Of course, one problem with the doctrine the inner witness was that it invited charges of fanaticism or, alternatively, complacency.

To provide safeguards against such charges, Wesley also spoke of the need for an indirect witness of our own spirit. As what Kenneth Collins calls "a composite of checks and balances that helped to inform believers of the soundness of their assurance," the indirect witness for Wesley included a good conscience, obedience to God's commands, the theological virtues as marks of the new birth, and the fruit of the Spirit.[25] Regarding the latter in particular, Wesley insisted that the inner witness of the Holy Spirit had to be accompanied by the fruit of the Spirit:

> let none ever presume to rest in any supposed testimony of the Spirit which is separate from the fruit of it. If the Spirit of God does really testify that we are children of God, the immediate consequence will be the fruit of the Spirit, even "love, joy, peace, long-suffering, gentleness, goodness, fidelity, meekness, temperance" [Gal 5:22–23].[26]

Emphasizing the fruit of the Spirit in this sense as the result of sanctification, Wesley therefore not only allows for assurance but actually identifies it as the privilege of all the children of God. Through the gracious presence and effects of the Holy Spirit indwelling those who believe, it is possible to be assured of one's pardon and acceptance by God.

For his part, Aquinas admits the possibility of a certain awareness of grace in the soul, but in a much more qualified way. In his discussion of grace in the *Summa*, he asks whether a person can know that he or she has received grace.[27] His answer, in brief, is

24. Sermon 11, *The Witness of the Spirit*, II, V.I, in Wesley, *Works*, ed. Outler, et al., 1:296.

25. Kenneth J. Collins, "Assurance," in William J. Abraham and James E. Kirby, eds., *The Oxford Handbook of Methodist Studies* (Oxford: Oxford University Press, 2009), 602–17, in particular 606.

26. *The Witness of the Spirit*, II, V.I, in Wesley, *Works*, ed. Outler, et al., 1:297.

27. *ST*, I–II, q. 112, a. 5.

no. So at a very basic level, Aquinas appears to deny what Wesley champions, namely, the possibility of the Christian's genuine assurance, through the Spirit, of being an adopted child of the Father by grace, a daughter or son in the Son. Yet a closer examination reveals a greater measure of common ground than this simple answer itself suggests.

Aquinas goes on to clarify that a thing can be known in three ways; and in two of those ways, some knowledge of the Christian's having grace is possible, even though this knowledge does not seem directly equivalent to the knowledge that one is a child of God as taught by Wesley. According to Aquinas, one way a person can know that he has received God's sanctifying grace is by revelation, when God reveals this knowledge "by a special privilege" (*ex speciali privilegio*) to a select few in accordance with their particular mission from God (e.g., St. Paul).[28] Another way is by means of signs, for in as much as a person perceives that she delights in God and has no mortal sin within her, it is possible for her to know that she has received sanctifying grace.[29] The second of these ways of knowing comes closest to the view that Wesley would later develop, but neither one fully equates to Wesley's doctrine of assurance. Indeed, for Aquinas, the other way in which we might know if we have received God's sanctifying grace is from our knowledge, although unlike Wesley on the certainty of faith in assurance, Aquinas maintains that in this way we simply cannot know with certainty that we have received grace. To understand this conclusion would require that we know the principle of grace, but Aquinas points out that God is thus nevertheless unknown to us in this life on account of his excellence, his light simply unapproachable by us given its immensity (cf. 1 Tm 1:17).[30] Clearly, there are some significant terminological differences between Wesley and Aquinas on the question of assurance.[31]

28. Ibid., q. 112, a. 5c.

29. Ibid.

30. Ibid., q. 112, a. 5c, ad 3.

31. A related issue concerns the relationship between grace and the person of

These differences may or may not in the end be resolvable—that question will be addressed more fully later—but what is worth pointing out now is that the position each takes on this issue is reflective in part of his primary approach to theology. Wesley's eminent concern for addressing the present status of a believer before God (a topic that Aquinas does not ignore, to be sure, even if it is not most characteristic of his thought) lends itself to an emphasis on the Spirit's gift of assurance to which Wesley believes the Scriptures bear witness. Aquinas's more speculative interests lead him to make nuanced distinctions on the matter that are at a conceptually deeper level while certainly not lacking a scriptural basis of their own.[32]

---

the Holy Spirit. Wesley practically identifies grace, the presence and power of God, with the Spirit, which is a view that bears certain similarities with the Eastern notion of uncreated grace (cf. Lycurgus M. Starkey Jr., *The Work of the Holy Spirit: A Study in Wesleyan Theology* [Nashville: Abingdon Press, 1962], 33–37; this parallel between Wesley and Eastern Christianity on grace has been pointed out by, among others, Daniel Luby, *The Perceptibility of Grace in the Theology of John Wesley: A Roman Catholic Consideration* [Rome: Pontifical University of St. Thomas, 1994], 129–30, and Maddox, *Responsible Grace*, 86). Aquinas, for his part, represents well the Catholic position of created grace as an infused *habitus* in which the Spirit certainly has a role to play but is not to be equated with grace in this sense because the Spirit is uncreated grace.

In a strict sense, Wesley and Aquinas appear to differ on this matter, but surely the interpretation of Aquinas on grace proffered by Nicholas M. Healy should resonate strongly with Wesley's interpreters: Aquinas's treatise on grace is "really … a treatise on the work of the Holy Spirit, for grace is the Spirit's loving and self-giving mission which, though often working incognito, is ever present in the Christian life" (*Thomas Aquinas: Theologian of the Christian Life* [Burlington, Vt.: Ashgate, 2003], 111). Moreover, readers of Wesley would be wrong to suggest (as Starkey seems to) that the metaphysical commitments of scholastic theology in general, and of Aquinas in particular, render God as "distant" to an extent that belies biblical notions of divine immanence and indwelling (Starkey, 35). To cite just one example, Aquinas's account of the work of the Holy Spirit in *ScG* IV, in which he explains biblical texts about the Spirit using the model of friendship (see the discussion of this passage in chapter 5), provides ample evidence to dispel such a misunderstanding. Clearly, Aquinas and Wesley both account for the intimacy of life with God through the indwelling of the Holy Spirit, and whatever their differences on understanding the relationship between the Spirit and grace, this common, underlying concern should not be overlooked.

32. Colón-Emeric posits that concerning the doctrine of assurance an appeal can

Merit

Merit is another issue on which their respective views at face value do not seem to agree. Aquinas speaks of merit in a positive sense as the effect of cooperative grace. In his study of grace and merit in Aquinas, Joseph Wawrykow traces the development of Aquinas's thought from the *Scriptum* to the *Summa* and finds that merit consistently denotes the establishment of a right in justice to a reward from God, a scripturally grounded view in as much as it elucidates the meaning of the biblical teaching that God gives a just reward for certain actions (e.g., Jer 31:16, Mt 5:12).[33]

Aquinas explains in his mature thought on the matter that the basis for God rewarding good deeds is found in God, since a person can receive as a reward from God only what God has given her the power to work for by her own effort.[34] More precisely, as Aqui-

---

be made to Otto H. Pesch's distinction between "existential" and "sapiential" modes of theology in his study of Luther and Aquinas, with Wesley representing the former and Aquinas the latter (Colón-Emeric, *Wesley, Aquinas, and Christian Perfection*, 171–72). Pesch explains what he means by those modes as follows: "Existential theology is the way of doing theology from within the self-actuation of our existence in faith, as we submit to God in the obedience of faith. Its affirmations are so formulated that the actual faith and confession of the speaker are not merely necessary presuppositions but are reflexively thematized. Sapiential theology is the way of doing theology from outside one's self-actuation in the existence in faith, in the sense that in its doctrinal statement the faith and confession for the speaker is the enduring presupposition, but is not thematic within this theology. This theology strives to mirror and recapitulate God's own thoughts about the world, men, and history, in so far as God has disclosed them" ("Existential and Sapiential Theology—The Theological Confrontation between Luther and Aquinas," in Jared Wicks, ed., *Catholic Scholars Dialogue with Luther* [Chicago: Loyola University Press, 1970], 61–81, in particular 76–77). While this is a creative and helpful distinction in certain respects, the accuracy of Pesch's application of sapiential theology to Aquinas, understood in this particular way, can be called into question. For to do theology "from outside one's self-actuation in the existence in faith" seems like the opposite of what Aquinas means by wisdom; cf. *ST*, I, q. 43, a. 5 ad 2.

33. Joseph P. Wawrykow, *God's Grace and Human Action: "Merit" in the Theology of Thomas Aquinas* (Notre Dame, Ind.: University of Notre Dame Press, 1995), esp. chs. 2 and 3.

34. *ST*, I–II, q. 114, a. 1c.

nas clarifies, what makes good deeds meritorious is ultimately God's prior ordination: "our own action is meritorious only by reason of a previous divine ordination. It does not follow, therefore, that God becomes a debtor to ourselves simply. Rather does he become a debtor to himself, in so far as it is a right that what he has ordained should be fulfilled."[35] In affirming that certain acts are meritorious, Aquinas does not mean that persons who perform good deeds have some claim on God independent of God's grace. God is not in our debt in this way; indeed, rather than claiming that God somehow owes us something, it is more accurate to say that God owes himself something because of his prior ordination. With this reference to divine ordination, Aquinas connects his understanding of merit to predestination. Simply put, for Aquinas, the one whose deeds are meritorious has been freely chosen by God to enjoy eternal life. Apart from grace, no one can merit eternal life.[36] Conversion cannot be merited, nor can perseverance in grace.[37] Salvation is, radically, a gift of God. Yet precisely as God's gracious gift, salvation is not entirely external to us, according to Aquinas; we have a role to play in the working out of our salvation, and in his discussion of merit Aquinas accounts for this role.

While Aquinas speaks of merit in a positive sense within the defined parameters (no meriting of conversion or of perseverance), Wesley characteristically repudiates the idea of good works as meritorious for salvation and instead locates merit solely in Christ.[38] Wes-

35. Ibid., I–II, q. 114, a. 1 ad 3.

36. Ibid., I–II, q. 114, a. 2.

37. Ibid., I–II, q. 109 (esp. aa. 1–2, 5–7) and q. 111, a. 2c (conversion to the state of grace is due to an operative *auxilium*, by which the will is moved and does not move itself); and I–II, q. 114, a. 9 and q. 109, a. 10 (the grace of perseverance cannot be merited, and one in grace needs the help of additional *auxilia* from God in order to persevere).

38. For example, Wesley is sure to point out in his sermon on the means of grace that what is meritorious is not the use of these means but the saving work of Christ: "We allow farther that the use of all means whatever will never atone for one sin; that it is the blood of Christ alone whereby any sinner can be reconciled to God [cf.

ley is not quite as precise as Aquinas, however, in his treatment of the subject. Wesley's writings provide evidence of two understandings of merit: what he calls a "strict" or "proper" sense and a "looser" sense. Regarding the former, Wesley avers that merit pertaining to salvation is to be found not in human works but only in Christ, by faith: "all merit is in the Son of God, in what he has done and suffered for us."[39] As he says in a letter to his brother Charles, "I have declared a thousand times, There is no goodness in man till he is justified; no merit, either before or after; that is, taking the word in its proper sense."[40] In a "looser" sense, though, Wesley admits—in a way like Aquinas—the equation of "meritorious" with "rewardable."[41]

It is apparently in this sense that Wesley speaks of the matter in the Conference Minutes of 1770, in the heat of a controversy with Calvinists over the place of good works in the Christian life.[42] After

Rom 5:10]; there being no other propitiation for our sins [1 Jn 2:2, 4:10], no other fountain for sin and uncleanness. Every believer in Christ is deeply convinced that there is no merit but in him; that there is no merit in any of his own works; not in uttering the prayer, or searching the Scripture, or hearing the Word of God, or eating of that bread and drinking of that cup [1 Cor 11:28]; so that if no more be intended by the expression some have used, 'Christ is the only means of grace,' than this—that he is the only meritorious cause of it—it cannot be gainsaid by any who know the grace of God.... I do expect that he will fulfil his Word, that he will meet and bless me in this way. Yet not for the sake of any works which I have done, nor for the merit of my righteousness; but merely through the merits and sufferings and love of his Son, in whom he is always well-pleased [Mt 3:17].... Settle this in your heart, that the *opus operatum*, the mere work done, profiteth nothing; that there is no power to save but in the Spirit of God, no merit but in the blood of Christ; that consequently even what God ordains conveys no grace to the soul if you trust not in him alone. On the other hand, he that does truly trust in him cannot fall short of the grace of God, even though he were cut off from every outward ordinance, though he were shut up in the centre of the earth" ("The Means of Grace," II.4, IV.2, V.4, in Wesley, *Works*, ed. Outler, et al., 1:382–83, 391, 396).

39. *A Farther Appeal to Men of Reason and Religion*, Pt. I, I.6, in Wesley, *Works*, ed. Outler, et al., 11:108.

40. Letter to Charles Wesley, August 3, 1771, in Wesley, *Letters*, 5:270.

41. "For in a loose sense, 'meritorious' means no more than 'rewardable'" (ibid.). Aquinas makes the same basic point in his claim that *meritum* is *praemium* (*ST*, I–II, q. 114, a. 1c).

42. For accounts of Wesley's struggles with Calvinist antinomianism, see Earl P.

stating that salvation is not by the merit of works, but by works as a condition, he proceeds to describe merit in the following way: "As to *merit* itself, of which we have been so dreadfully afraid: we are rewarded according to our works, yea, because of our works. How does this differ from *for the sake of our works*? And how differs this from *secundum merita operum*? As our works *deserve*? Can you split this hair? I doubt, I cannot."[43] Later, sensing a need to clarify, Wesley explained himself more fully by referring again to the different senses of merit as he understands it:

> And yet I still maintain ... there is no merit, taking the word strictly, but in the blood of Christ; that salvation is not by the merit of works; and that there is nothing we are, or have, or do, which can, strictly speaking, deserve the least thing at God's hand. And all this is no more than to say, Take the word merit in a strict sense, and I utterly renounce it; take it in a looser sense, and though I never use it (I mean, I never ascribe it to any man), yet I do not condemn it. Therefore, with regard to the word merit, I do not contradict myself at all.[44]

Wesley may not ultimately contradict himself, but he surely could have employed a greater measure of consistency and carefulness in his discussion of merit. Nevertheless, what is clear is that he locates all "strict" merit in Christ.

The important detail for now, however, is that even in his understanding of merit in the "looser" sense, Wesley does not speak of it in the sense of an autonomous human achievement that would somehow entitle us to an independent claim on God's grace (neither does Aquinas, as mentioned above). Rather, merit in this sense is properly located in the larger context of an affirmation of salvation

---

Crow, "John Wesley's Conflict with Antinomianism in Relation to the Moravians and Calvinists" (Ph.D. diss., University of Manchester, England, 1964); and Allan Coppedge, *John Wesley in Theological Debate* (Wilmore, Ky.: Wesley Heritage Press, 1988).

43. Wesley, *Works*, ed. Outler, et al., 10:393.

44. "Remarks on Mr. Hill's Farrago Double-Distilled," in Wesley, *Works*, ed. Jackson, 10:433.

as the work of God in which God freely grants us a certain role to play, such that our good deeds—which are only possible by God's grace—are graciously rewarded by God.

Although an extended dialogue between Aquinas and Wesley on merit would exceed the scope of this inquiry, it bears noting that, as is the case with assurance, upon closer examination a greater similarity between their positions on this issue can be discerned than what a surface-level reading would suggest. To be precise, Aquinas and Wesley both share two foundational concerns. First, they both want to safeguard the claim that all salvation is of God, which Aquinas does by emphasizing God's prior divine ordination and giving of gifts, and Wesley does by stressing the work of Christ as the meritorious cause of salvation—which actually complements the teaching of Aquinas on Christ as alone capable of meriting salvation for us.[45] Second, both wish to affirm that human beings have a certain role to play in salvation. To be sure, this role is secondary, dependent entirely upon God's gracious assistance, but it is a genuine role nonetheless. To point out these fundamental connections, however, is by no means to equate the two views fully, for obvious differences remain. Without question, additional careful theological reflection is needed to determine the extent to which these views are compatible.[46] As noted later, by revisiting a theme that was treated in chapter 4, it may be possible to discover a way forward on this disputed point through the pneumatological motif of gift in Aquinas.

Many other issues could certainly be mentioned, but this is not the place for a comprehensive assessment of the theological methods or teachings of Aquinas and Wesley. The main idea at this stage is not even to answer the question of whether the substantive differences between Aquinas and Wesley on assurance and merit finally

45. *ST*, I–II, q. 114, a. 6.

46. Toward that end, the Joint Declaration on the Doctrine of Justification, which became a tripartite agreement when the Methodists signed on in 2007, may be taken as a promising sign.

render their positions contradictory, although as the argument continues I will suggest that, without giving up their distinctive qualities but precisely by emphasizing them in a certain way, their views might be held in a creative tension. For now, the point is simply to recognize that there are some significant ways in which their works diverge, and to outline, in brief, the contours of their divergence; without such an acknowledgement any comparison of the two would be facile.

Yet notwithstanding their differences in approach, emphasis, and even, at times, the conclusions they reach, Aquinas and Wesley share a foundational interest in the promotion of love and holiness in the Christian life. Their common interest is significant enough to bring them into conversation on this issue in spite of the dissimilarities between them. In each case, a certain understanding of the Holy Spirit figures prominently, as the Spirit is identified as the cause of holiness and love in faithful Christians. The pneumatological parallels between Aquinas and Wesley suggest potential both ecumenically, for their theological heirs, and constructively, for those interested in the development of a more robust pneumatology. The fact that, in both Catholic and Methodist teaching, there is a clearly operative pneumatology with emphasis on love and holiness in Christian life has been observed in Catholic-Methodist ecumenical dialogue, and this basic similarity can be developed further through an assessment of Aquinas and Wesley on the Spirit. In addition, the recent interest shown in recovering the centrality of the doctrine of the Holy Spirit in theological inquiry and in the life of the church can be informed by an appreciation of the pneumatological thrust found in the works of these two figures, especially given the fervent concern for holiness typified by Wesley, which highlights the appropriated connection between the Spirit and sanctification, and the substantive trinitarian doctrine presented by Aquinas, which clarifies the proper depth and *telos* of holiness and love. This latter claim in particular brings into focus the problem of a general neglect of pneumatology in Christian theology.

The General Neglect of Pneumatology

In order to establish that Aquinas and Wesley can serve as sources for pneumatological recovery, which is one of the arguments of this final chapter, it is important to account for the problem that has created the need for such a recovery in the first place. This is therefore a fitting time to unpack the observation made in the introduction of the present work, where it was noted that the doctrine of the Holy Spirit has often been a relatively neglected subject in theological inquiry, perhaps especially in the modern West. What follows includes a more direct engagement with the aforementioned problem and the corresponding criticism of Western theology as a whole. To be sure, the history of Christian theology includes a number of quite sophisticated pneumatological expositions, and in at least some circles there seems to be a growing interest in pneumatology at present. Theologians, however, have generally devoted far less attention to the person and work of the Holy Spirit compared to the doctrine of Christ, for example. While affirming the inherent christocentricity of Christian theology, Gary Badcock explains that a major reason for the "hiddenness" of the Holy Spirit in Christian thought across the ages has been the "enormous elaboration" of the doctrine of Christ:

> Following both the Pauline theme that the Spirit is the Spirit of Christ, and above all the discourse of Jesus in John 14–16, the work of the Spirit has generally been understood to be somehow hidden beneath that of Christ, with the results, however, that the former has not received the degree of sustained treatment in the history of theology that the latter has been given.[47]

Thus one challenge facing theologians is the task of constructing a fuller and more explicit doctrine of the Holy Spirit, one that acknowledges the essential importance of the Spirit in relation to Christ but

47. Gary D. Badcock, *Light of Truth and Fire of Love: A Theology of the Holy Spirit* (Grand Rapids: Eerdmans, 1997), 1–2.

refuses to subordinate pneumatology to Christology. As an attempted corrective, Badcock proceeds to develop a theology of the Spirit that emphasizes the themes of truth and love and then relates this theology of the Spirit to the renaissance of trinitarian theology that began in the twentieth century and continues in various ways today. Later in this chapter, we will sketch the contours of a similar proposal to reevaluate the question of the work of the Spirit, in this case drawing from the insights of Aquinas and Wesley, and in which Christ's discourse on the Spirit in John 14–16, in particular his language of friendship and love in John 15, figures prominently—as an antidote, actually, to the very problem that Badcock identifies, and a site for pneumatological excavation. At present, though, what matters is simply to point out that the general neglect of pneumatology in Christian thought stems from a subordination, however implicit, of the work of the Spirit to the work of Christ.

The Alleged Pneumatological Deficiency of Western Theology

Furthermore, it is now widely claimed that the problem of insufficient attention to the doctrine of the Holy Spirit has left a significant lacuna in modern Western theology, and even in Western theology as a whole. Indeed, allegations of a pneumatological deficiency afflicting modern Western theology are made on the same grounds of overly concentrated christological formulations that leave nothing to be attributed to the Spirit, and those sweeping criticisms of Western theology across the ages are often fueled by this precise worry that the tradition accounts for the acts of the triune God without giving the Spirit anything to do. A case in point regarding the former is the pneumatological blind spot in the revival of trinitarian theology that began in the twentieth century. Eugene Rogers, for example, argues that the dearth of substantive reflection on the person and appropriated action of the Spirit in the modern West, in spite of a resurgence of interest in the doctrine of the Trinity, is a consequence of the Son overshadowing the Spirit. The basic problem seems to be the assumption that, in Rogers's clever formulation, "anything the Spirit can do, the Son can do better."[48] Eclipsed by the Son, the Spirit is necessarily reduced to a lesser role, given "the tendency in modern theology [especially modern *Western* theology, in Rogers's view] by which, to put it crudely, any way of talking appropriated to the Spirit might be better appropriated to the Son."[49] What Rogers is after in *After the Spirit* is revealed by the title itself, namely, a fuller understanding of the person and work of the Spirit in the context of a properly balanced and genuinely trinitarian mode of theology. Although Rogers pursues that goal in ways that lead beyond our focus here, it is telling that he turns primarily to the Eastern Christian tradition to resolve this characteristically Western difficulty.

As Rogers readily acknowledges, in his reading of historical theology as well as his own constructive pneumatological reflection, he builds on the work of Robert Jenson, specifically an influential article by Jenson entitled "You Wonder Where the Spirit Went."[50] The focus of Jenson's article is on the problem of the Spirit's apparent absence in the thought of Karl Barth in particular, but Jenson makes some pointed observations about Western trinitarian theology as a whole that have become representative of what is now a fairly common critique of theology in the West—that it evinces a dangerous tendency toward modalism or binitarianism rather than a genuine trinitarianism as a result of the Spirit again getting overlooked. As Jenson avers,

> Notoriously, traditional Western teaching has its drawbacks, in my judgment one principally. Any theologian for whom the doctrine of Trinity is

48. Eugene F. Rogers Jr., *After the Spirit: A Constructive Pneumatology from Resources Outside the Modern West* (Grand Rapids: Eerdmans, 2005), 33. Cf. ch. 1, entitled "Is There Nothing the Spirit Can Do That the Son Can't Do Better? Or, How the Spirit Puzzles a Trinitarian Revival" (19–32).

49. Ibid., 9.

50. Robert W. Jenson, "You Wonder Where the Spirit Went," in *Pro Ecclesia* 2/3 (Summer 1993): 296–304.

more than a relic, that is, any theologian who *uses* the doctrine of Trinity outside its own *locus*, is repeatedly led—indeed, compelled—to treat the three as *parties* of divine action, and that also "immanently." . . . The problem with the Western form of teaching is that it offers little or no justification for this necessary practice; indeed, it seems actually to have quenched the practice in Western theology. Notoriously also, difficulties of this sort are especially severe in the case of the Spirit—whether or not Eastern attribution of all Western problems to the *filioque* is correct. Augustine himself felt and remarked a special difficulty with the Spirit, and so have many successors.[51]

Here, Jenson also detects inherent difficulties in the characteristically Eastern approaches to the doctrine of the Trinity.[52] The additional charge that he issues against Western trinitarian theology, however, is an especially serious one. More specific to pneumatology, Jenson argues that the typical Western characterization of the Spirit as the *vinculum amoris* between the Father and the Son renders it difficult to account for the Spirit's authentic personhood and appropriated action in salvation history. As a result, the argument goes, the Spirit looks more like a thing—the bond of love uniting Father and Son—than a person; and, in contrast to the Father and especially the Son, there does not appear to be any action unique to the Spirit. As Jenson later posits in his *Systematic Theology*, "The common factor in Western problems with the Spirit, one may suggest, is a tendency of the Spirit simply to disappear from theology's description of God's triune action, often just when he might be expected to have the leading role."[53] Puzzlingly, Western theology seems to have the Spirit—"if we may put it so"—"abandon the action to the Father and the Son," which leaves the Spirit's role in the economy of salvation, and even very personhood, insufficiently clear.[54]

51. Ibid., 299.

52. "Moreover, Eastern forms of trinitarian teaching present equal if different drawbacks" (ibid.).

53. Robert W. Jenson, *Systematic Theology*, vol. 1: *The Triune God* (New York: Oxford University Press, 1997), 153.

54. Ibid., 156.

Assertions such as these from Rogers and Jenson have prompted the question as to what exact role the Spirit plays in the economy of salvation. If in fact the work of the Spirit is essentially eclipsed by a certain understanding of that of the Son, what is "left" for the Spirit to do? Indeed what *can* the Spirit do, if the Spirit's genuine personhood is obscured by overly zealous applications of the *vinculum* doctrine such that the Spirit is viewed mainly as impersonal "thing" (as bond or link, or even love in a sense) rather than as personal, acting "one"—as some*thing* but not some*one*? In the words of Bruce Marshall, "What does the Spirit have to do?"[55]

Marshall finds that, according to Aquinas's reading of the Gospel of John in particular, the Spirit actually has a great deal to do. Aquinas has no trouble attributing to the Spirit a number of significant actions and effects in the Trinity's economy of salvation, including the Spirit's adoptive action and teaching action. Each of these actions brings about a certain relationship between human beings and the Son, while being an action particular to the Spirit. The Spirit's adoptive action "makes those to whom he is sent like the one whose Spirit he is," which is to say, the Spirit makes them like Christ.[56] It is the Spirit who "has conformed us to the Son because he adopts us as children of God."[57] Thus, the Spirit imprints on us the very likeness of the Son, which is a motif that Aquinas develops in more detail elsewhere.[58] The Spirit's teaching action, a particularly prominent

55. Bruce D. Marshall, "What Does the Spirit Have to Do?" in Michael Dauphinais and Matthew Levering, eds., *Reading John with St. Thomas Aquinas: Theological Exegesis and Speculative Theology* (Washington, D.C.: The Catholic University of America Press, 2005), 62–77. Emery also has a fine article in the same volume touching on this theme, in which he observes that one of the key doctrinal principles at play in Aquinas's commentary on John is "the property of the Holy Spirit as Love: it is because he is personally Love that the Holy Spirit accomplishes the works of which love is the source" ("Biblical Exegesis and the Speculative Doctrine of the Trinity in St. Thomas Aquinas' Commentary on St. John," in ibid., 23–61, in particular 38).

56. *Ioan.*, 15, lect. 5, n. 2062.

57. Ibid., 14, lect. 6, n. 1957.

58. *ST*, III, q. 23 a.2, ad 3; and a. 1 ad 2.

theme in Aquinas's *Super Evangelium Sancti Ioannis Lectura*, teaches us the truth. To be precise, the Spirit teaches us the truth about the one who is the truth itself, that is, Christ.[59] While the Spirit is not unique among the trinitarian persons in having a teaching role—the Father and the Son each has such a role as well—and while the Trinity's teaching act is indivisible, this action is undertaken by the Spirit in a unique way, different from that of Father and Son. Aquinas distinguishes the teaching action undertaken by the Spirit from that undertaken by the Son, as he does concerning the mission of each as well, for "[j]ust as the effect of the mission of the Son was to lead us to the Father, so the effect of the mission of the Holy Spirit is to lead the faithful to the Son."[60] The Spirit's particular teaching act is to make known the Son, to enable us to grasp the teaching that Christ has given us about himself and about his Father.

Furthermore, in attributing particular roles to the Spirit, Thomas grounds these attributions in characteristics that are distinctive to this person, especially *amor* as a personal characteristic of the Spirit. In the *Summa*, of course, Aquinas investigates this problem in some detail, as recounted in chapters 3 through 5 above. Later in the present chapter, we will revisit several prominent themes from his account in the *Summa* in order to consider their implications for how Aquinas understands the appropriated work of the Spirit. Attentive to Aquinas's reading of John, Marshall observes a noteworthy connection between the divine act of forgiving sins—an act that is undertaken in a unique way by the Spirit, according to Aquinas—and his identification of the Spirit as love (or, as in his commentary on John, *amor ipse*).[61] It is quite fitting for God's act of forgiving sins, which is an act that occurs by love, to belong in particular to the Spirit who is love in person, and by whom love is given to us.[62] As in this example, not only does Aquinas designate certain actions

59. *Ioan.* 1, lect. 8, n. 188; 14, lect. 2, n. 1868.

60. Ibid., 14, lect. 6, 1958.

61. Ibid., 14, lect. 4, n. 1916.

62. Ibid., 20, lect. 4, n. 2541.

of the Trinity as actions specific to the Spirit; he also makes the appropriations on the basis of the Spirit's *propria*, especially *Amor*.[63]

So it appears that, at least in his commentary on John, Aquinas can answer the question of the work of the Spirit in rather substantive fashion. Not simply one isolated action or event, but in fact various aspects of the Trinity's work relate especially to the Spirit. Crucially, appropriate pneumatological attribution can be made in such a manner that shows the deep importance of the Spirit's role, not as merely a superfluous "extra" to that of the Son (or the Father) but as a genuine, personal agent in salvation history who is equally involved in achieving the world's salvation, as are the Father and the Son, and even in some sense uniquely so, in accordance with the Spirit's personally distinctive attributes, not least of which is love. As Marshall concludes, reading John's Gospel with Aquinas helps us see that the Spirit indeed has "a work of his own to do, yet not another work from that of the Father and the Son."[64] In this way, then, over against the common critique of Western theology as pneumatologically impoverished, with nothing for the Spirit to do, engagement with a classic figure like Aquinas suggests that there may be more substantive material on the doctrine of the Holy Spirit within the Western tradition that can be critically retrieved than has often been supposed.

Additional scrutiny is required, however, to substantiate such a claim. Specifically for our purposes here, it will be necessary to probe more deeply the significance of love as a personal *proprium* of the Spirit for the way in which Aquinas understands the appropriated work of the Spirit, with attention to question thirty-seven of the *pri-*

63. Marshall, "What Does the Spirit Have to Do?" 77.

64. Ibid. Aquinas's account of what the Spirit has to do raises problems about identity. To treat this complex issue adequately would exceed the scope of the present inquiry. Suffice it to say that while the notion of relative identity may shed some light on the matter, the second direction outlined by Marshall seems most promising even if the lack of a *modus significandi* according to our creaturely way of thinking about God limits us to a kind of apophaticism and a defensive posture in the sense that the "best we can do is block . . . unwanted inferences" (ibid., 71–77, in particular, 76).

ma pars of the *Summa theologiae* as well as book four of the *Summa contra Gentiles* and his sermon on the feast of Pentecost. Wesley also emerges as a surprisingly remarkable figure on this score given his emphasis on the personhood of the Spirit, for which reason, while not being equivalent to Aquinas in speculative rigor and sophistication, he is pneumatologically significant in his own right, and nonetheless based on his particular mission. In light of the above criticisms, the question of the extent to which a viable pneumatology can be retrieved from Western sources pertains directly to a central theme of this study, and thereby serves as a convenient transition to the next stage of inquiry in which a more detailed consideration of the Spirit in Aquinas and Wesley will take place.

The Spirit in Aquinas and Wesley

One reason that Aquinas's reflections on the Holy Spirit, whether in his commentary on John or elsewhere in his corpus, are notable is because of the connection that he discerns between the Spirit and love. The earlier exploration of that connection in chapters 3 through 5 makes it possible to bring together various themes related to love in Aquinas's pneumatology that can be used to establish Aquinas as an important source for contemporary efforts at pneumatological recovery. Furthermore, while Aquinas's linking of the Holy Spirit and love has its own particular nuances, he is not alone in this connection. It is clear in the theological writings of Wesley as well, for which reason Wesley is another Western thinker who in distinctive ways may also provide resources for developing a richer pneumatology, particularly in relation to love. The account of Wesley's doctrine of perfect love in chapter 2 highlighted his strong emphasis on the Holy Spirit as the gracious presence of God who restores in believers the image in which they were created, namely, the very image of the God who is love (cf. 1 Jn 4:16). Based on the conclusions reached in chapter 2 on Wesley, as well as those from chapters 3 through 5 on Aquinas, an assessment of these two figures on the Holy Spirit and love reveals not only a considerable degree of complementarity between them but also the potential contribution that each can make in the task of pneumatological recovery. In short, what positions both Aquinas and Wesley for this task is their common affirmation, with distinctive and yet strikingly compatible points of emphasis, that the Holy Spirit draws Christians into the life and love of the Trinity.

Aquinas's discussion of love as a *proprium* of the Spirit holds considerable significance for his way of understanding the appropriated work of the Spirit. This connection can be elucidated by some of the findings from the previous three chapters above. As shown in the earlier investigation of question thirty-seven of the *prima pars*, Aquinas's pneumatology of love consists of several phases: first, his identification of the Spirit as love in person or personal love (addressed in chapter 3).[65] Second is his account of the Spirit as the mutual love of the Father and the Son (chapter 4).[66] Then, in a third phase of his pneumatology, Aquinas explores the soteriological ramifications of the Spirit as love, with emphasis on the Spirit's gift of love in the economy of salvation, as presented in question thirty-eight of or which the *prima pars* and developed in various ways in book four of the *Summa contra Gentiles* and *Emitte Spiritum*, his sermon on Pentecost (chapter 5).[67] This three-part structure to his pneumatological reflection allows Aquinas to connect clearly love as a *proprium* of the Spirit with the theological virtue of charity that is central to the Christian life.

To summarize briefly, first Aquinas accounts for the Holy Spirit as personal love. In this sense, the Spirit is love precisely as the very person who proceeds as love within God's triune life. The Spirit's immanent procession occurs by way of the will, with God's goodness serving as the principle of love for himself, which gives rise to the imprint of love in God's will and the corresponding immanent

65. *ST*, I, q. 37, a. 1.

66. Ibid., I, q. 37, a. 2.

67. Ibid., I, qq. 38, 43; II–II, qq. 23–46.

procession of the Holy Spirit whom the Father and the Son breathe forth as love in person. By explicating the Spirit's procession in God, Aquinas is able to discern a relationship subsisting within the triune God. The Holy Spirit is love in person or personal love precisely as divine love proceeding. In this way, the Spirit is *in se* a subsistent relation that is produced by an immanent procession and characterized by love.[68]

Second, Aquinas then pursues the theme of the Spirit as mutual love or the love with which the Father and the Son love one another. The Holy Spirit is properly mutual love within God's own life in so far as the Spirit is love in person: there is expressed in the Spirit, as love, the relation of the Father to the Son, and vice versa, as that of the lover to the beloved. That is, the same love that the Spirit *in se* is, love in person, constitutes the Spirit's relation to the Father and the Son, a relation that is rooted in love. The Spirit is personal love and also mutual love, for the Father and the Son love one another by the Holy Spirit, love proceeding, as a tree flowers by its flowers (*arbor est florens floribus*).[69]

As an entry point into the third phase of his *amor*-based pneumatology, Aquinas makes a critical move by explaining that the love that the Father and the Son have for one another is actually the same love with which God loves us, that is, the Holy Spirit. With this move, Aquinas is able to attend to the soteriological import of the Spirit as love, and it is in this phase in particular that the connection between the Spirit's personal *proprium* of love and the appropriated work of the Spirit is clearly established. According to Aquinas, the same Spirit who is love—the Spirit who is love in person and the mutual love of the Father and the Son—is the one through whom God's love is poured out in the economy of salvation. *Caritas* is a matter of friendship with God that is established by the Spirit. Sent in time by the Father, the Holy Spirit takes up residence in the saints and fills them

68. Ibid., I, q. 37, a. 1. See chapter 3 above.

69. Ibid., I, q. 37, a. 1 ad 3; I, q. 37, a. 2. See chapter 4 above.

with the love that is constitutive of the Spirit's own person. *Caritas* is the soul's participation with the Holy Spirit.[70] This fact logically follows: in the friendship of charity, those in a state of grace become participants through the Holy Spirit in the triune God. For Aquinas, the same Spirit who proceeds eternally as the bond of love between the Father and the Son is sent in temporal mission to inhabit the hearts of the faithful in the gift of sanctifying grace, to make them like God by grace, and to draw them into the life and love of God.[71] In his two-part homily on the feast of Pentecost, Aquinas the preacher describes the Holy Spirit, whose property is love, as the giver of all life and the source of all being and of all motion, who has been freely sent into the world (part one).[72] With attention to the Spirit's omnipresence in Christian existence, Aquinas further identifies the Spirit as the cause of all holiness whose effects can be seen in the creation and renewal of the whole world and especially of the human being (part two).[73] These points suggest that the Christian life, marked by signs of the Spirit's work, is a gift of the Father through the Holy Spirit, a gift that conforms its recipients to the Son. Coming to dwell in us, the Spirit makes us friends of God in Jesus Christ (cf. Jn 15:12, 15) and kindles our love for God. Moreover, because every beloved is in the lover, for such is the intimacy of love, through the Holy Spirit the Father and the Son abide in us (Jn 14:23, 1 Jn 3:24), and we in them (1 Jn 4:16, 13). Through the Spirit, therefore, we become participants in the life of God.[74]

The theme of participation in God through the Spirit also figures prominently in the writings of Wesley, as noted earlier in chapter 2. Wesley developed the notion of the spiritual senses to account for human knowledge of God through the Spirit. He also placed a

70. Ibid., II–II, q. 23, a. 3 ad 3.

71. Ibid., I, q. 43, a. 3c; I, q. 43, a. 5 ad 2.

72. *Emitte Spiritum*, I.1–II.5.

73. Ibid., III.1–IV.5.

74. *ScG*, IV, ch. 21, par. 3. For more on the meaning of the Spirit as love for the soteriology of Aquinas, see chapter 5 above.

particular theological accent on the pursuit of personal and social sanctity in love. In a special way, this concern was related to his understanding of the doctrine of the Spirit, whom Wesley readily identified as the indwelling cause of all love and holiness in those who believe.[75] With this characteristic emphasis on sanctification of heart and life in and by the Spirit, Wesley taught that, through our experience of the living God by means of the spiritual senses, we come by grace to know and love God, to the end that the Christian life, which is a participation in God, expresses something of God's own holiness and love. Wesley's notion of perfection is animated by a participatory understanding of the doctrine of God in which the work of the Spirit is central. His approach to the doctrine of the Trinity shows a notably soteriological orientation, marked by a particular emphasis on the Holy Spirit, the personal presence of God whose immediate and ongoing work sanctifies those in Christ so that the image of God is more fully restored in their lives.[76]

This pneumatological dimension finds lyrical expression in a hymn on Pentecost published jointly by John and Charles Wesley:

> Granted is the Saviour's prayer,
> Sent the gracious Comforter;
> Promise of our parting Lord,
> Jesus to his heav'n restored.
>
> Christ, who now gone up on high
> Captive leads captivity,
> While his foes from him receive
> Grace, that God with man may live.
>
> God, the everlasting God,
> Makes with mortals His abode;
> Whom the heavens cannot contain,
> He vouchsafes to dwell in man.

75. *Letter to a Roman Catholic*, in Wesley, *Works*, ed. Jackson, 10:82.
76. See chapter 2 above.

Never will he thence depart,
Inmate of an humble heart;
Carrying on his work within,
Striving till he cast out sin.

There he helps our feeble moans,
Deepens our imperfect groans;
Intercedes in silence there,
Sighs th' unutterable prayer.

Come, divine and peaceful guest,
Enter our devoted breast;
Holy Ghost, our hearts inspire,
Kindle there the gospel-fire.

Crown the agonizing strife,
Principle, and Lord of life;
Life divine in us renew,
Thou the gift and giver too!

Now descend and shake the earth,
Wake us into second birth;
Now thy quick'ning influence give,
Blow—and these dry bones shall live!

Brood thou o'er our nature's night,
Darkness kindles into light;
Spread thy over-shadowing wings,
Order from confusion springs.

Pain and sin, and sorrow cease,
Thee we taste, and all is peace;
Joy divine in thee we prove,
Light of truth, and fire of love.[77]

Here the Wesleys teach that the Holy Spirit is sent into the world, thus fulfilling Christ's promise of a coming comforter or advocate who would establish and confirm his followers in the life of God (cf.

77. John Wesley and Charles Wesley, *Hymns and Sacred Poems* (London: William Strahan, 1739), "Hymn for Whitsunday," 213–14.

Jn 14:15–31). In this mystery of grace, God—whom not even heaven can hold—comes to dwell in human hearts through the Spirit. The Spirit is both gift and giver.[78] As such, the Spirit renews in us God's image and actual life.

With their own particular nuances and modes of presentation, therefore, Aquinas and Wesley specify that it is through the Spirit that those who believe come to partake in the life of the triune God. Aquinas brings together the speculative and the practical by accounting for the connection between the Spirit as love in person and the work attributed to the Spirit in the divine economy, in particular the establishment of a relationship between God and the faithful that is characterized by *caritas*, with the Spirit making us the friends of God and leading us to live as such. Wesley, for his part, stresses the importance of an experiential knowledge of God through the spiritual senses, and attributes to the Spirit the renewal of the divine image in believers as manifested in love for God and neighbor even unto perfection.[79] In each case, the association between love and the Spirit is vital, as in the various references or allusions to John 14–16 that Aquinas and Wesley make. Yes, Christ is the one who speaks of the Spirit here, thus implying a certain connection between the Spirit and Christ, but this connection need not lead to an overshadowing of the Spirit by the Son, since the Spirit has specific work to do. For both Aquinas and Wesley, the Spirit incorporates those who belong to Christ into the Trinity's own life.

It is also striking to point out that the Wesleys' hymn on Pentecost resonates with a number of the themes in Aquinas's sermon. For example, both mention the Spirit's temporal mission, though Aquinas refers to the Father as well as the Son, whereas here the Wesleys simply speak of the sending of the Spirit in reference to the Son (the Father may be implied as the one to whom the Son

78. Cf. Augustine, *De Trinitate*, XV, 19, as well as Aquinas's affirmation of this point in *ST*, I, q. 38, a. 2 ad 1.

79. For a similar understanding of experimental knowledge in Aquinas, cf. *ST*, I, q. 43 ad 2.

prays). Another common point of emphasis is the indwelling of the Spirit in God's people, an indwelling that produces in them the effect of love and holiness through the Spirit of love. Also, the notion of gift plays a role in the respective reflections on the meaning of Pentecost offered by Aquinas and (in this case) both Wesleys, with this motif as implicit in Aquinas's sermon but explicit in the *Summa theologiae*. To be sure, these and other similarities do not stem, primarily, from the direct influence of Aquinas on Wesley (which was minimal if perceptible at all).[80] They come more from the source of the knowledge of God's Spirit shared by Aquinas and Wesley, divine revelation. In regard to the operative understanding of the work of the Spirit, participation in God's life is key for both figures. It is this reality, through the Spirit, that Aquinas contemplated and described in his pneumatological writings and preaching, and about which Wesley also preached, wrote, and invited people to sing.

Having explicated this common affirmation and noted some corresponding elements of pneumatological and soteriological complementarity between Aquinas and Wesley, it is now fitting to return to the two prominent criticisms of the place of pneumatology in Western theology (or, more precisely, the lack thereof) mentioned earlier: first, the eclipse of the Holy Spirit by the Son; second, the obscuring of the Spirit's genuine personhood. Both of these criticisms have a bearing on how one understands the work appropriated to the Holy Spirit in salvation history. Now it is time to see how Wesley and Aquinas, respectively, measure up against these criticisms, and doing so will show the extent to which they are capable of contributing to the development of a constructive pneumatology of love.

Given their differences in theological method, Wesley will be

80. Wesley's few references to Aquinas in his entire corpus are rather general, and do not indicate any direct influence of the *doctor communis* on his thought. Clearly, however, he was familiar with Aquinas in at least a basic way. For example, he encouraged Methodist preachers to prepare themselves intellectually for their work in ministry by seeking to understand "metaphysics; if not the depths of the Schoolmen, the subtleties of Scotus or Aquinas, yet the first rudiments, the general principles, of that useful science" (Wesley, *Works*, ed. Jackson, 10:482).

discussed first, with an assessment of Aquinas and the more technical issues that he engages to follow. The first point of criticism raises the question of whether the Spirit's work is eclipsed by that of the Son. Is this true in Wesley? The fact that Wesley's writings are not systematized but more occasional in nature requires an understanding not simply of certain formulations mentioned here or there in his writing, but a more comprehensive understanding of the main contours of his thought. Three themes emerge from the above exploration of Wesley on sanctification that can be used to help answer the question about whether there is a christological eclipse of the Spirit in Wesley.

First, Wesley's conception of the spiritual senses is linked to a certain understanding of the work of the Spirit. While that connection has been mentioned already, at this stage it is important to clarify that Wesley did not claim that we perceive the particular manner in which the Spirit operates, but that we perceive the effects of the inspirations of the Spirit such as love, joy, and peace.[81] Still, these effects stem from what Wesley identified as the work specific to the Spirit, as a crucial part of the Spirit's redemptive mission, and the pneumatological basis is therefore clear. According to Wesley, the means through which human beings can perceive the effects of the Spirit's inspiration is through the spiritual senses. Graciously restored by the Spirit, these senses make us sensitive to internal or spiritual realities, and more precisely, to the peace, joy, and love that God grants those who believe.

Indicative of what is apparently a growing awareness of the role of the Spirit in his thinking, Wesley begins in some of his mature

81. As Wesley explains, the perception of which he speaks is not in the sense of "the *manner* in which [the Spirit] operates, but the *graces* which he operates in a Christian" (*A Farther Appeal to Men of Reason and Religion*, Pt. I, V.2, in Wesley, *Works*, ed. Outler, et al., 11:140; cf. ibid., I.6, in Wesley, *Works*, ed. Outler, et al., 11:108). In making this point, Wesley sounds much like Aquinas, for whom we cannot, of ourselves, know with certainty that we have grace because the principle of grace and its object, God, is fundamentally unknowable to us in this way (*ST*, I–II, q. 112, a. 5c).

writings to describe faith itself as a kind of spiritual sense. For example, in "The Witness of Our Own Spirit," Wesley speaks of faith as "that evidence, that conviction, that demonstration of things invisible, whereby the eyes of our understanding [are] opened, and divine light [is] poured in upon them."[82] In *The Scripture Way of Salvation*, he specifies that this understanding of faith is related to the work of the Holy Spirit. Faith in a general sense, which is how Wesley takes Hebrews 11:1,

> implies both a supernatural evidence of God and of the things of God, a kind of spiritual light exhibited to the soul, and a supernatural sight or perception thereof. Accordingly the Scripture speaks sometimes of God's giving light, sometimes a power of discerning it. So St. Paul: "God, who commanded light to shine out of darkness, hath shined in our hearts, to give us the light of the knowledge of the glory of God in the face of Jesus Christ" [2 Cor 4:6]. And elsewhere the same Apostle speaks "of the eyes of" our "understanding being opened" [Eph 1:18]. By this twofold operation of the Holy Spirit—having the eyes of our soul both *opened* and *enlightened*—we see the things which the natural "eye hath not seen, neither the ear heard" [1 Cor 2:9, Is 64:4]. We have a prospect of the invisible things of God.[83]

In a more particular sense, as Wesley goes on to explain, "faith is a divine evidence and conviction, not only that 'God was in Christ, reconciling the world unto himself' [2 Cor 5:19], but also that Christ 'loved *me*, and gave himself for *me*' [Gal 2:20]."[84] Therefore, Wesley's mature understanding of faith includes both christological and pneumatological dimensions, as Collins points out in his comments on justifying faith in particular: "justifying faith cannot be conceived in any full sense either apart from the redemptive nature of the life, death, and ministry of Jesus Christ, or apart from the

82. Sermon 12, "The Witness of Our Own Spirit" (1746), §8, in Wesley, *Works*, ed. Outler, et al., 1:304.

83. *The Scripture Way of Salvation*, II.1, in Wesley, *Works*, ed. Outler, et al., 2:160–61.

84. Ibid., II.2, in Wesley, *Works*, ed. Outler, et al., 2:161.

experiential trust and conviction graciously received by the believer through the ministrations of the Holy Spirit."[85] Wesley's description of faith in terms of the spiritual senses illumines the centrality of Christ, though not to the extent of being absorbed by it, such that faith would be entirely subsumed under the category of Christology. Instead, Wesley acknowledges, particularly in his later writings, the role of the Holy Spirit as he accounts for even such a christologically dense doctrine as faith. In this way, then, Wesley's concept of the spiritual senses serves to underline the work attributed to the Spirit in the divine economy.

Second, the notion of the *imago Dei* is a leading soteriological theme employed by Wesley, and his use of it reveals an important pneumatological element. As Jürgen Weissbach points out in his study on "the new humanity in the theological thought of John Wesley," Wesley is particularly attentive to the idea of the renewal of the divine image in believers.[86] Wesley describes salvation in terms of being renewed in God's image through the Spirit: "the love of God shed abroad in their hearts [cf. Rom 5:5 and its pneumatological reference], with love to every child of man, and a renewal in the whole image of God, in all righteousness and true holiness."[87] This renewal involves daily growth, with God, "the fountain of all holiness, continually filling thee with his own likeness.... Thy soul shall be renewed day by day after the image of him that created it."[88] Wesley describes sanctification as a matter of what God "*works in us* by his Spirit."[89] By doing so, Wesley attributes the work of renewing God's image in believers to the third person of the Trinity. The

85. Kenneth J. Collins, *The Theology of John Wesley: Holy Love and the Shape of Grace* (Nashville: Abingdon Press, 2007), 169.

86. Jürgen Weissbach, *Der neue Mensch im theologischen Denken John Wesleys* (Stuttgart: Christliches Verlagshaus, 1970).

87. Sermon 129, "Heavenly Treasure in Earthen Vessels" (1790), I.3; letter to John Oglevie, August 7, 1785, in Wesley, *Letters*, 7:283.

88. Sermon 28, "Upon Our Lord's Sermon on the Mount, VIII" (1748), §4, in Wesley, *Works*, ed. Outler, et al., 1:614.

89. "Justification by Faith," II.1, in Wesley, *Works*, ed. Outler, et al., 1:187.

sanctifying grace of the Spirit restores human persons to the image of God, and chiefly to what Wesley sometimes calls the moral image of God, that is, righteousness and holiness (cf. Eph 4:24).[90]

On the subject of sanctification, there is also in Wesley's doctrine of the Spirit a third theme, described throughout this study as participatory sanctification, that builds on the first two mentioned already. That is, the concept of participatory sanctification in Wesley is deeply pneumatological as well, assuming as it does the related motifs of the spiritual senses and renewal in the image of God, and extending the trajectory that they have begun. The union with the triune God that is made possible for all human persons by grace is related in a special way to the work of the Holy Spirit, for it is the Spirit whom Wesley identifies as the "immediate cause" of all the holiness that marks the lives of those who enjoy true fellowship with the Trinity.[91] In the communion of the Spirit we experience

90. Wesley describes the *imago Dei* in a threefold manner, for example, in his sermon "The New Birth." Picking up the language from Isaac Watts in his 1740 work *Ruin and Recovery of Mankind*, Wesley mentions that the image of God can be understood in three ways: the natural image, the political image, and the moral image. (Cf. Wesley's quotations from Watts in *The Doctrine of Original Sin, According to Scripture, Reason, and Experience: In Answer to Dr. Taylor* [1756], pp. 225, 261.) God has created human beings, Wesley says, "[n]ot barely in his natural image, a picture of his own immortality; a spiritual being, endued with understanding, freedom of will, and various affections; nor merely in his political image, the governor of this lower world, having 'dominion over the fishes of the sea, and over all the earth' [Gn 1:26–27]; but chiefly in his moral image, which, according to the Apostle, is 'righteousness and true holiness' [Eph 4:24]. In this image of God was man made" ("The New Birth," I.1 in Wesley, *Works*, ed. Outler, et al., 2:188). The gift of God creating us in his own image makes human beings, as Wesley says, "capable of God" ("The General Deliverance," I.5, III.6, 12 in Wesley, *Works*, ed. Outler, et al., 2:441, 448, 450). Yet the problem of sin, our tragic, willing rebellion against God, defaces this image in which God has made us. As a result, what is desperately needed is the renewal of God's image—one of Wesley's favorite descriptions of salvation, as in his sermon "The One Thing Needful" (Wesley, *Works*, ed. Outler, et al., 4:352–59). Such renewal touches all three dimensions of the image of God but deals chiefly with the area where it is needed most: the moral image of God, marred through the scandal of sin. Mercifully, God has made abundant provisions for the renewal of the divine image in us through Jesus Christ and the Holy Spirit.

91. *Letter to a Roman Catholic*, in Wesley, *Works*, ed. Jackson, 10:82.

constant communion with the Father and the Son, and this participation in God's life fills our hearts with love for God and neighbor. Elmer Colyer astutely observes that Wesley's soteriology is in the service of "a participatory Trinitarian understanding of salvation: our destiny in this life and the next is union and communion with the Triune God and with one another, indeed with all creation."[92] This communion, for Wesley, is a genuine communion of the sanctifying Spirit, through whom those who believe come to share in the life of God and are made holy by this participation in God.

Obviously, extended scrutiny of Wesley's pneumatology would allow for a more definitive conclusion than is possible here, but Wesley seems immune to the first critique of Western pneumatology. As these three important themes suggest, he speaks about the work of the Spirit to an extent that does not decline into the kind of christological eclipse that some say becomes characteristic of modern Western theology, but instead reflects a rather substantial pneumatology that stands alongside his claims about the person of Christ, and in a sense serves as a way into these claims, though without being usurped by them.

Concerning the second criticism of obscuring the Spirit's genuine personhood, again one should keep in mind Wesley's method and aims as a practical theologian or (as was suggested before) a soteriologist.[93] Wesley does not say much about the person of the Spirit in terms of God's immanent life, but is content appealing to mystery on this score.[94] Rather, he focuses on the Spirit in the econ-

92. Elmer M. Colyer, "Trinity," in William J. Abraham and James E. Kirby, eds., *The Oxford Handbook of Methodist Studies* (Oxford: Oxford University Press, 2009), 508. On this last point about communion with all creation, the reference is to Wesley's conclusion of his sermon "The New Creation": "And to crown all, there will be a deep, an intimate, an uninterrupted union with God; a constant communion with the Father and his Son Jesus Christ, through the Spirit; a continual enjoyment of the Three-One God, and of all the creatures in him!" ("The New Creation," §18, in Wesley, *Works*, ed. Outler, et al., 2:510).

93. See chapter 2 above.

94. Cf. his distinction between fact and manner in *On the Trinity*, where he plainly affirms the *fact* that God is three in one, but makes no claim for understand-

omy of salvation as recounted in Scripture and affirmed in creedal form. In a strict sense, therefore, his precise understanding of the person of the Spirit within the Godhead (to the extent that he actually developed such an understanding) remains unclear, rendering the criticism of Jenson on the Western problems concerning the doctrine of the Spirit as mutual love, for example, largely inapplicable by default.

Nevertheless, it is still possible to address the overall question of whether sufficient attention is paid in this case to the person of the Spirit. Even though Wesley does not engage in detailed consideration of the Spirit *ad intra*, he speaks of the work of the Spirit in a way that affirms the Spirit's authentic personhood. This affirmation can be seen in what Wesley says about the themes identified above, along with other dimensions of God's saving action in which the person of the Spirit figures prominently (e.g., adoption, which will be revisited later). There is no need to elucidate these themes again here, but suffice it to say that, in agreement with the findings of William Arnett, sanctification represents the broadest category for understanding Wesley's pneumatology, a category in which the Spirit's personal presence and agency are central.[95] Moreover, as Outler explains, throughout Wesley's writings there is an intimate relationship between "Spirit" and "spirituality," further indicating the importance of the Spirit in his thought.[96] It is for such reasons that Wesley is generally acknowledged to emphasize in his pneumatology the personhood of the Spirit in an outstanding way, particularly for a Western figure.[97] Implicit in such an observation is the assertion that Wesley

ing the precise *manner* in which this is so (*On the Trinity*, §15, in Wesley, *Works*, ed. Outler, et al., 2:384). Here as elsewhere Wesley's reflections are driven by his underlying soteriological concerns, for which reason he concentrates on the actions of God in the divine economy.

95. William M. Arnett, "The Role of the Holy Spirit in Entire Sanctification in the Writings of John Wesley," *Wesleyan Theological Journal* 14/2 (Fall 1979): 15–30.

96. Albert C. Outler, "A Focus on the Holy Spirit: Spirit and Spirituality in John Wesley," *Quarterly Review* 8/2 (1988): 3–18.

97. E.g., F. LeRon Shults and Andrea Hollingsworth, *The Holy Spirit* (Grand Rapids: Eerdmans, 2008), 62.

not only avoids this second pitfall, deemed to be characteristic of Western theology, but may actually provide resources to help recover a richer pneumatology. Indeed, our findings here affirm that this is the case, particularly in regard to his understanding of the relationship among the Holy Spirit, sanctification, and love in the Christian life.[98]

The above account of Wesley, following Wesley's theological method, has provided a more extensive response to the first problem commonly associated with Western pneumatology than to the second. Aquinas, however, is well suited to take on both criticisms directly, given the depth and breadth of his speculative approach.

In response to criticism of a certain tendency for the Son to overshadow the Spirit, one should acknowledge from the start that Aquinas comments quite extensively on the work of the Spirit, even if this aspect of his thought is relatively little studied. Earlier in this chapter it was noted that Aquinas offers a substantial account of the Spirit's work in his commentary on John, where he establishes that numerous aspects of the economy of salvation relate in particular to the Spirit. In fact, in his reading of John, far from leaving nothing for the Spirit to do, Aquinas attributes action to the Spirit that is differentiated from, but one with, that of the Son and the Father, action that is undertaken by the Spirit in a way that is unique on the basis of the *propria* distinctive to this person, principally love. In this respect, then, rather than reflecting an eclipse of the Spirit by the Son, Aquinas's thought seems nothing less than fully trinitarian.

Of course, Aquinas reflects on the person and work of the Spirit not only in his biblical commentaries but also in his other works. He does so in a way that relates to his doctrine of the Son while also being distinct from it, as illustrated by his account of the processions and missions in the *prima pars* of the *Summa theologiae*. After observing that procession exists in God only according to an internal action, Aquinas is able to establish that, since such action

98. A fuller exposition of Wesley's pneumatology, with attention to these and related themes, is found in Starkey, *The Work of the Holy Spirit*.

in an intellectual nature is by way of either the intellect or the will, there are two processions in God, that of the Word by way of the intellect and that of love by way of the will.[99] The two processions share a certain similarity in that they are the only two processions within God.

Yet the divine processions are also distinguishable in several respects, one being what each can properly be named. The procession of the Word is rightly called generation, Aquinas deduces, because by this procession the object understood—the Word—resides according to its own likeness in the intellect, that is, by way of similitude.[100] The Word proceeding also subsists in the same nature as the Father, since in God the act of understanding and existing are the same.[101] The procession of love in God, however, is not properly called generation. Whereas the procession of the Word is by way of similitude in the intellect, the procession of love in God is an act of the will, and the will is made actual not by having the object willed reside in the will according to its likeness but by having a certain inclination to the object willed. This procession is by way of impulse and movement toward an object. "So what proceeds in God by way of love does not proceed as begotten, or as son, but proceeds rather as spirit, a name that expresses a certain vital movement and impulse, accordingly as anyone is described as moved or impelled by love to perform an action."[102] The procession of the will in God has no proper name, but can be called spiration since it is the procession of the Spirit.[103] In his discussion of the procession of the divine persons, therefore, Aquinas reflects on the person of the Spirit by associating the Spirit with the Son in one sense (as the two persons proceeding in God) while also distinguishing the Spirit from the Son in important ways (the precise nature and name of each procession).

99. *ST*, I, q. 27, a. 3c.
100. Ibid., I, q. 27, a. 2c.
101. Ibid., I, q. 27, a. 2 ad 2; cf. I, q. 14, a. 4.
102. Ibid., I, q. 27, a. 4c.
103. Ibid., I, q. 27, a. 4 ad 3.

Aquinas uses this same approach of making a certain association between the Spirit and the Son and then introducing a set of key distinctions between the two in his subsequent account of the missions, which is based on his doctrine of the processions.[104] As a result, he is able to specify the sense in which actions can be attributed to the Spirit in particular. The connection between the Spirit and the Son that Aquinas makes in his account of the missions relates to the general conclusions that he reaches in the opening articles of question forty-three, including the suitability for a divine person to be sent (a. 1), the temporal nature of the mission (a. 2), and the fittingness of the Son and Spirit being sent, but not the Father (a. 4). In these articles, Aquinas establishes that the Son and Spirit are sent in time for certain work in the world.

Beyond this basic similarity, the more particular aspects of the mission of each of these divine persons allow Aquinas to distinguish them in a way that promotes a greater understanding of each. While considering whether it is fitting for the Son to be sent invisibly (a. 5), Aquinas raises an objection that is pertinent to the question of whether the Spirit's work is subsumed by that of the Son. The objection is that the mission of the divine person is a procession, as he has pointed out earlier.[105] Further, because the procession of the Son differs from that of the Spirit, then so too must their missions be distinct—to the effect, it would seem, that one of the missions alone would suffice for the creature's sanctification, thus making the other superfluous.[106] Assuming that the mission of the Son would be deemed all sufficient and that of the Spirit therefore rendered redundant, this objection sounds much like the first contemporary criticism of Western theology as a whole, that the Son outshines the Spirit.

In his reply to the objection, however, Aquinas makes a decisive distinction. He explains that the missions of the Son and the Spirit

104. As Aquinas explains, mission includes the eternal procession with the addition of a temporal effect (ibid., I, q. 43, a. 2 ad 3).

105. Ibid., I, q. 43, aa. 1, 4.

106. Ibid., I, q. 43, a. 5 obj. 3.

can be distinguished when one is speaking of mission according to origin, as generation is distinguished from procession. Considering mission in regard to the effect of grace, the two missions are united in their basis, which is grace, but distinguished in the effects of grace, which in the case of the mission of the Son is the illumination of the intellect and in the case of the mission of the Spirit is the kindling of affection.[107] Pointing back to the account of the processions, Aquinas is able to show that some distinction is possible while also affirming that one mission cannot be without the other, since each mission produces an effect that is distinctive to that particular mission. Specific to the Spirit is the effect of stirring the soul's desire for God, an effect that is fitting for one who is love proceeding eternally and one who is sent visibly in time, as Aquinas later explains, as the gift of sanctification.[108]

As in his doctrines of procession and mission, Aquinas relates his reflection on the person and work of the Spirit to the doctrine of the Son, but he also distinguishes the two clearly enough to speak in distinctive ways about the person and work of the Spirit. His manner of doing so suggests that the Spirit is not eclipsed by the Son in Aquinas's thinking but rather plays an equally vital role as the Son (and the Father) in the Trinity's economy of salvation.

Whether in commentating directly on Scripture, as in his commentary on John, or in outlining his scripturally informed speculative theology, as in his account of the processions and missions, Aquinas does not hesitate to attribute particular actions to the Spirit. The Spirit's work, for example, of establishing us as God's friends, forgiving our sins, and sanctifying God's people by inhabiting them in a special way, is grounded in the Spirit's own *propria*, especially the personal characteristic of *Amor*. Rather than overlooking the work of the Spirit in a manner that some have deemed characteristic of Western theology, Aquinas is duly attentive to the unique

107. Ibid., I, q. 43, a. 5 ad 3.
108. Ibid., I, q. 43, a. 7c.

actions associated with the third person of the Trinity, actions that are deeply related, as the *doctor communis* shows, to the Spirit's *proprium* of love.

The second critique of Western theological reflection, concerning the question of the authentic personhood of the Spirit, is one that Aquinas stands especially well positioned to deal with given his understanding of *sacra doctrina* and specifically its speculative depth. Again, Jenson argues that the doctrine of the Spirit as the bond of love uniting the Father and the Son obfuscates the Spirit's authentic personhood and action in salvation history, to the effect that the Spirit ends up resembling more a thing than a person. Jenson is certainly right that ascribing undue weight to an understanding of the Spirit as *vinculum* is a problem. If the primary characteristic distinguishing the third person of the Trinity is that this person is the bond of love uniting the Father and the Son, then the Spirit hardly sounds like a person at all, but more like an impersonal thing. The question in this case is whether Aquinas contributes to the problem, and if so, to what degree.

Based on the conclusions reached in chapters 3 through 5 above, however, a strong argument can be made that Aquinas is actually part of the solution and not the problem. For just as surely as an imbalanced emphasis on the Spirit as *vinculum* causes major trinitarian trouble, this principle can also be expressed in a balanced way that does not detract from, but rather affirms, an understanding of the Spirit's genuine personhood and the action appropriated to the Spirit in salvation history. To recall once more the previous three chapters, Aquinas achieves the necessary balance with his carefully presented, three-phase pneumatology of love, covering, first of all, the Holy Spirit as love in person; second, the Spirit as mutual love; and third, the soteriological implications of the Spirit as love.

In his investigation of *Amor* as a proper name of the Holy Spirit, Aquinas does consider the sense in which the Spirit is the mutual love or *vinculum* uniting the Father and the Son, but this topic is not his point of departure. He begins on a related note with an account of the Spirit as personal love or love in person, based on the Spirit's immanent procession by way of the will in God. That is, the Holy Spirit is love in person specifically as divine love proceeding. As that divine person who is love by his own relation of origin to the Father and the Son, the Spirit is not an impersonal thing, but in fact a genuine person whose *proprium* is love. Aquinas's discussion of love in God taken personally therefore clarifies the personhood of the Spirit.[109]

Moreover, by showing explicit attention to the person of the Spirit at the start of his inquiry into the Spirit as love, Aquinas also sets the terms for understanding the Spirit as mutual love, which represents the second stage in his *amor*-based pneumatology. The idea of the Spirit as the bond of love between the Father and the Son shares an important connection with that of the Spirit as personal love. Sometimes Aquinas even appeals to the doctrine of mutual love in order to explain how the Spirit can be thought of as love in person, as in his statement that "there is expressed in the Holy Spirit, as Love, the relation of the Father to the Son, and conversely, as that of the lover to the beloved."[110] While such language might cause some interpreters to suspect a depersonalizing of the Spirit, Aquinas's main point here is actually that the Spirit cannot be reduced to the mutual love of the Father and the Son, but rather is the product of that love; and the Spirit is this product precisely as love in person. In those cases that may seem to call into question an argument for the priority of personal love over mutual love in Aquinas's pneumatology in the *prima pars*, the latter is not understood in isolation from the former. For this reason, even when discussing the Spirit as the *amor Patris et Filii*, Aquinas never loses sight of the fact that the Spirit is a genuine divine person and not a thing.

Mostly, however, Aquinas's argument moves from personal love

109. Ibid., I, q. 37, a. 1.
110. Ibid., I, q. 37, a. 1 ad 3.

to mutual love, which suggests that the latter is a second stage in the journey that builds on the first. Grasping the Spirit's immanent procession as love in person makes it possible to conceive of a relationship that subsists within the Trinity, a relationship that is the very person of the Spirit. In other words, the Spirit is *in se* a subsistent relation within the triune God that is produced by an immanent procession and characterized by love as a matter of relation of origin to the Father and the Son. Yet the Spirit is *vinculum* precisely as love in person. Or from another angle, proceeding from the Father and the Son as love in person, the Spirit is also their mutual love, in whom is expressed their relation as that of the lover to the beloved.[111] The Holy Spirit is properly mutual love because the very love that the Spirit *in se* is, love in person, constitutes the Spirit's own relation to the Father and the Son, a relation of origin. Thus the Spirit, as personal love proceeding in a way analogous to a tree flowering with the flower, is also mutual love—the love that the Father and the Son have for one another.[112]

As Aquinas explains, his understanding of the Spirit as love uniting Father and Son also serves as a transition into the third phase of his pneumatology of love. That is because the love that the Father and Son have for one another is actually the same love with which God loves us. The affirmation of the Spirit as mutual love, though primarily a claim pertaining to God's immanent life as Trinity, also implies, secondarily, God's relation to creatures. What logically follows, therefore, is an exploration of the soteriological ramifications of the Holy Spirit as love, which Aquinas conducts by placing particular emphasis on such themes as gift, friendship, and charity, all in relation to the Spirit's *proprium* of love.[113]

In sum, mutual love serves to advance Aquinas's account while also recalling and reaffirming his earlier remarks about love tak-

111. Ibid.

112. Ibid., I, q. 37, a. 2c.

113. Ibid., I, q. 38; cf. *ScG*, IV and *Emitte Spiritum*.

en in God personally. The advance comes in the form of a greater depth of inquiry into the notion of relation in God. At the same time, however, mutual love cannot be isolated from personal love, since the Spirit is both love in person and love of the Father and the Son. The same Spirit who is the subsistent relation between the Father and the Son, which is to say, their mutual love, is love in person proceeding by way of the will in God. An affirmation of the Spirit's personhood is essential to an account of the Spirit in terms of *vinculum*. Yet Aquinas's identification of the Spirit as mutual love not only points back to the foundational claim of the Spirit as love in person but also looks ahead, as it were, by serving as the basis for the Spirit's temporal mission.

For these reasons, the way in which Aquinas accounts for the Spirit as the love of the Father and the Son is balanced enough to avoid the pitfall against which Jenson rightly warns. The Spirit is first and foremost a genuine person, the divine person whose *proprium* is love by relation of origin to the Father and the Son. Precisely as the one who proceeds eternally as love in person, the Spirit is also the bond of love uniting Father and Son, and the very person sent in time to establish the church, inhabit the saints, and kindle in human hearts love for God and love for neighbor in God and because of God. In all this, the Spirit's personhood is not strangely buried or concealed but rather confirmed and illuminated.

In light of the call for retrieving a richer pneumatology that is fueled by such criticisms as the overshadowing of the Spirit's work by that of the Son and the obscuring of the Spirit's authentic personhood, Aquinas and Wesley are two possible Western contributors to a rehabilitated doctrine of the Spirit. While not necessarily the only two, they are noteworthy because they both show the kind of attentiveness to matters of the Spirit that is essential for a fully operative pneumatology, and in particular, a pneumatology of love. Each reflects on the Spirit with his own nuances, but there is a basic complementarity in their works, touching on such critical themes as the centrality of love and sanctification in the Christian life, with each understood in direct relation to the Spirit. On the subject of pneumatology, Aquinas stands poised to contribute in characteristically speculative fashion, or on the basis of what Jacques Maritain calls a "speculatively practical science," and Wesley in a "practically practical" way.[114] What they can say together, with distinctive points of emphasis, is that the Holy Spirit draws Christians into the life and love of the Trinity. Different as they may be, these are two Western figures whose approaches supplement one another, and who thus provide resources that can be used to recover a fuller understanding of the person and work of the Holy Spirit, specifically in reference to love. As they help us see, it is specifically life in the Spirit that is life in loving communion with the triune God.

THOMISTS AND WESLEYANS: MUTUAL ENRICHMENT ON AND IN THE SPIRIT

Given the pneumatological resonance and compatibility emerging from their common association between the Holy Spirit and love in the Christian life, the scope of significance for assessing Aquinas and Wesley on the Spirit and love also includes those who inherit these theological traditions. Additional consideration suggests the potential for mutual enrichment of and in the Spirit for Wesleyans, on the one hand, and Thomists, on the other.

114. "It is important to understand that, with respect to that most eminent of actions, to wit, the passion of things divine and contemplative union with God, there is not only a speculatively practical science which is the science of the theologian, but that there is also a practically practical science which is not so much interested in telling us what perfection is, as leading us to it. This is the science of the master of spirituality, the practitioner of the soul, the artisan of sanctity, the man who stoops to our wretched hearts, which he wants at all costs to lead to their supreme joy" (Jacques Maritain, *The Degrees of Knowledge*, trans. Gerald Phelan, in *The Collected Works of Jacques Maritain*, ed. Ralph McInerny [Notre Dame, Ind.: University of Notre Dame Press, 2002], 7:335–36).

Aquinas for Wesleyans?

In response to recent appeals to rethink sanctification in more compelling theological terms, Wesley's heirs stand to benefit from the approach that Aquinas takes in several respects. The first sense concerns Aquinas's doctrine of the Holy Spirit as love and its implications, while a second insight expressed by Aquinas that may be of interest to Wesleyans comes in his doctrine of grace. First and foremost, three features of Aquinas's *amor*-based pneumatology, as elucidated in chapters 3 through 5, now stand out as being potentially instructive for Wesleyans as they address the problem of interpreting and reclaiming Wesley's doctrine of Christian perfection. To be specific, Wesleyans may find an understanding of Aquinas's doctrine of the Holy Spirit useful in this regard because of, first, the trinitarian context in which he places his pneumatology; second, his deep association of the Holy Spirit with love; and third, the trinitarian foundation on which he constructs his account of the Christian life. With this approach, Aquinas clarifies the proper basis and *telos* of love and holiness by relating them positively to the doctrine of God and to the doctrine of the Holy Spirit in particular. Since Wesley's own understanding of sanctification was implicitly trinitarian, in this way Aquinas could help Wesleyans become more authentically Wesleyan. In an attempt to substantiate this admittedly unusual claim, each of these features of Aquinas's thought will now be reviewed in turn, and their implications for an updating of Wesley on Christian perfection explored.

As noted earlier in chapter 3, Aquinas's discussion of the Holy Spirit as love is deeply related both in context and content to the doctrine of the Trinity. The fact that Aquinas situates this discussion in the midst of his larger exposition of God as Trinity allows for a fruitful exploration of the connection between the doctrine of the Spirit and other doctrines, including the doctrines of processions, relations, persons, and missions. By placing his inquiry into the person of the Holy Spirit in an explicitly trinitarian context, Aquinas demonstrates that the proper basis of pneumatology is the doctrine of the Trinity.

Granted, following Wesley's practical orientation, most if not all Wesleyans would likely show little interest in developing a full-blown speculative doctrine of the Trinity in the manner of Aquinas, and would prefer instead to emphasize the practical meaning of this doctrine for Christian living. This inclination toward praxis is surely in keeping with the spirit of Wesley. Nevertheless, the fact that in the *prima pars* Thomas grounds his pneumatology in the doctrine of the Trinity is not without significance even for those who would follow Wesley. More precisely, Wesley's implicitly trinitarian understanding of sanctification could be enriched by an appeal to Aquinas on this point, because locating pneumatology within the broader context of the doctrine of the Trinity means that the work attributed to the Holy Spirit must also be understood in clearly trinitarian terms.

Sanctification, of course, is a doctrine in which the Holy Spirit has traditionally played a central role. The pneumatological focus of sanctification is certainly a mark of Wesley's thought, as shown in chapter 2. In part because of the connection in his writings between sanctification and the Spirit, one conclusion reached in that same chapter was that the more substantive theological account of Christian perfection called for by a number of Wesley's interpreters can indeed be developed with considerable support from Wesley. What should be of particular importance toward that end is a greater appreciation for the embedded trinitarianism in Wesley's doctrine of sanctification.

Wesleyans must therefore recover from Wesley a clearer sense of what John Deschner calls Wesley's "presupposed theology," including the trinitarianism that was "fundamental in his theology" even if he "did not emphasize [it] when he preached at street corners."[115]

115. John Deschner, *Wesley's Christology: An Interpretation*, 2nd ed. (Grand Rapids: Zondervan, 1988), xii.

Earlier, the observation was made that Wesley seems to have assumed a trinitarian grounding for his conception of holiness. His implicitly trinitarian doctrine of Christian perfection is enough to suggest a certain relation between holiness and love, on the one hand, and the doctrine of God, on the other. Although he does not exhaustively develop this trinitarian content in his writings, the problem of interpreting Wesley's doctrine of Christian perfection calls for a deep retrieval and constructive updating of it.

It is precisely on this point that someone like Aquinas can help Wesleyans build on Wesley by accounting more explicitly for the trinitarian depth and *telos* of sanctification. Identifying the properly trinitarian context of pneumatology, as Aquinas does, is a step in that direction because it entails understanding the work attributed to the Holy Spirit in trinitarian terms, which would mean in the case of Wesley connecting sanctification more clearly to the doctrine of the triune God—not in a total departure from Wesley but precisely as an affirmation and extension of his own spiritual and theological insights.

In the midst of appeals for a more theological account of sanctification, Wesleyans may also find Aquinas's doctrine of the Holy Spirit enlightening because of his association between the Holy Spirit and love, by which he makes explicit that love is an irreducibly theological term. In Aquinas, this association extends to the point that he identifies *Amor* as a name proper to the Spirit, so deeply theological is his understanding of love.[116] The connection between God and love is a significant one in Aquinas's thought, whether in terms of *Amor* as a *proprium* of the Spirit or the theological virtue of *caritas*, which is a virtue infused in the soul by God.[117] Simply put, for Aquinas, love is about God, and one could even say that in the Christian life, love takes on its clearest and most profound meaning when it is viewed in light of what the faith teaches about God.[118]

116. *ST*, I, q. 37.

117. Ibid., I–II, q. 62, a. 1c.

118. E.g., "We know love by this, that [Christ] laid down his life for us—and we

Of course, Wesley also closely associated love with God, as in his naming of love as God's "darling" attribute.[119] The pneumatological element animating Wesley's account of sanctification holds promise for the development of a theology of holiness and love that is related especially closely to the Spirit of holiness and love, and this element may be supplemented by crucial insights from someone like Aquinas. At a very basic level, Aquinas and Wesley are able to discern a connection between God and love through the plain teaching of Scripture, as in 1 John 4:7–8, 13 and Romans 5:5, each of which suggests a link between the love of God and the gift of the Holy Spirit.

Yet in a largely therapeutic age such as the present, in which love is sometimes reduced to a matter of mere human feeling or simply meaning well, love can easily be misconstrued and even cheapened through a dumbing down or stripping away of its essential theological elements. One challenge for those seeking to retrieve and update Wesley's doctrine of Christian perfection is precisely to avoid this tendency. If love is to be made perfect, which Wesley tirelessly propagated as a genuine possibility under grace, then the operative understanding of love must itself be sufficiently theological, or else it is by definition something other than love in its truly Christian sense. For this to be the case, love cannot be understood as somehow independent of knowledge and truth.

Wesley is sometimes championed as one who encouraged Methodists to "think and let think," but quoting this phrase in isolation from its proper context is misleading since the principle in its entirety reads, "as to all opinions which do not strike at the root of Christianity, we 'think and let think.'"[120] On points that do not threaten essential truth, Wesley is glad for Methodists to have liberty as to opinions and to grant others the same. Well aware that Wesley's epigram has

---

ought to lay down our lives for one another.... In this is love, not that we loved God but that he loved us and sent his Son to be the atoning sacrifice for our sins" (1 Jn 3:16, 4:10).

119. Wesley, *Explanatory Notes*, 1 Jn 4:8.

120. *The Character of a Methodist*, §1, in Wesley, *Works*, ed. Outler, et al., 9:34.

often been distorted, Outler offers this candid observation: "If Methodism may rightly be charged with theological indifferentism, this has no valid grounds in Wesley himself."[121] One place where Wesley emphasizes the unity of truth and love in especially noteworthy fashion is his sermon "An Israelite Indeed."[122] Here Wesley critiques the proposal of Francis Hutcheson in *An Inquiry into the Original of Our Ideas of Beauty and Virtue* (1725) that the essence of virtue is benevolence or love of our fellow creatures, a claim that is representative of Hutcheson's autonomous ethical theory divorced from any theological ground. Against Hutcheson, Wesley insists on the love of God as "the true foundation both of the love of our neighbour and all other virtues," in accordance with Christ's own designation of this commandment as the "first and greatest" (Mt 22:38).[123] He further asserts that truth and love are to be understood as integrally united, and in a direct correlation with holiness:

> This then is real, genuine, solid virtue. Not truth alone, nor conformity to truth. This is a property of real virtue, not the essence of it. Not love alone, though this comes nearer the mark; for "love" in one sense "is the fulfilling of the law" [Rom 13:10]. No: truth and love united together are the essence of virtue or holiness.[124]

Benevolence, as Wesley goes on to say, is surely part of the good life, but must be fixed on "its right foundation, namely, the love of God, springing from faith, from a full conviction that God hath given his only Son to die for my sins."[125] Here Wesley states plainly the connection between truth and love that is vital to genuine virtue and holiness.

This is a connection, however, that Wesley does not always make explicit in what he says about love, which opens the door to distortions and misunderstandings similar to the one about his putative

121. Wesley, *Works*, ed. Outler, et al., 1:220, fn. 7.

122. Sermon 90 (1755), in Wesley, *Works*, ed. Outler, et al., 3:278–289.

123. Ibid., §2, in Wesley, *Works*, ed. Outler, et al., 3:280.

124. Ibid., II.11, in Wesley, *Works*, ed. Outler, et al., 3:289.

125. Ibid.

indifferentism mentioned above.[126] Thus, while thorough engagement with Wesley can certainly help preserve a properly theological vision of love, more potent medicine than what he provides may be necessary.

As someone who reflects on the unity of truth and love in a substantive way, Aquinas offers no shortage of such an antidote. To adumbrate the integration of knowledge of God and love in Aquinas's thought, we will turn to an excellent study by Michael Sherwin, *By Knowledge and By Love: Charity and Knowledge in the Moral Theology of St. Thomas Aquinas.* Sherwin's treatment of Aquinas is guided by a twofold question: "[W]hat is charity's relationship to knowledge, and what are the implications of this relationship for one's theology of charity as a virtue?"[127] For the present inquiry, the first part of the question has the most direct relevance. Over against interpretations of Aquinas according to which charity's act independently precedes practical reasoning (as posited by "theologians of moral motivation," in Sherwin's lingo), Sherwin demonstrates that, for Aquinas, will and intellect work cooperatively in every human act.[128] In addition, love and knowledge are interconnected in a way that is analogous to the relation between intellect and will.[129]

126. E.g., "Though we can't think alike, may we not love alike?" ("Catholic Spirit," §4, in Wesley, *Works*, ed. Outler, et al., 2:82). This rhetorical question is also susceptible to misinterpretation as an endorsement of glossing over disagreements on matters of essential truth, such as the ones that he lists elsewhere "concerning the incarnation of our Lord, concerning the ever blessed Trinity, and every other doctrine contained in the oracles of God" ("The Way to the Kingdom," I.6; by "the oracles of God," Wesley means the Scriptures taken as a coherent whole; cf. Rom 3:2, Heb 5:12, 1 Pt 4:11, Acts 7:38). In the context of this rhetorical question, Wesley is talking specifically about differences in opinions or modes of worship, which he considered important but ultimately nonessential matters.

127. Michael Sherwin, OP, *By Knowledge and By Love: Charity and Knowledge in the Moral Theology of St. Thomas Aquinas* (Washington, D.C.: The Catholic University of America Press, 2005), xxii.

128. As in his mature description of human choice in *De malo* 6; cf. *ST*, I–II, q. 9, a. 1 ad 3 on how the intellect and will move each other in the human act, the intellect on the level of specification, and the will on the level of exercise.

129. In Aquinas's account of the interdependence of knowledge and love, the

Therefore, charity is not something that exists independently of knowledge of God, and neither can the movement of charity be independent of practical reasoning and concrete action. Rather than being separated, intellect and will are reciprocally related in the moral theology of Aquinas, as are knowledge and love, such that, in Sherwin's helpful summary, "knowledge has priority in attaining the beloved, while love has priority in moving toward the beloved."[130] Similarly, Aquinas's account of the theological virtues displays an interpenetration and integration in the case of knowledge and love, since charity's act presupposes the knowledge of faith while charity animates faith and directs it toward its end of union with God.[131]

Aquinas's account of knowledge and love as mutually dependent obviously bears the marks of his own sophisticated moral psychology and moral theology, which may or may not hold much appeal to readers of Wesley. Yet they do not have to trace all the subtle intricacies of Aquinas's thought in order to appreciate something of the significance of the conclusions that he reaches in regard to knowledge and love. In particular, the insight that knowledge and love are inextricably intertwined could help orient Wesleyans toward a theological conception of love that is illuminated by the light of faith and thus rooted profoundly in God and in the knowledge of God that faith gives.

---

will moves the intellect toward greater knowledge of the beloved while the will's desire for deeper knowledge is itself dependent on the intellect already having come to know something about the beloved (e.g., *ST*, I–II, q. 28, a. 2c, where Aquinas addresses love's dependence on knowledge, and his reference to cognition's dependence on love in his discussion of ecstasy in I–I, q. 28, a. 3c, especially his remark that "love makes the lover dwell on the beloved ... and to dwell intently on one thing draws the mind from other things").

130. Sherwin, *By Knowledge and By Love*, 120.

131. E.g., *ST*, II–II, q. 4, a. 7: "the last end must be in the intellect before it is in the will, because the will does not move toward anything except in so far as it is apprehended by the intellect." Aquinas affirms faith's structural priority over charity while ascribing to charity a greater dignity than faith: "Since to love God is something greater than to know him, especially in this state of life, it follows that love of God presupposes knowledge of God" (ibid., II–II, q. 27, a. 4 ad 2). Meanwhile, charity has priority in moving faith to its end (ibid., II–II, q. 4, a. 5c).

Although Wesley did not synthesize his works into a comprehensive system of thought, he relates love and God in more or less direct ways throughout his writings, and in that association the Holy Spirit figures prominently. This aspect of Wesley's thought can be highlighted through a careful and extensive engagement with his corpus as a whole. It can also be amplified through an appreciation of Aquinas on the Spirit as love, which provides in fuller form a pneumatological grammar of love that connects with and extends some of Wesley's own spiritual and soteriological intuitions. In these ways, Wesleyans could discover the rich resources necessary to safeguard a properly theological understanding of love, over against cheapened, superficial, or sentimentalized versions, and to ensure that the love in question is really the love that "rejoices in the truth" of God (cf. 1 Cor 13:6). A constructive retrieval and updating of Wesley's doctrine of perfect love must be informed by knowledge of the truth, illumined by the light of faith, if the love under consideration is to be the love of the God of Jesus Christ—the love that Wesley attributes repeatedly to the Holy Spirit and, as Aquinas would say, the love that the Holy Spirit in a certain sense *is*.

The trinitarian foundation that Aquinas establishes in his identification of the Spirit as love and the broader doctrinal heading under which it comes, namely, the doctrine of the Trinity, is the same foundation on which he proceeds to construct his account of the Christian life. As he states in the *prima pars* of the *Summa theologiae*, one implication of grasping that the Father and the Son love one another by the Holy Spirit is the insight that the Father loves not only the Son by the Spirit but also loves himself, and even us, by the Spirit as well. This is true when love is taken in a notional sense, by which it denotes to "spirate love," as to speak is to produce a word and to flower is to produce flowers. As a tree flowers by its flowers, so the Father and the Son love each other and us by the Holy Spirit, who is love proceeding.[132] In this sense, love imports a relation to creatures in a secondary way. God loves himself and every creature

132. Ibid., I, q. 37, a. 2c.

by the Holy Spirit, who proceeds as the love of God's own goodness, whereby God loves above all himself, since God is the greatest good, and loves us in relation to himself.[133] The upshot is the profound soteriological affirmation that God loves us with the very same love with which God loves himself—the Holy Spirit. Through the Spirit, nothing less than God's own love is poured out upon us, immersing us in God's life. Aquinas later explains in his treatment of the mission of the divine persons that by the gift of sanctifying grace, God actually comes to dwell in us as in his own temple.[134] With these rich notions of God loving us by the Holy Spirit, and dwelling in us as in a place consecrated to God, Aquinas speaks to the depth of participation in God's triune life that is made possible for us by grace.

In Aquinas's thought, dogmatic theology and moral theology share a vital and direct connection. As in the case of his doctrine of the Trinity and his account of the Christian life in participatory terms, his moral theology rests on the foundation of dogmatic theology. The soteriological import of this clear connection is quite substantial, and calls attention to the motifs of divine indwelling and participation.

While Aquinas develops these themes in his own way, they are not unique to him, but rather represent an important strand of the scriptural witness to salvation in Jesus Christ. Indeed, Wesley also espouses a participatory understanding of the Christian life as life with and in God by the illuminating and sanctifying work of the Holy Spirit. Wesley was obviously not an explicit Thomist, but he shared in common with Aquinas, and much of the broader Christian tradition, what D. Stephen Long has called a metaphysics of illumination and participation.[135] Placing Wesley in the tradition of moral theology exemplified by Aquinas, Long shows how both Aquinas and Wesley account for the Christian life in sufficiently

133. Ibid., I, q. 37, a. 2 ad 3.

134. Ibid., I, q. 43, a. 3.

135. Long, *John Wesley's Moral Theology*, 188–94.

theological terms that preserve the appropriate manner of speaking about sanctification as participation in the triune God.[136] Wesley, of course, does not use the same technical language as Aquinas, but Long is quite right that certain dogmatic themes are discernible in his reflections on life in Christ, notably that of partaking in the divine nature (2 Pt 1:4). This kind of fruitful engagement with Aquinas can help Wesleyans better understand both Wesley and themselves. By relating love and holiness in specific ways to the doctrine of God and to the doctrine of the Holy Spirit in particular, Aquinas can be used to highlight some of the underlying theological elements of Wesley's thought, such as the trinitarian basis of sanctification and salvation as participation in God.

Aquinas's *amor*-based pneumatology, particularly as he develops it in the *Summa*, is marked by a trinitarian context, a deep association of the Holy Spirit with love and the development of a theology of love in which the Spirit has an important role, and a trinitarian foundation that serves as the basis for his account of the Christian life. These three topics represent one area in which Aquinas's thought provides the kind of theological substructure that could be useful for Wesleyans in their quest to recover and revitalize Wesley's implicitly trinitarian view of sanctification.

A second potential benefit of turning to Aquinas would be to gain clarity on one of the perennial problems associated with the interpretation of Wesley on Christian perfection, the question of how best to balance the instantaneous and gradual dimensions in his thought. As deftly pointed out by Colón-Emeric in his study of Christian perfection in Wesley and Aquinas, Aquinas's nuanced account of grace may also help overcome the apparent impasse between the two main interpretive camps on this disputed question. Both groups, each with its representative contemporary scholar, acknowledge that Wesley's soteriology allows for instantaneous as well as gradual dimensions, but the debate hinges on understand-

136. Ibid., 174.

ing the relationship between these two motifs and whether (and if so, how) one assumes priority over the other. On the one hand, Maddox posits the concept of "responsible grace" in an attempt "to preserve the vital tension between two truths that [Wesley] viewed as co-definitive of Christianity: without God's grace, we *cannot* be saved; while without our (grace-empowered, but uncoerced) participation, God's grace *will not* save."[137] Based on the observation that for Wesley God's grace is personal and co-operant, Maddox concludes that salvation is best understood as a process.[138] While he recognizes that Wesley speaks of entire sanctification occurring at a single moment in time, and that the possibility of entire sanctification might have been "*distinctive*" in Wesley, more than the instantaneous element Maddox stresses the theme of gradual growth in holiness, for as he sees it "the conception of sanctification (as a whole) as the progressive journey in responsive co-operation with God's empowering graces was most *characteristic* of Wesley."[139] God takes the initiative and then acts in concert with and in the context of a grace-enabled, yet genuinely free human response to God's grace in the ongoing journey in which salvation consists.

On the other hand, Collins acknowledges that gradual growth certainly occupies a place in Wesley's soteriology but maintains that, in itself, the claim that God and humanity ever work together in the process of redemption "does not represent the full range of Wesley's understanding of grace."[140] In particular, such a claim fails to express the emphasis that Wesley places on grace as understood to denote the sole activity of God or what Collins calls "free grace."[141] According to Collins, "not only did Wesley view grace as co-operant ... but also he considered grace, in a very *conjunctive* way, as indicative of divine favor and therefore, in a real sense, as the work of God *alone*."[142] So any paradigm expressing both divine and

137. Maddox, *Responsible Grace*, 19.
138. Ibid., 87.
139. Ibid., 190.
140. Collins, *The Theology of John Wesley*, 12.
141. Ibid.
142. Ibid.

human acting in the process of redemption must be balanced by adequate attention to the operation of God alone and the corresponding instantaneous elements of salvation in Wesley's view. In short, what is needed is the subsuming of Maddox's perspective into an "*even larger conjunction*" where the sole—and instantaneous—work of God is also sufficiently factored in.[143]

Based on the illuminating observation of Colón-Emeric, a possible resolution to the problem of interpreting Wesley on sanctification can be discerned in Aquinas's distinction between operative grace and cooperative grace. These interpretive lenses for reading Wesley have noteworthy parallels to Aquinas's division of grace into the categories of operative and cooperative, habitual and actual. A brief explanation of these important concepts in Aquinas is necessary in order to elucidate the connection. When the will is moved and not moving, but God is the sole mover, this is called *gratia operans*, whereas when the will is both moved and moving this is called *gratia cooperans*.[144] In the former, the operation is attributed only to God. In the latter, it is attributed to the human will as well as to God. Bernard Lonergan clarifies with reference to the corresponding concepts of habitual and actual grace: "In habitual grace divine operation infuses the habit, to become cooperation when the habit leads to free acts; in actual grace divine operation effects the will of the end to become cooperation when this will of the end leads to an efficacious choice of means."[145] Colón-Emeric then explains:

> With this distinction between *gratia operans* and *gratia cooperans* the Gordian knot tying the instantaneous versus gradual debate is undone. On the one hand, as operating grace, all divine operation is instantaneous. The infusion of virtue in habitual operating grace and the reducing of the will to action in actual operating grace take place in an instant.

143. Ibid.

144. *ST*, I–II, q. 111, a. 2.

145. Bernard Lonergan, *Grace and Freedom: Operative Grace in the Thought of St. Thomas Aquinas* (Toronto: University of Toronto Press, 2000), 147 (as cited by Colón-Emeric).

On the other hand, as cooperating grace all divine operations are gradual. The exercise of virtue and willing of acts are not instantaneous, not because of any deficiency in God, but because our willing and doing are temporal acts.[146]

Even though Wesley did not himself use the technical language of operative and cooperative grace, it brings into focus some of his main concerns with regard to the relationship between the instantaneous and gradual dimensions in his doctrine of sanctification. By means of conceptual clarity from a new vantage point and an appropriate emphasis on divine sovereignty in salvation, Aquinas's twofold division of grace casts light on a possible way forward for the interpreters of Wesley.

The language of operating and cooperating grace gives a conceptual clarity to the debate over Wesley on Christian perfection because of the important distinction between what happens in an instant and what is gradual. Again, as Aquinas teaches, operating grace denotes an operation attributed to God as sole mover, and as such it is instantaneous, as in the infusion of virtue in the soul (habitual operating grace) and the reducing of the will to action (actual operating grace).[147] Cooperating grace, meanwhile, refers to the gradual operations of God with which human beings cooperate.[148] To make more apparent the connection with Wesley that Colón-Emeric has identified, Collins's interpretive hermeneutic of "free grace" finds a certain analogy with operant grace (*gratia operans*) in the thought of Aquinas, the similarities being twofold: God as sole mover and instantaneous effect. With his emphasis on responsible grace as crucial for interpreting Wesley, Maddox exhibits an understanding of grace that corresponds to Aquinas's notion of cooperating grace (*gratia cooperans*) in two notable ways, with each approach allowing for (1) the cooperation of human beings with God,

146. Colón-Emeric, *Wesley, Aquinas, and Christian Perfection*, 175.
147. *ST*, I–II, q. 111, a. 2c.
148. Ibid.

in response to the divine initiative, and (2) cooperation that takes the form of gradual operations and effects.

By helping to clarify the main features of the debate, Aquinas's terminology serves to isolate the distinctive merit of each position, that is, grace as the work of God alone as stressed by Collins; and the opportunity for genuine human cooperation with God, by grace, in Maddox. It also makes possible an affirmation of the fundamental complementarity between these two points of emphasis when they are set within a wider conceptual framework. Collins's more recent call for a "larger conjunction" in which to understand Wesley on salvation is a noble attempt to balance more effectively such conjunctions as (1) divine-human cooperation and the work of God alone and (2) the gradual and instantaneous elements of sanctification in Wesley.[149] The primary concern for such an approach—clearly affirming divine sovereignty in salvation—is also met by Aquinas as demonstrated in his distinction between operating and cooperating grace.[150]

In addition, Aquinas's language attains this clarity from a new vantage point that may be precisely what is needed to drive forward the discussion regarding how best to interpret Wesley. Collins and Maddox have had numerous extended exchanges over the last twenty years, with little give or take. By this point the lines in the debate have become so clearly drawn that it may take the introduction of a fresh voice, even if from outside the Methodist fold, to help resolve the interpretive dilemma. To be sure, the appeal to Aquinas to understand Wesley is not without difficulty, for example, in regard to the problem of predestination, which the two do not approach in the same way (although Colón-Emeric outlines the contours for a possible rapprochement on this issue).[151] Yet the analogy in Aqui-

149. Collins, "The State of Wesley Studies in North America: A Theological Journey," *Wesleyan Theological Journal* 44/2 (Fall 2009): 7–38, in particular 38; Collins, *The Theology of John Wesley*, 76.

150. Cf. Colón-Emeric, *Wesley, Aquinas, and Christian Perfection*, 264 fn. 124.

151. Ibid., 176–78.

nas represents a potentially fruitful line of inquiry for Wesleyans on sanctification because of the parallels between Aquinas's twofold division of grace (operative and cooperative, habitual and actual) and the positions staked out and defended by Collins and Maddox.

In sum, in their ongoing attempt to rethink sanctification in more compelling theological terms, Wesley's heirs can learn from Aquinas on several fronts. First of all, there are lessons to be gleaned from Aquinas's pneumatology, given its trinitarian context in the structure of the *Summa*, his exposition of the Holy Spirit as love (*Amor*) and corresponding theology of charity, and the trinitarian foundation on which he constructs his account of the Christian life. Such an approach relates love and holiness to the doctrine of God and in particular to the doctrine of the Holy Spirit, and with this move Aquinas elucidates the depth and *telos* of love and holiness and provides a backdrop against which Wesley's own implicitly trinitarian understanding of salvation could be situated, to the effect of Aquinas helping Wesleyans become more authentically Wesleyan. Second, given disputes over the relationship between the instantaneous and gradual dimensions in Wesley's thought, an appeal to Aquinas's distinction between *gratia operans* and *gratia cooperans* can lead beyond the stalemate between Collins's "free grace" and Maddox's "responsible grace" by clarifying the terms of the debate and integrating the merits of each position into a more balanced account, one that clearly affirms both the primacy of divine sovereignty in salvation and the authenticity of human response and cooperation. Thus, Aquinas provides the conceptual clarity necessary for a better understanding of Wesley, which is the second sense in which an appreciation of Aquinas could help Wesleyans become better Wesleyans.

Wesley for Thomists?

Meanwhile, Catholics may benefit from Wesley's passionate emphasis on the pursuit of personal and social sanctity in love as being essential for all Christians, whether lay or clergy. In fact an understanding of Wesley's theological message can serve to call attention to the same kind of concern in Catholic theology and spirituality, particularly as represented by Aquinas. Sanctification is a prominent theme in Aquinas's vision of life in Christ, and it is capable of further development among his interpreters.[152] The pairing of Aquinas and Wesley is instructive on this point because it shows that an account of perfect love in Wesley can serve as a catalyst for a reappraisal of Aquinas on sanctification, *caritas*, and the Holy Spirit. For like Wesley, Aquinas was also attentive to the practical implications of salvation, even though that aspect of his thought is sometimes underappreciated. Thus, Wesley can contribute to a recovery of this important strand in Aquinas's works, and could help Thomists become more authentically Thomistic.

Wesley was not a speculative theologian, but a practical theologian, a soteriologist one might say, who advocated in his work of preaching, writing, teaching, and pastoral oversight what he called "practical divinity."[153] Colón-Emeric argues that precisely as such, Wesley offers Catholics an example of the pursuit of perfection, a practitioner "next to St. John of the Cross, who applies the speculatively practical theology of Thomas Aquinas in a practically practical way, a way leading not up Mount Carmel to a life of contemplation but down the plain to a life of action."[154] Wesley saw it as his mission, and the mission of Methodism, to offer people the hope of

152. Cf. the increasingly influential reading of Aquinas as first and foremost a theologian, not a philosopher, as reflected in the work of Torrell, especially his two-volume biography, *Initiation à saint Thomas d'Aquin: Sa personne et son oeuvre*, 2nd ed., Vestigia, Pensée antique et médiévale, 13 (Fribourg: Éditions du Cerf–Éditions Universitaires de Fribourg, 2003; ET: *Saint Thomas Aquinas*, vol. 1: *The Person and His Work*); and *Saint Thomas d'Aquin, maître spirituel: Initiation à saint Thomas d'Aquin*, 2nd ed., Vestigia, Pensée antique et médiévale, 19 (Fribourg: Éditions du Cerf–Éditions Universitaires de Fribourg, 2003; ET: *Saint Thomas Aquinas*, vol. 2: *Spiritual Master*).

153. E.g., preface to *A Collection of Hymns for the Use of the People Called Methodists*, §4, in Wesley, *Works*, ed. Outler, et al., 7:74.

154. Colón-Emeric, *Wesley, Aquinas, and Christian Perfection*, 8–9.

life in Christ, and he propagated the message of this hope as widely as he could through his preaching in parish churches, at Methodist preaching houses, and even in the fields and by the coal mines. Wesley recognized that in their everyday lives, people could experience the transforming presence and power of God, enlightening our understandings, forgiving our sins, renewing our natures, guiding us when we are perplexed, consoling us in our sorrows, deepening our faith, conforming us to the image of Christ, and producing in our lives the fruit of the Holy Spirit. Speaking as he does *ad populum*, Wesley is one who "does not only define perfection but leads others to it," a practitioner who propagates the universal call to holiness that is central to the Gospel.[155]

Along those lines, something that Thomists could pick up on from Wesley is an emphasis on holiness of heart and life through the ongoing work of God in the lives of the faithful—work that can be attributed in a special way to the Holy Spirit. Aquinas shows a keen awareness of the transformative work of the Spirit, as in his remarkable passage about friendship with God through the Spirit in *Summa contra Gentiles* IV, and in his reading of the Sermon on the Mount as well.[156] While this emphasis on holiness has not exactly

155. On Wesley speaking *ad populum*, see Wesley, *Works*, ed. Outler, et al., 1:103. Colón-Emeric describes Wesley as a practitioner and teacher of perfection in *Wesley, Aquinas, and Christian Perfection*, 181.

156. See chapter 5 above on *ScG* IV. In addition, Aquinas's reading of the Sermon on the Mount in conversation with Wesley is ably narrated by Long and Colón-Emeric with attention to the virtues and Beatitudes (Long, *John Wesley's Moral Theology*, 141–65; Colón-Emeric, *Wesley, Aquinas, and Christian Perfection*, 125–47). The latter in particular finds some significance in the fact that for Aquinas, the distinction between counsels for the religious and precepts for ordinary Christians is less apparent in his reading of the Beatitudes than it is elsewhere, and does not belie that, as he explains in the *Summa*, "the perfection of divine love is a matter of precept for all without exception, so that even the perfection of heaven (*perfectio patriae*) is not excepted from this precept" (*ST*, II–II, q. 184, a. 3 ad 2). In other words, while Aquinas posits that the perfection required for salvation is less perfect than the perfection that is a matter of counsel, he also insists that the life of holiness and even perfection (cf. Mt 5:48) as described by Christ in this sermon is the Lord's call for all who would

been ignored by Thomists, it is arguably capable of further development. Wesley's commitment was to spreading scriptural holiness through the promotion of nothing less than "the life of God in the souls of men."[157] Given that commitment, a basic understanding of Wesleyan theology may serve to enrich the study of Aquinas by calling renewed attention to sanctification and other aspects of Aquinas's rich spiritual theology that is generally underemphasized by his interpreters.

Catholics may find in Wesley, with his sanctification-based soteriology, an exemplar of a similar soteriological orientation characteristic of Catholic theology and spirituality, to which Aquinas gives ample (if somewhat overlooked) expression. The Christian life as described by Aquinas is, by its nature, a life of holiness through creaturely participation in God. The topic of the Spirit, *caritas*, and sanctification is a relatively understudied motif among Thomists, and one that is worthy of additional attention. For all its apparent incommensurability, the juxtaposition of Wesley and Aquinas on the Holy Spirit and the Christian life brings to the fore, particularly given Wesley's doctrine of perfect love, the question of the relationship between the Spirit and love, which is a question that interested Aquinas as well. As a possible entry point into a more sustained examination of Aquinas on the Spirit as love, an understanding of Wesley can serve to promote a retrieval of this aspect of Aquinas's thought, and Wesley could thus help Thomists become more authentically Thomistic.[158]

follow him and not simply for some (Colón-Emeric, *Wesley, Aquinas, and Christian Perfection*, 138–40).

157. Cf. Wesley's letter to Samuel Walker, September 3, 1756: "I have one point in view—to promote, so far as I am able, vital, practical religion; and by the grace of God to beget, preserve, and increase the life of God in the souls of men" (Wesley, *Letters*, 3:192).

158. The relative brevity of this section on Wesley for Thomists can be explained in large part by the methodological differences between Aquinas and Wesley. In terms of technical theological distinctions, which are crucial to an account of the doctrine of the Holy Spirit such as the one pursued in this study, it is my contention

Merit and Assurance Revisited: Mutual Enrichment for Thomists and Wesleyans?

Up to this point, a number of parallels between Aquinas and Wesley on the Christian life have been noted and explored, including the centrality of love, a connection between love and the Spirit, the human person's transformation through divine indwelling, and the universal call for the embodiment of holiness through the Spirit. Such parallels, it has been argued, invite common study and create the possibility for a fruitful exchange between Thomists and Wesleyans on the Spirit, love, and sanctification. Even with these areas of nuanced compatibility between Aquinas and Wesley, however, the question still remains concerning the extent to which their respective thinking on merit and assurance poses problems for the kind of jointly conducted inquiry outlined above. In a manner of speaking, given the apparent contradictions between Aquinas and Wesley on these two significant issues, can an account such as this be said to "merit" the "assurance" of mutual enrichment for Thomists and Wesleyans? Or does their divergence on merit and assurance in fact render such a proposal inherently problematic, perhaps even hopelessly naïve?

There is no denying that, at least verbally, Aquinas and Wesley

that Wesleyans have more to learn from Aquinas than Thomists have to learn from Wesley. This contention is not meant to criticize Wesley but to recognize the outstanding thoroughness and rigor shown by Aquinas as well as the particular charism entrusted to Wesley. Wesley's contribution comes less in the area of theological acumen or sophistication than in evangelical zeal for the spreading of the Gospel and the promotion of holiness of heart and life through our communion with the triune God. This experiential component is also, of course, vital for a robust pneumatology, although there is a sense in which less can be said about this dimension in terms of precise dogmatic formulations because it is meant ultimately not so much to be defined as to be lived. Here again one may think of Wesley as exemplifying Maritain's notion of "the practically practical science which is not so much interested in telling us what perfection is, as leading us to it" (Maritain, *The Degrees of Knowledge*, 336). The importance of such an emphasis on actual praxis can hardly be overstated, even if it takes considerably less space to establish this point than it does to explain that Methodists stand to gain additional clarity on certain technical doctrinal matters from an understanding of Aquinas.

reach different conclusions in regard to the topics of merit and assurance. Again, Wesley rejects merit in the "strict" sense, and admits the legitimacy of a "looser" understanding even while stating his own preference to avoid the term altogether.[159] The sense in which Wesley has no objections to the term is not exactly the same as what Aquinas means by merit. Conversely, Aquinas allows for the knowledge of having received grace by way of revelation or through a certain sweet experience and a perception of delighting in God, but denies the possibility of such knowledge for human beings with certainty on the basis of God's transcendence.[160] The sense in which Aquinas allows for knowledge of having received grace does not seem quite the same as what Wesley means by assurance. There may be, however, a more substantial degree of agreement between them than what appears to be the case at first. Beyond these differences, or rather beneath them, it is worth considering whether there is any common ground between Aquinas and Wesley on merit and assurance that would make possible some degree of mutual affirmation and even enrichment among their interpreters on the subject of the Holy Spirit and the Christian life.

Concerning merit, Aquinas's account of the Spirit as gift may provide a fresh vantage point for considering this disputed issue. One foundational assertion stands out in particular: as the *doctor communis* clarifies, human power on its own avails nothing for participation in God; rather, the human being's participation in God must be freely given from above.[161] Thus the Christian life is rightly identified as a gift, and indeed the gift of the Spirit, which is what Aquinas enables his readers to see as pointed out in the previous chapter. The Spirit's gift to human beings of their participation in God is the theological context in which Aquinas discusses merit, with his question on this theme coming, fittingly enough, under

159. Cf. Wesley's letter to his brother Charles, August 3, 1771, in Wesley, *Letters*, 5:270.

160. *ST*, I–II, q. 112, a. 5.

161. Ibid., I, q. 38, a. 1c.

the heading of grace and its effects. In fact, apart from this context his account of merit would simply be unintelligible, for any talk of merit as Aquinas understands it assumes the prior and free gift of a genuine sharing in God's own life for the faithful through the Spirit.

After stating in particular that merit is the effect of cooperating grace, Aquinas considers whether a person in grace can merit eternal life condignly, that is, according to the inherent value of an action.[162] He avers that a person's meritorious action, in so far as it is the outcome of human free will, is not a matter of condign merit simply because of the "extreme inequality" between God and any human person, but rather pertains to the congruous merit (i.e., the ordained value of an action) by which it is fitting for God to reward such an act according to the excellence of God's power.[163]

Admittedly, the position that Wesley would later take on merit, at best, does not clearly conform with Aquinas's conclusion here, not least because Wesley made no such distinction between condign and congruous merit. Despite their verbal differences, however, a closer analysis of the substance of their positions may indicate a deeper level of compatibility than is generally supposed to be the case between Methodists (and Protestants more broadly) and Catholics. Granted, in his relatively few discussions of merit, Wesley often stressed the idea of human unworthiness over against perceived Roman Catholic teaching, as in his treatise *Popery Calmly Considered* (1779):

> The Church of Rome teaches, that "good works truly merit eternal life."
>
> This is flatly contrary to what our Saviour teaches: "When ye have done all those things that are commanded you, say, We are unprofitable servants: We have done that which was our duty to do." [Lk 17:10] A command to do it, grace to obey that command, "and a far more exceeding

162. Ibid., I–II, q. 114, a. 3.

163. Ibid., I–II, q. 114, a. 3c. Cf. q. 114, a. 1c, where Aquinas explains that there is a "very great inequality" between God and humankind, and that "all the good that is in a man is due to God."

and eternal weight of glory" [2 Cor 4:17], must for ever cut off all pretence of merit from all human obedience.[164]

Wesley seems to assume in Catholic teaching the idea of justification by works, and therefore distances himself from it. When Aquinas speaks of merit, though, he is not speaking of justifying grace, which cannot be merited in any sense, but of the value of certain actions.[165] That God freely gives a value to our good works is a principle that Wesley actually affirms in commenting on Luke 17:10 in his *Explanatory Notes Upon the New Testament*:

When ye have done all, say, We are unprofitable servants—For a man cannot profit God. Happy is he who judges himself an unprofitable servant: miserable is he whom God pronounces such. But though we are unprofit-

164. *Popery Calmly Considered*, II.2, in Wesley, *Works*, ed. Jackson, 10:143. Wesley's views of Catholicism more broadly were complex and varied, ranging from the stinging criticism that was common among Anglicans of his day (e.g., *A Roman Catechism, faithfully drawn out of the allowed writings of the Church of Rome: With a Reply thereto* [1756], which is Wesley's abridgement of *A Catechism Truly Representing the Doctrines and Practices of the Church of Rome with an Answer thereunto*, published by John Williams in 1686) to a remarkably conciliatory spirit (e.g., *A Letter to a Roman Catholic* [1749]). David M. Chapman offers a detailed and candid examination of Wesley and Roman Catholicism in the opening chapter of *In Search of the Catholic Spirit: Methodists and Roman Catholics in Dialogue* (Peterborough, U.K.: Epworth Press, 2004), 6–43. For a brief discussion of Wesley's alliance with opponents of the Catholic Relief Act of 1778 on the grounds that, while he professed no desire to persecute, his perception was that Catholics would always need to be restrained by penal laws to ensure that they did not harm Protestants, see Colin Haydon, *Anti-Catholicism in Eighteenth-Century England, c. 1714–80: A Political and Social Study* (Manchester, U.K.: Manchester University Press, 1993), 63–65, 210–11. Outler notes that even with Wesley's concerns about "popery" and criticisms of "the errors of the Church of Rome," which he had inherited from a long tradition of Anglican anti-Catholic polemics, Wesley "had always considered the piety and devotion of Roman Catholics like De Renty, Lopez, Fénelon, *et al.*, authentic; thus, he always insisted that truly 'catholic spirit' must also include the Romans" (Wesley, *Works*, ed. Outler, et al., 2:71, fn. 32). David Butler provides a fuller account of Wesley's relationship to and views of the Catholic Church in *Methodists and Papists: John Wesley and the Catholic Church in the Eighteenth Century* (London: Darton, Longman & Todd, 1995).

165. *ST*, I–II, q. 114, aa. 2, 5.

able to *Him*, our serving Him is not unprofitable to *us*: for He is pleased to give by His grace a value to our good works, which, in consequence of His promise, entitles us to an eternal reward.[166]

Wesley's interpretation of this verse here suggests a greater degree of substantive similarity between Wesley and Aquinas on the question of merit than the verbal contradiction would seem to allow. Specifically, Wesley's emphasis on God assigning a value to our good works and, on the basis of God's promise, granting us an eternal reward, closely resembles some of the points made by Aquinas. Thus, there is a depth of theological consensus between Aquinas and Wesley on this issue that is noteworthy, and this consensus is truly theological in the sense that it has as its subject God.

Later in the same question, Aquinas elucidates the motif of gift and the centrality of the Spirit in the Christian life in a way that is even more explicitly amenable, in terminology as well as substance, to Wesley and his interpreters. Aquinas proceeds to explain that a meritorious work can also be considered in so far as it proceeds from the grace of the Holy Spirit, and he concludes that when it is considered from this perspective, the act in question merits eternal life condignly:

For the degree of its merit then depends on the power of the Holy Spirit which moves us to eternal life, according to John 4:14: "... shall be in him a well of water springing up into everlasting life." A man's work is therefore rewarded according to the worth of the grace by which he is made a partaker of the divine nature, and adopted as a son of God to whom the inheritance is due by right of adoption, according to Rom. 8:17: "... and if children, then heirs."[167]

Viewed from this perspective, a work is rewarded according to the sheer gift of God's grace and the power of the Holy Spirit. Dwelling in the faithful, the Spirit is the efficient cause of eternal life.[168] It is

166. Wesley, *Explanatory Notes*, Luke 17:10.

167. *ST*, I–II, q. 114, a. 3c.

168. Ibid., I–II, q. 114, a. 3 ad 3.

precisely through the Spirit's presence and power that one is given a share in the life of God, is adopted by grace, and thus comes to receive the inheritance associated with this divinely endued identity.

The very notion of meritorious works, then, can be recast as—far from a matter of bare human achievement—fundamentally an outworking of the free gift of God's grace. The same holds true even in the more particular case of congruous merit as well, in so far as it rests on the foundation of God's work in justification and in the ongoing provision of grace to which human beings respond.[169] Aquinas's account clarifies the important point that God has not only made human beings with the capacity to perform works that God will reward but also provides the grace necessary for such works. Therefore, the significance of good works can be affirmed without claiming that God owes anything to those in grace or that God somehow incurs a debt to them because, strictly speaking, God is a debtor only to the one who is the source of the gift of grace—which is to say that God owes only himself.[170] With this move, Aquinas provides a grammar for describing the works themselves not as grounds for any independent or autonomous claim on grace but as gifts in a certain sense, manifestations of the power of the indwelling Spirit in the faithful as a result of the sheer and abundant goodness of God, for as Aquinas plainly states, all the good in us is finally attributable to God.[171]

Accounting for the place of works in the broader context of an affirmation of God's goodness is also an underlying concern for Wesley. According to Wesley, while salvation is at root by grace

169. The way in which Aquinas speaks of justification is significant, and serves as a helpful reminder of the absolute necessity of God's grace for human salvation: Aquinas identifies justification as not only God's work but also God's "greatest work" (*maximum opus Dei*; ibid., I–II, q. 113, a. 9). Again, the account of merit that Aquinas goes on to provide makes sense only in the context of such an affirmation of the gift of God's grace that exceeds the worthiness of an ungodly person.

170. Ibid., I–II, q. 114, a. 1 ad 3.

171. Ibid., I–II, q. 114, a. 1c.

through faith, works are in some sense necessary for final salvation. As he explains in "On the Wedding Garment," holiness is necessary in a secondary sense for salvation, and its importance only makes sense in the context of what is alone sufficient, which is precisely God's own righteousness as revealed in the person of Jesus Christ:

> The righteousness of Christ is doubtless necessary for any soul that enters into glory: But so is personal holiness too, for every child of man. But it is highly needful to be observed, that they are necessary in different respects. The former is necessary to entitle us to heaven; the latter to qualify us for it. Without the righteousness of Christ we could have no claim to glory; without holiness we could have no fitness for it. By the former we become members of Christ, children of God, and heirs of the kingdom of heaven. By the latter "we are made meet to be partakers of the inheritance of the saints in light" [Col 1:12].[172]

With this distinction between the righteousness of Christ and Christian holiness in his vision of salvation, Wesley is able to maintain the essential quality of both while grounding the latter in the former. In this way, the "rewardable" nature of works comes clearly into focus in the light of God's grace in the person of Christ.[173] Furthermore, given Wesley's precise formulation that "[w]ithout the righteousness of Christ we could have no claim to glory," he seems to assume that, in fact, we do have a claim, one that is in Christ, of course—and this is essentially merit in Aquinas's sense.[174]

Although they work out this concern in different ways, with Aquinas affirming merit by way of nuanced distinctions that Wesley does not explicitly draw, the two figures nevertheless share common ground in their respective views of the place of good works in the Christian life, placing a fundamental emphasis on the goodness and gratuitous grace of God in Jesus Christ. A consideration

172. Sermon 127, "On the Wedding Garment" (1790), §10, in Wesley, *Works*, ed. Outler, et al., 4:139–48, in particular 144.

173. On Wesley's "loose" sense of the term merit, in which he allows for works as "rewardable," see his letter to Charles Wesley, August 3, 1771, in Wesley, *Letters*, 5:270.

174. E.g., *ST*, I–II, q. 114, a. 6 on only Christ as capable of meriting salvation for us.

of Aquinas's account of merit in the context of his treatise on grace, and with particular attention to the motif of gift, can therefore help shed light on a basic but noteworthy conviction that Aquinas and Wesley both affirm. While this common ground may or may not be enough to lead to a final resolution of their differences on the notion of merit (that question need not be definitely answered here), it does allow Thomists and Wesleyans to discover more in common than what might have been initially supposed in relation to this subject, and thus may hold promise for further progress that is yet to be achieved.

In regard to assurance, here again the theme of gift, used somewhat more broadly, can be used to illumine a jointly held foundational concern about a topic on which strict agreement may seem unlikely given the verbal contradictions between Wesley and Aquinas. For Wesley, assurance is the work of the Holy Spirit and, as such, it is a gift of God through the Spirit who bears witness with our spirit that we are children of God, adopted by grace (cf. Rom 8:16–17).[175] That God grants such a gift at all is due in no way to any obligation on the part of God toward those who receive, but simply to God's abundant goodness and mercy as shown in Christ. Wesley pursues the question of a believer's present status before God with a greater intensity than Aquinas, which is again reflective of their different theological methods. Given his practical orientation, Wesley focuses his preaching and theological teaching on the lived reality of Christian existence under grace, part of which, he believes, is the gracious privilege of the assurance of God's pardon and love shed abroad in the heart. Indeed, so strong is Wesley's belief in assurance that at one point he describes it as "one grand part of the testimony which God has given [the Methodists] to bear to all mankind."[176]

175. Wesley explicates this scriptural notion in his two discourses on this very passage, "The Witness of the Spirit, I and II," in Wesley, *Works*, ed. Outler, et al., 1:269–98.

176. *The Witness of the Spirit*, II, I.4, in Wesley, *Works*, ed. Outler, et al., 1:285.

Such assurance has a clear pneumatological basis in that it is conveyed through the spiritual senses, which are awakened and piqued by the activity of the Holy Spirit, convicting persons of their sin, leading them to repentance, pointing them to redemption in Christ, and guiding them toward ever deepening love of God and neighbor in holiness of heart and life, to the point that they can be assured of their new identity as the beloved children of God. All of this, Wesley stresses, is God's free gift, and so, too, is the role in working out their salvation that God grants those who believe.[177]

As noted above, on the perceptibility of grace Aquinas allows for a certain knowledge of having received grace, but not in exactly the same way as Wesley would later propose. Thomists cannot affirm the full sense in which Wesley speaks of assurance out of concern to defend God's transcendence—for God, as God, cannot be comprehended and thus is not known by us in this particular way.[178] Nevertheless, there is still a similarity between Wesley on assurance and Aquinas on knowledge by experience that may allow for the resolution of this verbal contradiction. Aquinas's notion of *cognitio experimentalis* represents a point of contact with Wesley because of the relationship between the missions of the Son and the Spirit, on the one hand, and creaturely union with God, on the other.[179] Aquinas's way of connecting these two important themes with his

177. Cf. "On Working Out Our Own Salvation," where in explicating Philippians 2:12–13 Wesley couches the human role in the context of the gifts of God's priority and enabling power: "there is no opposition between these—'God works; therefore do ye work'—but on the contrary the closest connection, and that in two respects. For, first, God works; therefore you *can* work. Secondly, God works; therefore you *must* work" (Sermon 85, "On Working Out Our Own Salvation" [1785], III.2, in Wesley, *Works*, ed. Outler, et al., 3:199–209, in particular 206).

178. *ST*, I–II, q. 112, a. 5c.

179. In addition to *ST*, I, q. 43, a. 5 ad 2, as discussed earlier, Aquinas establishes this connection in the *Scriptum*: "non qualiscumque cognitio sufficit ad rationem missionis, sed solum illa quae accipitur ex aliquo dono appropriato personae, per quod efficitur in nobis conjunctio ad Deum, secundum modum proprium illius personae, scilicet per amorem, quando Spiritus Sanctus datur. Unde cognitio ista est quasi experimentalis" (*In I Sent.*, d. 14, q. 2, a. 2 ad 3).

appeal to *cognitio experimentalis* shows a striking resemblance to what Wesley would later say about assurance, specifically the way in which Wesley grounds the doctrine in the missions of the Son and the Spirit and stresses the union with God that these missions make possible, a union that is ours to experience through the experimental knowledge in which practical divinity consists.[180] Therefore, Wesley's conception of the certainty of faith in assurance of our adoption as God's children seems basically to correspond to what Aquinas means by *cognitio experimentalis* and not what he means by *certitudo fidei*, the terminological discrepancy notwithstanding.[181]

At the very least, however, a student of Aquinas should be able without much difficulty to resonate with what appears to be Wesley's deeply practical, and pastoral, motivating concern in his doctrine of assurance. For Aquinas, too, teaches that theology is not a mere intellectual activity alone; while in a Thomistic sense it surely involves contemplation of God, it also involves practicing the faith through disciplined and godly living aimed precisely at salvation. What Thomists may be able to appreciate in Wesley is his attentiveness to matters of the Spirit, based on the shared affirmation that the message of the Gospel is actually true: God really has opened his life to human beings in Christ and, through the Holy Spirit, gives us a share in it. Wesley's understanding of assurance rests on this basic conviction, which is central to Aquinas's thought as well, even if he develops it in his own way.

Therefore, while juxtaposing Aquinas on merit and Wesley on assurance does not totally dissolve the differences between them, it does allow for the identification of shared underlying concerns, and

180. Again, as expressed in Wesley's designation of the 1780 *Collection of Hymns for the Use of the People Called Methodists* as "a little body of experimental and practical divinity" (Preface to *A Collection of Hymns for the Use of the People Called Methodists*, in Wesley, *Works*, ed. Outler, et al., 7:74).

181. This is a point that will need to be elaborated upon elsewhere. I am indebted to Bruce Marshall for helping me to see this degree of agreement between Aquinas and Wesley.

this common ground serves to cast the perspectives represented by Aquinas and Wesley on these issues in a new light. Despite the verbal inconsistencies between them, there is a certain connection between Aquinas on merit and Wesley on assurance. The connection stems from the fact that each underscores the work of the Holy Spirit—Aquinas on merit, and specifically on condign merit, which is due to the gift of grace through the Spirit; and Wesley on assurance, which accentuates the point that the identity conferred upon an adopted child of God is given and comes to be embodied in and through the Spirit. If Aquinas's understanding of merit rests on the gift of God's grace in Christ through the Spirit, and thereby leads to the related themes of participation in God and adoption by God, then in one sense Wesley's doctrine of assurance can be seen as an extension of the trajectory begun by Aquinas. Wesley's orientation is practical and even (recalling Pesch) existential.[182] Because of this orientation, Wesley is especially concerned, to a greater degree and in a different but not necessarily incompatible way than Aquinas, to emphasize that a positive answer to the question of one's status before God—the question of whether or not one is in a state of grace—is actually attainable through the gift of the gracious witness of the Holy Spirit, the effects of which are evident not only through an inward perception of delighting in God but also objectively in the fruit of the Spirit that proceeds from lively faith and from the operations of the indwelling God on the soul.

With that last point, a final observation on this subject can be made. Both Aquinas's account of merit and Wesley's understanding of assurance, despite their differences, nevertheless are ultimately directed toward a similar end, namely, a certain way of life that bears the marks of sanctification. In other words, they share not only common ground, expressed through the themes of divine goodness and

182. Cf. Otto H. Pesch, "Existential and Sapiential Theology—The Theological Confrontation between Luther and Aquinas," in Jared Wicks, ed., *Catholic Scholars Dialogue with Luther* (Chicago: Loyola University Press, 1970), 61–81.

gift, but also a common goal that is life in the Spirit to the praise of the triune God. For Aquinas, as is suggested by the context of his account of merit (i.e., his treatise on grace) and especially by the direction in which it points, establishing the legitimacy of merit within its proper parameters per se is not really the ultimate goal, but rather serves the greater purpose of elucidating the goodness of the God who freely justifies the ungodly and then graciously gives them a share in working out their salvation.[183] In this way, Aquinas's account of merit promotes life lived to the glory of God. Similarly, for Wesley, the doctrine of assurance is not an end in itself, but must be understood in its larger context in what Wesley called the way of salvation. Genuine assurance, as Wesley often stressed, will naturally lead to the manifestation of the Spirit's fruit, so that those who are given this gift will bear witness in word and deed to the life-transforming power of God.[184] In each case, then, the goal is ultimately holiness through faithful living that glorifies God, who is the source of all that is good and the giver of all grace.

Unqualified agreement on the nuances of merit and assurance may be beyond reach, but the common ground and common goal shared by Aquinas and Wesley make possible what is perhaps a surprising degree of mutual enrichment by Thomists and Wesleyans. Given the doxological thrust in the thought of each figure, their differences do not exactly dissolve but can be put in proper perspective against the larger backdrop of life lived to the praise of God, for that alone is a genuinely good life and one that befits all who are adopted children of God. In that sense, Aquinas and Wesley can sing the doxology together. By following the position of each to its logical end, so too can their heirs.

Even if certain difficulties concerning the questions of assurance

183. *ST*, I–II, q. 113 (on justification as an effect of operative grace), q. 114 (on merit as the effect of cooperative grace).

184. E.g., "The Witness of the Spirit, I and II," in Wesley, *Works*, ed. Outler, et al., 1:269–98.

and merit remain, Wesleyans and Thomists can affirm several areas of common concern that underlie the respective positions of Wesley and Aquinas on these issues and orient them to similar practical and doxological ends. Moreover, these two figures share a number of core convictions about the Spirit and the Christian life, touching on not only the signature importance of love for Christian living but also an association between the Spirit and love that relates to human transformation through divine indwelling as embodied in the life of holiness. Parallels such as these create the potential for Thomists and Wesleyans to discover in one another something about themselves. Colón-Emeric makes the point concisely as he reflects on having placed Wesley and Aquinas in dialogue on Christian perfection: "Reading Thomas can help Methodists be better Wesleyans. Conversely, reading Wesley can help Thomists be better Catholics."[185] As suggested by the precisely ecclesial references in that observation, what ultimately is at stake here pertains not simply to two traditions of academic theology, but also to the ecclesial traditions represented thereby. Because there are important ecclesiological implications raised by the study of Aquinas and Wesley on the Holy Spirit, a closer consideration of Catholic-Methodist ecumenical dialogue is now in order. For this task, the notion of gift can profitably be employed once more.

THE HOLY SPIRIT AND THE SHARING OF GIFTS IN CATHOLIC-METHODIST DIALOGUE

The pneumatological and soteriological complementarity between Aquinas and Wesley outlined above has important implications not only for the ongoing work of pneumatological recovery and for the study of Aquinas and of Wesley, but also for ecumenical dialogue between the theological heirs of these two figures. As it

185. Colón-Emeric, *Wesley, Aquinas, and Christian Perfection*, 181.

has been pointed out in Catholic-Methodist bilateral dialogue, the doctrine of the Holy Spirit represents a point of contact between these two Christian traditions. The basis for that connection derives to a considerable degree from the commitments and emphases of Aquinas and Wesley, each of whom is a leading figure in his respective tradition. As we will see, the measure of pneumatological compatibility between Catholics and Methodists that has already been recognized in ecumenical dialogue can be extended through the insights of Aquinas and Wesley. Following an overview of the international Catholic-Methodist dialogue, this section will explore the topic of the Holy Spirit and the sharing of gifts, which represents a convenient heading under which to consider both recent ecumenical progress between Methodists and Catholics and the possibility of further advancement in this dialogue under the Spirit's agency and direction.

A Brief Overview of the International Catholic-Methodist Dialogue

Since 1967, Roman Catholics and Methodists have engaged in formal ecumenical dialogue with one another on an international level through the work of the Joint Commission for Dialogue between the World Methodist Council and the Roman Catholic Church. The results of this dialogue have come in the form of a report, issued once every five years, addressing the chosen theme of that five-year session in conversation with previous reports and other relevant ecumenical and theological texts as appropriate. The international dialogue between Catholics and Methodists is notable for its steady growth in convergence between two communities with more in common than has often been supposed.[186]

186. Chapman presents a comprehensive account of the dialogue between Methodists and Roman Catholics from John Wesley to the present day in his study *In Search of the Catholic Spirit*.

The dialogue began with a period of mutual acquaintance and the preliminary discussion of doctrinal, ethical, and pastoral issues of shared interest, including spirituality, the Christian home and family, Eucharist, and ministry and authority (1971 and 1976 reports). After this initial stage of the dialogue, the Joint Commission sought to develop, through sketching broad theological perspectives, a doctrinal framework that could make possible the eventual resolution of the doctrinal and structural differences that continue to divide Methodists and Catholics.[187]

Significantly, the first doctrine employed in the construction of such a framework was pneumatology, in the 1981 report entitled *Towards an Agreed Statement on the Holy Spirit*.[188] This report illustrates a considerable measure of convergence in regard to the person and work of the Spirit. Together, Catholics and Methodists affirm the Spirit's full divinity and personhood: "The Spirit is God's Gift of Himself to His people. He is Lord and Giver of Life. He is the love of God reaching out to humankind for its transformation and salvation."[189] While the doctrine of the person of the Holy Spirit has never been an area of division between Catholics and Methodists, the Joint Commission's conversations have demonstrated that "differing traditional emphases and forms of expression are comple-

187. In the conclusion to the 1996 report, *The Word of Life: A Statement on Revelation and Faith*, the Joint Commission summarized the dialogue by referring to its progression in terms of these two stages (i.e., first, mutual acquaintance and the preliminary consideration of doctrinal, ethical, and pastoral issues of shared interest; and second, the sketching of broad theological perspectives as a framework for treating divisive matters). The conclusion also outlines the contours of a third stage of the dialogue, which would treat in a more detailed way some salient questions emerging from earlier conversations (*The Word of Life: A Statement on Revelation and Faith*, Report of the Joint Commission for Dialogue between the Roman Catholic Church and the World Methodist Council [Lake Junaluska, N.C.: World Methodist Council, 1996], §§131–32).

188. *Towards an Agreed Statement on the Holy Spirit*, Report of the Joint Commission for Dialogue between the Roman Catholic Church and the World Methodist Council (Lake Junaluska, N.C.: World Methodist Council, 1981).

189. Ibid., §11.

mentary and mutually enriching, rather than divisive or a cause of dissension."[190] The discovery of new meanings in the similarities between Wesley and the mainstream of Catholic spirituality have led to the acknowledgement that

> [t]his convergence could have significant implications for our own growing spiritual awareness of 'oneness in Christ' and for the future of the cause of Christian unity. Thus we have agreed that a reclamation of our complex heritage by both sides would benefit our respective communities and also enhance our present experience of unity in the Spirit.[191]

Indeed, the present investigation of Aquinas and Wesley on the Holy Spirit and the Christian life represents one attempt at pneumatological retrieval toward the goal of deepening the unity experienced already by Catholics and Methodists in the Spirit. In that way, it seeks to build on the foundation laid in *Towards an Agreed Statement on the Holy Spirit.*

In the 1986 report on ecclesiology, *Towards a Statement on the Church*, the final goal of the dialogue was clearly formulated: "full communion in faith, mission and sacramental life."[192] In view of that goal, subsequent reports have covered the Apostolic Tradition (1991), revelation and faith (1996), teaching authority (2001), and a further reflection on the church (2006) that includes specific principles and proposals for developing relations between Catholics and Methodists along the lines of the "exchange of gifts" called for by Pope John Paul II in his encyclical letter of 1995, *Ut Unum Sint.*[193] The most recent report, *Encountering Christ the Savior: Church and Sacraments* (2011), deals with the sacraments of the church and the sacramental nature of the church itself.[194]As the reports readily ac-

190. Ibid., §7.
191. Ibid., §25.

192. *Towards a Statement on the Church*, Report of the Joint Commission for Dialogue between the Roman Catholic Church and the World Methodist Council (Lake Junaluska, N.C.: World Methodist Council, 1986), §20.

193. *Ut Unum Sint*, §28.

194. *Encountering Christ the Savior: Church and Sacraments*, Report of the Joint

knowledge, some significant obstacles to full, visible unity between Catholics and Methodists remain. Yet in light of the substantial convergence on pneumatology and Christian spirituality that has already been achieved in this dialogue, as well as the pneumatological parallels between Aquinas and Wesley explored above, it seems quite possible for Catholics and Methodists to continue building on the steady progress of this dialogue. In keeping especially with the theme of the 2006 report, additional consideration of the Holy Spirit and the sharing of gifts may be able to provide a way forward for Catholics and Methodists toward greater unity in love and, indeed, toward the one who, in Christ, has shown the whole world a love that is far greater than any other (cf. Jn 15:12): the God who is Father, Son, and Holy Spirit.

Catholics, Methodists, and a Sharing in the Gifts of the Spirit

The sharing of gifts in Catholic-Methodist dialogue is a subject that has been addressed in detail in the 2006 report, which merits a careful reading by theologians in these two traditions and even more widely.[195] Given the focus of the present study, what is particularly noteworthy about this topic is the joint affirmation of the ecclesial location of the gift of participation in God through the Spirit, as can be seen in the considerable agreement on ecclesiology that leads to a mutual recognition of one another's ecclesial character.

The 2006 report explores the "very considerable agreement" reached over the years of the dialogue, an agreement that indicates "that Catholics and Methodists do, in fact, hold in common many

---

Commission for Dialogue between the Roman Catholic Church and the World Methodist Council (Lake Junaluska, N.C.: World Methodist Council, 2011).

195. For a discussion of the report, see Kenneth M. Loyer, "Progress and Possibility: Ecumenism at the 2006 World Methodist Conference," in *Ecumenical Trends* 35/9 (October 2006): 9–14, in particular 11–14. In what follows, I am drawing from parts of this article.

beliefs and priorities regarding the Church."[196] Especially pertinent to the topic of the Holy Spirit and the Christian life is the fact that this common understanding finds expression in a robustly trinitarian account of the nature and mission of the church. Together, Catholics and Methodists affirm that the church shares in the life of the Holy Trinity.[197] The triad of subject headings are indicative of this shared affirmation.[198] In the first, the church is the "People and Family of God the Father."[199] The second is the "Body and Bride of Jesus Christ, God the Son Incarnate."[200] And the third is the "Living Temple of God the Holy Spirit."[201] The church is drawn into the eternal fellowship of the Holy Trinity—the invisible *koinonia* that constitutes the very life of God—and so is itself a visible *koinonia* of Christ's disciples.[202] The church is marked with signs of the Holy Trinity, including signs of Christ's life, death and resurrection.[203] The church is marked as well with signs of Pentecost.[204] Having been thus claimed and gifted by God, the church shares the divine mission, which aims at nothing less than the salvation of the world.[205] Indeed, to share in God's life is to share in the Father's saving purposes in the sending of his Son and in the outpouring of the Holy Spirit upon the apostles at Pentecost. Methodists and Catholics already share "an extensive agreement" regarding the nature and mission of the church.[206] The marvelous trinitarian statements concerning the church reveal a substantial depth of consensus that is now enjoyed among Catholics and Methodists. That degree of consensus is the fruit of many years of dialogue, and is itself a gift of the Holy Spirit.

196. *The Grace Given You in Christ: Catholics and Methodists Reflect Further on the Church*, Report of the International Commission for Dialogue between the Roman Catholic Church and the World Methodist Council (Lake Junaluska, N.C.: World Methodist Council, 2006), §97.

197. Ibid., §51.

198. Ibid., §§54–59.

199. Ibid., §54.

200. Ibid., §§55–57.

201. Ibid., §§58–59.

202. Ibid., §§60, 51.

203. Ibid., §§67–71.

204. Ibid., §72.

205. Ibid., §51.

206. Ibid., §141.

Following this agreement on ecclesiology, a crucial step is taken in the third chapter of the report: a mutual recognition of one another's ecclesial character. In the words of the report, "It is time now to return to the concrete reality of one another, to look one another in the eye, and with love and esteem to acknowledge what we see to be truly of Christ and of the Gospel, and thereby *of the Church*, in one another."[207] This mutual appraisal constitutes "a significant achievement" in Methodist-Roman Catholic dialogue, as the dialogue partners proceed to state—for the first time—"what we recognise to be truly of the Church in each other."[208] The purpose is to call attention to the gifts with which the Holy Spirit has endowed Roman Catholics and Methodists, respectively, and that Catholics and Methodists might suitably offer one another in the service of Christ in the world.[209] The principle ways in which Methodists and Catholics can recognize one another's ecclesial character are then identified, with an eye toward that "exchange of gifts" which ecumenical dialogue, in some way, always is.[210] A Methodist perspective of the exchange of gifts indicates that, much more so than was commonly credited in the past, Methodists now recognize Roman Catholics as fellow Christians and partners in a shared trinitarian faith. Furthermore, whereas the Roman Catholic Church was not always viewed so positively by Methodists, Methodists can now recognize the Roman Catholic Church as "a true church" and so as a means of grace for salvation.[211] Also, Methodists recognize ordained ministers of the Roman Catholic Church as "agents of God" who exercise "a graced and fruitful ministry."[212] While certain dif-

207. Ibid., §97. Cf. *Lumen Gentium*, §8.

208. Report of the Joint Commission for Dialogue, *The Grace Given You in Christ*, §141.

209. Ibid., §97.

210. Ibid. Cf. *Ut Unum Sint*, §28.

211. Report of the Joint Commission for Dialogue, *The Grace Given You in Christ*, §107.

212. Ibid., §108.

ferences concerning the sacraments remain, Methodists recognize that baptism in the Roman Catholic Church constitutes entry into the one, holy, catholic, and apostolic Church.[213] Methodists further identify in the Roman Catholic Church an emphasis on holiness, both personal and social, which is similarly valued in Methodism, as are various other ecclesial elements and endowments to which Catholics attach importance.[214]

A Catholic perspective on the exchange of gifts also indicates ecumenical progress with Methodists. Following the Decree on Ecumenism in the Second Vatican Council, Catholics recognize "Methodist churches themselves as being of significance and importance in the mystery of salvation" and acknowledge God's use of these communities—both in the past and at present—as means of salvation that derive their efficacy "from the very fulness of grace and truth that Catholics believe has been entrusted to the Catholic Church."[215] Catholics identify in Methodists "a vigorous Trinitarian faith" and "a great attachment" to Jesus Christ, the incarnate Word of God, who calls us to a life of holiness in communion with God and with others in God.[216] Catholics hold as precious some of the core features of Methodism, including the pursuit of holiness, commitment to mission, and the characterization of the Christian life in terms of communion or connection.[217] Catholics acknowledge the ecumenical commitment shown by Methodists, and they resonate deeply in this commitment.[218] Regarding these vital areas of trinitarian faith, quest for holiness, commitment to mission, and pursuit of visible Christian unity, Catholics recognize that they and Methodists would "surely be strengthened by one another in the full communion of our

213. Ibid., §109.

214. Ibid., §110.

215. Ibid., §121. Cf. *Unitatis Redintegratio*, §3; *Lumen Gentium*, §8.

216. Report of the Joint Commission for Dialogue, *The Grace Given You in Christ*, §122.

217. Ibid., §121.

218. Ibid., §125.

churches."[219] Moreover, in one of the more forthright declarations of the entire text, "Catholics can unhesitatingly state that they would gain from such a communion."[220] That kind of a statement serves to indicate the growing appreciation among Catholics for their Methodist siblings in the faith.

The report goes on to identify specific points of potential gain for both sides. Methodists, for instance, can learn from both the diversity in unity and the universality of the Roman Catholic Church, and they would also benefit from a more developed theology of the Eucharist such as can be found in Catholic teaching.[221] Meanwhile, Catholics can learn from Methodists' devotion to reading the Scriptures "with a vivid sense that God speaks to us personally as we do so" and to singing the faith in hymns, as well as from the Methodist understanding and practice of lay ministry.[222] While these and other points leave us with much to ponder, the simple fact that they have been mentioned is itself an indication of progress.

As a result of the bilateral dialogue, Methodists and Catholics have learned more about one another, have discovered considerable agreement on the doctrine of the church, and have come by God's grace to recognize signs of Christ—and so of the church—in one another. The two dialogue partners have moved closer to one another as they have moved closer to Jesus Christ, whose will it is that "they may all be one ... so that the world may believe" (Jn 17:21). The stated goal of the dialogue is "full visible unity in faith, mission and sacramental life."[223] Although this goal has not yet been achieved, *The Grace Given You in Christ* highlights some very important progress that has recently taken place in the Methodist-Roman Catholic international dialogue.

The results of this study of Aquinas and Wesley on the Holy

219. Ibid., §126.

220. Ibid.

221. Ibid., §111.

222. Ibid., §126.

223. Ibid., §12; cf. Report of the Joint Commission for Dialogue, *Towards a Statement on the Church*, §20.

Spirit and the Christian life affirm and could serve to extend the common declaration among Catholics and Methodists that the church shares in God's life. These results affirm this conclusion particularly because of the ways in which Aquinas and Wesley stress such themes as the centrality of love in the life of faith, an association between the Holy Spirit and love, Eucharist as a means of sanctification, and sanctification as participation in God through the Spirit. Their accounts of Christian living point to a way of life that is a reality in the church, as expressed concisely in a statement from the 1986 report that Jean-Marie Tillard has said "deserves to take its place among the most beautiful definitions of the Church":[224] "Because God so loved the world, he sent his Son and the Holy Spirit to draw us into communion with himself. This sharing in God's life, which resulted from the mission of the Son and the Holy Spirit, found expression in a visible *koinonia* of Christ's disciples, the Church."[225] The conclusions reached above on Aquinas and Wesley strongly support such expressions of the communion with God that is made available in Christ and through the Spirit.

In addition, these conclusions could extend the joint affirmation of the ecclesial location of participation in God by facilitating a deeper description of this life with reference to arguably the central figure in each tradition. There is much about Wesley's doctrine of sanctification that Catholics can appreciate, and there is much about Aquinas's doctrine of the Spirit as love that could resonate with Methodists. At the heart of each is the assertion that the Father presents Christians with life in the Spirit of love, which is life in his Son and in his body the church. Additional light is thrown on the definition of the church from the 1986 report, for example, by Aquinas's account of the Spirit as love, which speaks to the depth of God's

224. J. M. R. Tillard, "Commentary on 'Towards a Statement on the Church,'" *One in Christ* 22 (1986), 259–66, in particular 260.

225. Report of the Joint Commission for Dialogue, *Towards a Statement on the Church*, §1.

love for the world by the Holy Spirit, the same love with which the Father loves the Son. Thus, as Wesley in particular emphasizes, the loving communion with God and with other faithful Christians that is ours in the life of grace is truly transforming for us, renewing in us God's image through the gracious ministrations of the indwelling Spirit. The result is a closer union with Christ and thereby with his body the church, where the greatest possible participation in God in this life is to be found and enjoyed. In one sense, such participation is a gift that Catholics and Methodists already share, along with the whole church. In another sense it is a gift not yet fully shared, for the final goal of "full communion in faith, mission and sacramental life" lies still ahead, and exactly how far remains to be seen.[226]

Without glossing over the differences between Methodists and Roman Catholics, the reports of the international Catholic-Methodist dialogue sound a hopeful note in identifying the ongoing work of the Holy Spirit as the way to full, visible Christian unity. In particular, in the 2006 report the Commission expresses well the pneumatological foresight necessary to envision this gift of the Holy Spirit, and does so with appropriate emphasis on the call for each tradition to move by grace toward a deeper union with the triune God:

> Separated Christian communities must eventually grow toward one another if they grow closer to Christ. They are formed by the Spirit to be one and not divided. Methodists and Catholics are kept from full communion by still unresolved doctrinal matters that the churches each believe are vital to the Gospel of Jesus Christ. Nevertheless, we are conscious of the Holy Spirit drawing us towards deeper *koinonia*. All separations, therefore, are ever only temporary for those who seek to follow Christ, and can never be definitive. Christ alone knows the timing for the coming together of his followers. They only need to wait upon him and to respond whole-heartedly to the movements of the unifying Spirit.[227]

226. Ibid., §20.

227. Report of the Joint Commission for Dialogue, *The Grace Given You in Christ*, §44.

The way to full visible unity in Christ is through the Holy Spirit. Only by the Spirit of love can the wounds of Christian division be healed.

As Methodists and Catholics, indeed as all Christians, grow closer to the Trinity, they will grow closer to one another. The work of the Spirit drawing us into the life of God is, after all, a vital truth that both Aquinas and Wesley repeatedly affirm, in distinctive and yet largely complementary fashion. Aquinas provides conceptual tools to account for the Holy Spirit as love in person who proceeds from the Father and the Son in God's own life.[228] The Holy Spirit is the love by whom, analogous to a tree flowering by its flower, the Father and the Son love each other eternally and love us in the economy of grace.[229] For Wesley, the association between the Spirit and love is best celebrated by invocation and ultimately doxology in song:

Come, Holy Ghost, our hearts inspire,
 Let us thy influence prove;
Source of the old prophetic fire,
 Fountain of life, and love.

Expand thy wings, prolific Dove,
 Brood o'er our nature's night;
On our disordered spirits move,
 And let there now be light.

God through himself we then shall know,
 If thou *within us* shine,
And sound, with all thy saints below,
 The depths of love divine.[230]

Underpinning and informing the teachings of both Wesley and Aquinas on the Holy Spirit and the Christian life is, of course, the

228. *ST*, I, q. 37, a. 1c.

229. Ibid., I, q. 37, a. 2c.

230. John and Charles Wesley, *Hymns and Sacred Poems* (London: W. Strahan, 1740), stanzas 1, 3, and 4, 42–43.

scriptural witness that belongs to the church as a whole. This common divine source links the Spirit and love in ways that not only fueled the theological works of these two figures, but may well inspire fresh insights from theologians in these Christian traditions as well as others into a critical but sometimes relatively neglected doctrine, namely, the person and work of the Holy Spirit. "God's love has been poured into our hearts through the Holy Spirit that has been given to us" (Rom 5:5). "Beloved, let us love one another, because love is from God; everyone who loves is born of God and knows God. Whoever does not love does not know God, for God is love.... By this we know that we abide in [God] and he in us, because he has given us of his Spirit.... God is love, and those who abide in love abide in God, and God abides in them" (1 Jn 4:7–8, 13, 16).

LESSONS FROM WESLEY AND AQUINAS ON THE SPIRIT: THE POLITICS OF PARTICIPATION IN THE LIFE AND LOVE OF GOD

In light of the preceding material, we are now ready to return to the problem identified in chapters 1 and 2—the pressing need for a deeper theological foundation for the Methodist doctrine of sanctification that avoids the pitfalls of both subjective spiritualities and reductionist political partisanship. Having examined Wesley's doctrine of sanctification, the intricacies of Aquinas's *amor*-based pneumatology, and their distinctiveness and compatibility, we are better positioned to assess this problem by applying to it the insights gleaned from Aquinas and Wesley on the Holy Spirit as love.

Contemporary theology in the Wesleyan tradition faces challenges on several fronts. From one direction, this tradition has long been threatened by subjective spiritualities that distort Wesley's teaching on sanctification into something it is not—individualistic or static. From another direction, a deep-seated concern for social and political impact or relevance has driven certain strands of Methodist theology toward reductionist political partisanship. In at least these two ways, contemporary Methodism runs the risk of losing the theological core of its own tradition if it has not in fact lost it already. While there is no quick fix in either case, perhaps the best prospects for renewing Methodist theology lie in the effort to make this theological tradition more explicitly theological through a greater attentiveness to the person and work of the Holy Spirit.

Regarding the first of these challenges, the appeals to recast sanctification in richer theological (as opposed to overly anthropological) terms that many of today's Methodist and Wesleyan theologians have issued reflect an awareness of the problem and an understandable keenness to overcome spiritually truncated misreadings of Wesley's doctrine of holiness. As noted above in chapter 2, we can help to ensure a sufficient theological grounding and orientation to Wesleyan teaching about sanctification by describing Christian perfection as a participation in God's perfect love in Jesus Christ through the indwelling of the Holy Spirit in the lives of believers. Over against individualistic misinterpretations of holiness, such participation grants us a sharing in Christ's body the church. So the Christian life is not simply an individual encounter with Jesus but has a necessary communal component. The mistake of espousing a static understanding of Christian perfection can be corrected by recalling Wesley's insistence that perfection is dynamic and ongoing, with God's love continually filling the human heart and then even expanding our capacity to love God and neighbor.

At the same time, Wesley's implicitly trinitarian understanding of sanctification can profitably be made more explicit, and here is where the kind of approach to the Holy Spirit and the Christian life taken by Aquinas can provide further theological depth and richness. For example, Aquinas sees in the Eucharist, in which Christ gives himself to his people for their nourishment and sanctification, a sign of their mutual love, which is the love shared by members of Christ's body. Christ's faithful are drawn into the larger reality of his own life and, thus, into the larger reality of love uniting them with one another in the journey toward God. The fact that this is an ongoing journey in community can serve as a corrective to both individualistic and static renderings of sanctification, which suffer from a diluted understanding of the Spirit's work. With the material covered earlier in this study, by this point the need in contemporary Methodist and Wesleyan theology for a fuller doctrine of sanctification to avoid individualistic, static, or otherwise simplistic alternatives has been amply addressed.

What requires a more thorough probing is a tendency toward overlooking the doctrine of sanctification or considerably revising it in search of a certain social and political impact or relevance for theology in the Methodist tradition. In this respect, Methodist theology would also benefit from becoming more clearly theological, in particular by retrieving and developing the doctrine of the Holy Spirit.

Such retrieval and expansion efforts can actually serve to enrich a Methodist political theology. With a richer doctrine of the Spirit, when talking about poverty, justice, human rights, the environment, and other pressing social issues, Methodist theologians and ethicists will have more theological substance from which to draw, to the effect of clarifying, deepening, and strengthening their conclusions about confronting injustices and working for positive social change in ways that Christian faith empowers and demands. Rather than the downplaying or substantial revision of theological claims on the basis of potentially predetermined political convictions, a critical retrieval of those claims, including their pneumatological force and dynamism, holds more promise for renewing this theological tradition and unearthing its genuine political implications as shaped by the Gospel of Jesus Christ. The lessons from Aquinas and Wesley on the doctrine of the Holy Spirit show that participation in the life and love of God is a more theologically solid and promising motif than are political projects per se. A politics of participation, to characterize the former, makes good on the reduction of the Spirit's work that is so common in the latter.

In chapter 1, consideration of the strand of Methodist theology that draws from liberation traditions identified two key theological themes: the continuation of God's work in the world and the promotion of life. Each of these themes can be extended and enriched through what might be called a politics of participation, that is, an account of Christian existence founded on the concept of human participation in God's life and love through the Spirit. A commitment to the continuation of God's work in the world takes on a new light when the deeper question of participation in God's own life is carefully explored. What we then find is that sharing in God's life constitutes the grounds and impetus for our mission of doing God's work, which is work that we cannot achieve on our own, despite our inclinations to trust in our own abilities or try to take matters into our own hands. Such work can only be done through power from God, power that is made available to us by our sharing in God's life through Christ and in the Holy Spirit.

Likewise, concern for advancing teachings, practices, and social structures that promote life can be informed by renewed attention to the doctrine of God and especially the doctrine of the Holy Spirit. The creedal designation of the Spirit as "giver of life" associates the person of the Spirit in a particular way with the Trinity's work of creating and sustaining life. Eternally proceeding from the Father and the Son, the Spirit is worshiped and glorified with them. In the economy of salvation, appropriation is creedally made to the Spirit for having "spoken through the prophets" and brought into being the one, holy, catholic, and apostolic church. As the body of Christ, the community of God's love and justice graciously sustained by the life-giving work of the Spirit, the church is called to be itself that paradigmatic social structure promoting life in its teaching and practice and thus sharing in the Spirit's work throughout the world—a sharing that is funded through a participation in God's own life.

The theological principles highlighted by Wesley and Aquinas in their respective accounts of the Holy Spirit and the Christian life provide a vision of such participation in the divine nature, which is life-giving in the deepest possible way. Wesley makes at least two contributions in this respect. First, Wesley's theology is infused with a lively sense of God's presence and activity through the Holy Spirit. A particularly prominent example is Wesley's doctrine of the spiritual senses, according to which a genuine Christian "feels, is inwardly sensible of, the graces which the Spirit of God works in his heart."[231] Those gifts imparted by God's Spirit include a "peace which passeth all understanding" [Phil 4:7]; "such a joy in God as is 'unspeakable and full of glory'" [1 Pt 1:8]; and "the love of God shed abroad in his heart by the Holy Ghost which is given unto him" [Rom 5:5].[232] Through the exercise of the spiritual senses, a Christian then grows in grace through a sharing in God's own life:

> By the use of these he is daily increasing in the knowledge of God, of Jesus Christ whom he hath sent, and of all the things pertaining to his inward kingdom. And now he may properly be said *to live*: God having quickened him by his Spirit [cf. 1 Pt 3:18], he is alive to God through Jesus Christ [Rom 6:11]. He lives a life which the world knoweth not of, a "life" which "is hid with Christ in God" [Col 3:3]. God is continually breathing, as it were, upon his soul, and his soul is breathing unto God. Grace is descending into his heart, and prayer and praise ascending to heaven. And by this intercourse between God and man, this fellowship with the Father and the Son [1 Jn 1:3], as by a kind of spiritual respiration, the life of God in the soul is sustained: and the child of God grows up, till he comes to "the full measure of the stature of Christ" [Eph 4:13].[233]

As this passage suggests, particularly with the italicized words (which are original to Wesley), central to Wesley's understanding of the Christian life is the influence of the Holy Spirit making us alive to God through Jesus Christ.

231. "The New Birth," II.4, in Wesley, *Works*, ed. Outler, et al., 2:193.
232. Ibid.
233. Ibid.

Second, Wesley grounds his doctrine of sanctification in pneumatology. For example, in his *Letter to a Roman Catholic*, he makes clear the connection between holiness and the Holy Spirit. He confesses faith in "the infinite and eternal Spirit of God, equal with the Father and the Son, to be not only perfectly holy in himself, but the immediate cause of all holiness in us."[234] Then Wesley describes the Spirit's sanctifying work in stirring terms: "enlightening our understandings, rectifying our wills and affections, renewing our natures, uniting our persons to Christ, assuring us of the adoption of sons, leading us in our actions, purifying and sanctifying our souls and bodies to a full and eternal enjoyment of God."[235] For Wesley, what makes us holy as God is holy, and truly happy and full of life in God, is our personal communion with God through the Spirit, who is the agent of sanctifying grace.

Aquinas, for his part, contributes to a doctrine of participation in God by pinpointing the trinitarian context in which pneumatology is rightly located. This context not only illuminates the trinitarian basis of the doctrine of the Holy Spirit but also gives sanctification, the Spirit's appropriated work, its proper ground and goal in the triune God. Here again findings from the above inquiry into Aquinas's pneumatology are noteworthy, as they were in the discussion of its implications for Wesleyans earlier in this chapter. Contemplating the place of the Holy Spirit in the life of the Trinity, as in question thirty-seven of the *prima pars* of the *Summa theologiae*, Aquinas shows that grasping the Spirit's immanent procession makes it possible to conceive of a relationship subsisting within the triune God, a relationship that is the person of the Holy Spirit. The subsequent insight that the Father and the Son love one another by the Holy Spirit leads Aquinas then to convey yet another crucial point: the Father loves not only the Son by the Spirit but also loves himself,

234. *Letter to a Roman Catholic*, in Wesley, *Works*, ed. Outler, et al., 10:82.

235. Ibid.

and even us, by the Spirit as well.[236] In other words, God loves us with the same love with which God loves himself, and that love is the person of the Holy Spirit. Furthermore, as Aquinas articulates in his account of the missions of the divine persons, through the gift of sanctifying grace God dwells in us as in God's own temple.[237] We are thus consecrated to God, and made holy in and by the Holy Trinity. Loving us by his Spirit and actually dwelling in us through sanctifying grace, God has made possible for us a participation in his triune life through the Spirit.

Given Wesley's passionate concern for holiness in and through the gracious ministrations of the Holy Spirit, as well as Aquinas's careful attentiveness to the properly trinitarian context for pneumatology and therefore sanctification, the thought of each figure reflects a participatory understanding of the doctrine of salvation in which the Holy Spirit plays a prominent role. This politics of participation in God's life provides a grammar of true holiness, bestowed in ever deepening ways by the Spirit of holiness (a characteristic theme of Wesley) who makes us God's friends (a concept delineated by Aquinas). It also stresses the genuine communion with God that is the privilege of all faithful Christians, as they encounter Christ in the life of faith and especially in the Eucharist—that "*sacramentum caritatis*" (as termed by Aquinas) in which, through the Spirit, Christ's body is imparted, his blood is transmitted, and his people are filled "with all the life of God" (as the Wesley brothers would have us sing) before being sent forth in service to God's world.[238] In these ways, the insights gleaned from Wesley and Aquinas on the Spirit indicate that any political relevance of the Trinity, and of theology as a whole, is rooted in nothing other than the life of God

236. *ST*, I, q. 37, a. 2c and ad 3.

237. Ibid., I, q. 43, a. 3.

238. Aquinas calls the Eucharist the "*sacramentum caritatis*" in *ST* III, q. 73, a. 3 ad 3 and III, q. 78, a. 3 ad 6. The Wesleys refer to God filling his people, through this sacrament, "with all the life of God," in *HLS*, 57:1.

and our communal participation in this life, a participation made possible for us all by the personal indwelling and power of the Holy Spirit, the Spirit of love.

Aquinas's approach in particular has the added benefit of making explicit theological content that remains simply implicit in Wesley. That is, as in the various ways described throughout this study, Wesley's implicitly trinitarian account of sanctification can be enriched by the kind of substantive, explicitly trinitarian foundation presented in the theology of Aquinas. The potential for such enrichment, and the persistent difficulties without it, together constitute precisely what is to be gained by learning from Aquinas and what is at stake in neglecting him. A sympathetic appropriation of the theological attentiveness of Aquinas by Methodist and Wesleyan theologians can aid them in developing a deeper and more distinctively theological basis for the doctrine of sanctification that is so urgently needed today, and without which historic Methodist teaching on holiness will likely remain little more than a dead letter or mere historical artifact. That kind of renewal of Methodism's doctrinal core, accelerated by external help from Aquinas, could in turn contribute to making Methodism a more vibrant and coherent theological tradition in its own right through a clearer focus on what is central, namely, God and our life in God.

Ultimately, what Aquinas and Wesley discover and in turn describe—each with his own emphases, but in strikingly complementary fashion—is a truth transcending their times and even ours, a truth powerful enough to reinvigorate theological speech and practice in the Catholic and Methodist traditions and beyond: the connection among love, holiness, and the work of the Holy Spirit is so beautiful and so profound that it takes us to the heart of the Gospel and, indeed, to the very heart of God. "For this reason I kneel before the Father, from whom every family in heaven and on earth derives its name. I pray that, according to the riches of his glory, he may grant that you may be strengthened with power through his

Spirit in your inner being, and that Christ may dwell in your hearts through faith, as you are being rooted and established in love. I pray that you may have power, together with all the saints, to grasp what is the breadth and length and height and depth, and to know the love of Christ that surpasses knowledge, so that you may be filled with all the fullness of God" (Eph 3:14–21).

Conclusion

FURTHER PATHS TO MUTUAL THOMIST AND METHODIST ENRICHMENT

THE POSSIBILITY for Thomists and Methodists to continue to grow in mutual understanding and advancement is by no means exhausted within the pages of this book. By way of conclusion, the following five avenues represent further paths to such enrichment.

First, and rather generally, an immersion in primary texts will help foster greater familiarity across traditions. Rooted in the sources, a sympathetic reading in each direction—Methodists and Wesleyans reading Aquinas and Thomists reading Wesley, as well as Methodists reading Wesley and Thomists reading Aquinas—holds promise for identifying new areas of inquiry that can be fruitfully investigated.

Second, a probing of the sources behind each of these figures should also prove illuminating. The same would no doubt hold true for the study of each figure on his own; in fact, it already has done so, for example, in research on Aquinas in the Augustinian tradition and on Wesley in that same tradition, respectively.[1] Exploring

1. For example, Michael Dauphinais, Barry David, and Matthew Levering, eds., *Aquinas the Augustinian* (Washington, D.C.: The Catholic University of America

both their uses of common sources, including possible divergences as well as convergences, and each figure's role in the development of those shared traditions would be a worthwhile next step.

Another mutually enriching way forward for Thomists and Methodists is a critical comparison of prominent interpreters of primary texts and exemplars within each tradition. On the Methodist side, key figures include John and Mary Fletcher, Richard Watson, and William Burt Pope, while on the Thomistic side, the works of Cajetan, John of St. Thomas, Réginald Marie Garrigou-Lagrange, and Jacques Maritain are among the many places to turn. In a similar vein, already Edgardo Colón-Emeric has creatively paired the Methodist Jane Cooper with Aquinas and the Catholic Gregorio López with Wesley, and has found characteristic points of emphasis from one tradition at work in the other.[2] An additional variation of this approach would be to bring into extended conversation an outstanding interpreter or practitioner from either tradition with the other tradition's main figure directly, such as an examination of John Fletcher, who introduced scholastic distinctions into Wesley's theology, and Aquinas on a topic of mutual interest like nature and grace; or St. John of the Cross, whose experiential insights complement Aquinas's speculative approach to *sacra doctrina*, and John Wesley on experimental or practical divinity.[3]

Press, 2007); and John W. Wright, "'Use' and 'Enjoy' in John Wesley: John Wesley's Participation within the Augustinian Tradition," *Wesley and Methodist Studies* 6 (2014): 3–36.

2. Edgardo A. Colón-Emeric, *Wesley, Aquinas, and Christian Perfection An Ecumenical Dialogue* (Waco, Tex.: Baylor University Press, 2009), 185–98.

3. A helpful source concerning the second example would be Réginald Marie Garrigou-Lagrange, *Perfection chrétienne et contemplation selon S. Thomas d'Aquin et S. Jean de la Croix* (Saint-Maximin, *éd.* de La Vie Spirituelle [1923]; ET: *Christian Perfection and Contemplation, According to St. Thomas Aquinas and St. John of the Cross*, trans. Sr. M. Timothea Doyle [St. Louis: Herder, 1937]), in which he synthesizes the conceptually sophisticated writings of Aquinas with the experiential writings of St. John of the Cross and in so doing provides a theologically rich account of the spiritual life, an account that should resonate in various respects with Methodists and Wesleyans.

Fourth, scholars could take a topical approach as the basis for a joint study of Aquinas and Wesley, while attending to both similarities and difference in style and substance, along with their potential implications for advancing the Catholic and Methodist theological traditions. Some work has been done already on eucharistic theology pertaining to these two traditions.[4] There are related aspects of sacramental theology yet to be taken up, such as questions of eucharistic presence and practice in Aquinas, Wesley, and their respective theological heirs.

While this list is certainly not all-encompassing, a fifth possibility involves intentionally relating the common study of the Thomistic and Wesleyan traditions to ecumenical dialogue and the reception and advancement of such dialogue. One example concerns the recent convergence on the doctrine of justification as a result of the Methodist Statement of Association (with the Catholic Church and the churches of the Lutheran World Federation) with the *Joint Declaration on the Doctrine of Justification.* An analysis of justification in Aquinas and in Wesley could not only gain from the ecumenical work done already, but could also serve to deepen the degree of convergence already reached on that crucial doctrine. Whatever the particular focus, born out of the conviction that theology is for the church, this approach would have the benefit of being able to learn from the many fine and carefully produced ecumenical documents (which, unfortunately, tend to receive little attention even among professional theologians) while also potentially working to renew our pursuit of the visible Christian unity for which Christ prayed

4. See my article on the threefold temporal reference of the Eucharist, in which the Wesleys' *Hymns on the Lord's Supper* are found to match the teaching of Aquinas on the Eucharist as an efficaciously commemorative, demonstrative, and prognostic sign ("Memorial, Means, and Pledge: Eucharist and Time in the Wesleys' *Hymns on the Lord's Supper*," *Proceedings of the Charles Wesley Society* 11 [2006–2007]: 87–106). See also Stephen B. Sours, "Eucharist and Anthropology: Seeking Convergence on Eucharistic Sacrifice between Catholics and Methodists" (Ph.D. thesis, Duke University, 2010), which includes a comparison of eucharistic teaching in Thomas Aquinas and in John Wesley.

(Jn 17:20–23). By more clearly connecting academic theology with ecumenical theology, perhaps progress toward the reinvigoration of ecumenism could be achieved.

These are some paths, by turns historical, constructive, and ecumenical, to discovering ways in which the Wesleyan spirit and the Thomistic spirit are in fact the same Spirit—a common divine source—the Holy Spirit, and to unearthing the significance for Catholics, Methodists, and other interested parties going forward.

BIBLIOGRAPHY

PRIMARY SOURCES FOR THOMAS AQUINAS

Aquinas, Thomas. *The Aquinas Prayer Book: The Prayers and Hymns of St. Thomas Aquinas.* Translated and edited by Robert Anderson and Johann Moser. Manchester, N.H.: Sophia Institute Press, 2000.

———. *Commentaire de L'Épître aux Romains.* Translated by Jean-Éric Stroobant de Saint-Éloy, OSB. Paris: Les Éditions du Cerf, 1999.

———. *Compendium theologiae.* Vol. 42, *Opera omnia*, Leonine edition, Cura et studio fratrum praedicatorum. Rome and Paris: 1882–present.

———. *De caritate.* ET: *On Charity.* Translated with an introduction by Lottie H. Kendzierski. Milwaukee: Marquette University Press, 1960.

———. *Emitte Spiritum.* Translated by Jeremy Holmes and Peter Kwasniewski. *Faith and Reason* 30, nos. 1–2 (2005): 108–39.

———. *Expositio et lectura super epistolas Pauli apostoli.* Edited by R. Cai. Rome: Marietti, 1953.

———. *In duo praecepta caritatis et in decem legis praecepta, expositio.* Vol. 16, *Opera omnia.* Parma: Typis Petri Fiaccadori, 1865.

———. *Liber de veritate catholicae fidei contra errores infidelium seu Summa contra Gentiles*, t.2–3. Edited by P. Marc, C. Pera, P. Caramello. Marietti: Taurini-Romae, 1961.

———. *Quaestiones disputatae.* Rome: Marietti, 1965.

———. *Sancti Thomas de Aquino opera omnia iussu Leonis XIII P.M. edita.* Rome: Typographiapolyglotta, 1882ff.

———. *Scriptum super Sententiis magistri Petri Lombardi*, t. 1. Edited by P. Mandonnet. Paris: P. Lethielleux, 1929.

———. *Summa contra Gentiles.* Translated by A. C. Pegis, et al. Notre Dame, Ind.: University of Notre Dame Press, 1975.

———. *Summa Theologiae.* Matriti: Biblioteca de Autores Cristianos, 1961–1965.

———. *Summa Theologiae.* Vol. 7: Father, Son and Holy Ghost (1a. 33–43). Translated and notes by T. C. O'Brien. London: Blackfriars, 1976.

———. *The Summa Theologica of St. Thomas Aquinas.* Translated by Fathers of the English Dominican Province. Allen, Tex.: Christian Classics, 1948.

———. *Super Evangelium Sancti Ioannis Lectura*. Edited by R. Cai, OP. Turin: Marietti, 1952. ET: *Commentary on the Gospel of St. John*. Translated by Fabian R. Larcher, OP. Albany: Magi Books, 1998.

PRIMARY SOURCES FOR JOHN AND CHARLES WESLEY

Wesley, Charles. *Hymns on the Trinity*. Bristol: Pine, 1767; facsimile reprint, Madison, N.J.: Charles Wesley Society, 1998.

Wesley, Charles, and John Wesley. *Hymns and Sacred Poems*. London: Strahan, 1740. http://www.divinity.duke.edu/wesleyan/docs/jwmoderncollections/05_Hymns_and_Sacred_Poems_(1740)_mod.pdf. Accessed March 1, 2010.

———. *Hymns on the Lord's Supper*. Bristol: Felix Farley, 1745; facsimile reprint, Madison, N.J.: Charles Wesley Society, 1995.

Wesley, John. *Explanatory Notes Upon the New Testament*. London: William Bowyer, 1755; reprint edition, London: Epworth Press, 1954.

———. *The Letters of John Wesley*. Edited by John Telford. 8 vols. London: Epworth Press, 1931.

———. *A Plain Account of Christian Perfectionas Believed and Taught by the Reverend Mr. John Wesley, From the Year 1725, to the Year 1777*. Bristol, 1777; reprint edition, London: Epworth Press, 1952.

———. *The Works of John Wesley*. Edited by Thomas Jackson. 14 vols. Grand Rapids: Zondervan, 1958–1959.

———. *The Works of John Wesley*. Edited by Albert C. Outler, et al. 35 vols. Nashville: Abingdon Press, 1984ff.

OTHER SOURCES

Abraham, William J. "Christian Perfection." In William J. Abraham and James E. Kirby, eds., *The Oxford Handbook of Methodist Studies*. Oxford: Oxford University Press, 2009, 587–601.

Albin, Thomas R. "Experience of God." In William J. Abraham and James E. Kirby, eds., *The Oxford Handbook of Methodist Studies*. Oxford: Oxford University Press, 2009, 379–97.

The Apostolic Tradition. Report of the Joint Commission for Dialogue between the World Methodist Council and the Roman Catholic Church. Lake Junaluska, N.C.: World Methodist Council, 1991.

Arnett, William M. "The Role of the Holy Spirit in Entire Sanctification in the Writings of John Wesley." *Wesleyan Theological Journal* 14 no. 2 (1979): 15–30.

Augustine. *De Trinitate libri XV*, Cura et studio W. J. Mountain, auxiliante Fr. Glorie, Corpus Christianorum Series Latina. Vol. LA, Aurelli Augustini Opera, Pars XVI, 2. Turnholti: Typographi Brepols Editores Pontificii, 1968. ET: *The Trinity*. Translated by Edmund Hill, OP. Hyde Park, N.Y.: New City Press, 1991.

Badcock, Gary D. *Light of Truth and Fire of Love: A Theology of the Holy Spirit*. Grand Rapids: Eerdmans, 1997.

Baker, Frank. "John Wesley and Practical Divinity." *Wesleyan Theological Journal* 22 no. 1 (1987): 7–15.

Bourassa, François. "Adoptive Sonship: Our Union with the Divine Persons." *Theological Studies* 13 (1952): 309–35.

———. "Dans la communion de l'Esprit Saint: Étude théologique I." *Science et Esprit* 34 (1982): 31–56.

———. "Dans la communion de l'Esprit Saint: Étude théologique II." *Science et Esprit* 34 (1982): 135–49.

———. "Dans la communion de l'Esprit Saint: Étude théologique III." *Science et Esprit* 34 (1982): 239–68.

———. "L'Esprit Saint, 'Communion' du Père et du Fils (I)." *Science et Esprit* 29 (1977): 251–81.

———. "L'Esprit Saint, 'Communion' du Père et du Fils (II)." *Science et Esprit* 30 (1978): 5–37.

———. *Questions de théologie trinitaire*. Rome: Presses de l'Université Grégorienne, 1970.

———. "Le Saint-Esprit unité d'amour du Père et du Fils." *Sciences ecclésiastiques* 14 (1962): 375–415.

———. "Sur la propriété de l'Esprit, Questions disputées (I)." *Science et Esprit* 28 (1976): 243–64.

———. "Sur la propriété de l'Esprit, Questions disputées (II)." *Science et Esprit* 29 (1977): 23–43.

Boyle, John F. "The Ordering of Trinitarian Teaching in Thomas Aquinas' Second Commentary on Lombard's *Sentences*." In E. Manning, ed., *Thomistica*. Recherches de Théologie ancienne et médiévale, Supplementa 1. Leuven: Peeters, 1995, 125–36.

Boyle, Leonard E. "Alia lectura fratris Thome." *Mediaeval Studies* 45 (1983): 418–29.

Butler, David. *Methodists and Papists: John Wesley and the Catholic Church in the Eighteenth Century*. London: Darton, Longman & Todd, 1995.

Browne, Peter. *Limits of Human Understanding*. London: William Innys, 1728.

Burgess, Stanley M. *The Holy Spirit: Medieval Roman Catholic and Reformation Traditions*. Peabody, Mass.: Hendrickson, 1997.

Campbell, Ted A. *John Wesley and Christian Antiquity: Religious Vision and Cultural Change*. Nashville: Kingswood Books, 1991.

Carter, David. "*The Grace Given You in Christ*: Some Reflections." *Ecumenical Trends* 36, no. 2 (February 2007): 6–12.

———. "Spiritual Ecumenism in the Wesleyan Tradition." *Ecumenical Trends* 37, no. 4 (April 2008): 1–4.

Catechism of the Catholic Church. New York: Image Books, 1995.

Cell, George Croft. *The Rediscovery of John Wesley*. New York: Henry Holt, 1935; reprint, Lanham, Md.: University Press of America, 1983.

Chapman, David M. "Forty Years On: Catholic-Methodist Dialogue, 1967–2007." *Ecumenical Trends* 36, no. 3 (March 2007): 5–10, 15.

———. *In Search of the Catholic Spirit: Methodists and Roman Catholics in Dialogue*. Peterborough, U.K.: Epworth Press, 2004.

———. "Methodism and the Future of Ecumenism." In William J. Abraham and James E. Kirby, eds., *The Oxford Handbook of Methodist Studies*. Oxford: Oxford University Press, 2009, 449–67.

Clapper, Gregory S. *John Wesley on Religious Affections: His Views on Experience and Emotion and Their Role in the Christian Life and Theology*. Metuchen, N.J.: Scarecrow Press, 1989.

Collins, Kenneth J. "Assurance." In William J. Abraham and James E. Kirby, eds., *The Oxford Handbook of Methodist Studies*. Oxford: Oxford University Press, 2009, 602–17.

———. "The State of Wesley Studies in North America: A Theological Journey." *Wesleyan Theological Journal* 44 no. 2 (2009): 7–38.

———. *The Theology of John Wesley: Holy Love and the Shape of Grace*. Nashville: Abingdon Press, 2007.

Colón-Emeric, Edgardo A. *Wesley, Aquinas, and Christian Perfection: An Ecumenical Dialogue*. Waco, Tex.: Baylor University Press, 2009.

Colyer, Elmer M. "Trinity." In William J. Abraham and James E. Kirby, eds., *The Oxford Handbook of Methodist Studies*. Oxford: Oxford University Press, 2009, 505–21.

Congar, Yves. *I Believe in the Holy Spirit*. Vo1. 1. Translated by David Smith. New York: The Seabury Press, 1983.

Coppedge, Allan. *John Wesley in Theological Debate*. Wilmore, Ky.: Wesley Heritage Press, 1988.

Crow, Earl P. "John Wesley's Conflict with Antinomianism in Relation to the Moravians and Calvinists." Ph.D. diss., The University of Manchester, England, 1964.

Cubie, David L. "Wesley's Theology of Love." *Wesleyan Theological Journal* 20 no. 1 (1985): 122–54.

Dabney, D. Lyle. "Pneumatology in the Methodist Tradition." In William J. Abraham and James E. Kirby, eds., *The Oxford Handbook of Methodist Studies*. Oxford: Oxford University Press, 2009, 573–86.

Deschner, John. *Wesley's Christology: An Interpretation*. 2nd ed. Grand Rapids: Zondervan, 1988.

Dondaine, H. F. "'Alia lectura fratris Thome'? (Super I Sent.)." *Mediaeval Studies* 42 (1980): 308–36.

———. "Saint Thomas et la Procession du Saint-Esprit." In *Saint Thomas D'Aquin, Somme Théologique, La Trinité*, I. Paris: Desclée & Cie, 1962, 387–409.

Emery, Gilles, OP. "Biblical Exegesis and the Speculative Doctrine of the Trinity in St. Thomas Aquinas' Commentary on St. John." In Michael Dauphinais and Matthew Levering, eds., *Reading John with St. Thomas Aquinas: Theological Exegesis and Speculative Theology*. Washington, D.C.: The Catholic University of America Press, 2005, 23–61.

———. "The Doctrine of the Trinity in St Thomas Aquinas." In Thomas Weinandy, Daniel Keating, and John Yocum, eds., *Aquinas on Doctrine: A Critical Introduction*. London: T&T Clark, 2004, 45–65.

———. "Trinitarian Theology as Spiritual Exercise in Augustine and Aquinas." In Michael Dauphinais, Barry David, and Matthew Levering, eds., *Aquinas the Augustinian*. Washington, D.C.: The Catholic University of America Press, 2007, 1–40.

———. *The Trinitarian Theology of Saint Thomas Aquinas*. Translated by Francesca Aran Murphy. Oxford: Oxford University Press, 2007.

———. "Trinity and Creation." In Rik Van Nieuwenhove and Joseph Wawrykow, eds., *The Theology of Thomas Aquinas*. Notre Dame, Ind.: University of Notre Dame Press, 2005, 58–76.

———. *Trinity, Church, and the Human Person: Thomistic Essays*. Faith and Reason. Studies in Catholic Theology and Philosophy. Naples, Fla.: Sapientia Press, 2007.

———. *Trinity in Aquinas*. Ann Arbor, Mich.: Sapientia Press, 2003.

Encountering Christ the Savior: Church and Sacraments. Report of the Joint Commission for Dialogue between the Roman Catholic Church and the World Methodist Council. Lake Junaluska, N.C.: World Methodist Council, 2011.

Fuchs, Lorelei F. *Koinonia and the Quest for an Ecumenical Ecclesiology: From Foundations through Dialogue to Symbolic Competence for Communionality*. Grand Rapids: Eerdmans, 2008.

The Grace Given You in Christ: Catholics and Methodists Reflect Further on the Church. Report of the International Commission for Dialogue between the World Methodist Council and the Roman Catholic Church. Lake Junaluska, N.C.: World Methodist Council, 2006.

Growth in Agreement. Report of the Joint Commission for Dialogue between the World Methodist Council and the Roman Catholic Church. Lake Junaluska, N.C.: World Methodist Council, 1971.

Growth in Understanding. Report of the Joint Commission for Dialogue between the World Methodist Council and the Roman Catholic Church. Lake Junaluska, N.C.: World Methodist Council, 1976.

Hammond, Geordan and Peter S. Forsaith, eds. *Religion, Gender, and Industry: Exploring Church and Methodism in a Local Setting*. Eugene, Ore.: Wipf and Stock, 2011.

Haydon, Colin. *Anti-Catholicism in Eighteenth-Century England, c. 1714–80: A Political and Social Study*. Manchester: Manchester University Press, 1993.

Healy, Nicholas M. *Thomas Aquinas: Theologian of the Christian Life*. Burlington, Vt.: Ashgate, 2003.

Heitzenrater, Richard P. "God with Us: Grace and the Spiritual Senses in John Wesley's Theology." In Robert K. Johnston, L. Gregory Jones, and Jonathan R. Wilson, eds., *Grace Upon Grace: Essays in Honor of Thomas A. Langford*. Nashville: Abingdon Press, 1999, 87–109.

———. *Wesley and the People Called Methodists*. Nashville: Abingdon Press, 1995.

Hulley, Leonard D. "An Interpretation of John Wesley's Doctrine of Perfect Love." *Theologia Evangelica* 23 (March 1990): 21–29.

Hütter, Reinhard. "The Directedness of Reasoning and the Metaphysics of Creation." In Paul J. Griffiths and Reinhard Hütter, eds., *Reason and the Reasons of Faith*. New York: T&T Clark, 2005, 160–93.

Jenson, Robert W. *Systematic Theology*. Vol. 1: *The Triune God*. New York: Oxford University Press, 1997.

———. "You Wonder Where the Spirit Went." *Pro Ecclesia* 2 no. 3 (Summer 1993): 296–304.

John Paul II. *Ut Unum Sint*. Boston: Pauline Books and Media, 1995.

Johnson, Mark. "'Alia lectura fratris Thome': A List of the New Texts of St Thomas Aquinas found in Lincoln College, Oxford, MS. Lat. 95." *Recherches de Théologie ancienne et médiévale* 57 (1990): 34–61.

John of St. Thomas, *Cursus theologicus*. ET: *Gifts of the Holy Ghost*. Translated by Dominic Hughes, OP. London: Sheed & Ward, 1951.

Jones, Scott J. *John Wesley's Conception and Use of Scripture*. Nashville: Kingswood Books, 1995.

Jordan, Mark D. "Theology and Philosophy." In Norman Kretzmann and Eleonore Stump, eds., *The Cambridge Companion to Aquinas*. Cambridge: Cambridge University Press, 1993, 232–51.

Keaty, Anthony. "The Holy Spirit as Love: A Study in the Pneumatology of Thomas Aquinas." Ph.D. diss., University of Notre Dame, 1997.

———. "The Holy Spirit Proceeding as Mutual Love: An Interpretation of Aquinas' *Summa Theologiae*, I.37." *Angelicum* 77 (2000): 533–57.

Krapiec, Albertus. "Inquisitio circa Divi Thomae doctrinam de Spiritu Sancto prout amore." *Divus Thomas* 27 (1950): 474–95.

Kwasniewski, Peter. "Aquinas's Sermon for the Feast of Pentecost: A Rare Glimpse of Thomas the Preaching Friar." *Faith and Reason* 30, nos. 1–2 (2005): 99–107.

Langford, Thomas A. "John Wesley's Doctrine of Sanctification." *Bulletin of the United Church of Canada Committee on Archives and History* 29 (1980–1982): 63–73.

———. *Practical Divinity: Theology in the Wesleyan Tradition*. 2 vols. Nashville: Abingdon Press, 1998.

Lee, Hoo-Jung. "Experiencing the Spirit in Wesley and Macarius." In Randy L. Maddox, ed., *Rethinking Wesley's Theology for Contemporary Methodism*. Nashville: Kingswood Books, 1998, 197–212.

Lessman, Thomas. *Rolle und Bedeutung des Heiligen Geistes in der Theologie John Wesleys*. Stuttgart: Christliches Verlagshaus, 1987.

Lindström, Harald. *Wesley and Sanctification: A Study in the Doctrine of Salvation*. Stockholm: Nya Bokförlags Aktiebolaget, 1946.

Lonergan, Bernard. *Grace and Freedom: Operative Grace in the Thought of St. Thomas Aquinas*. Toronto: University of Toronto Press, 2000.

Long, D. Stephen. *John Wesley's Moral Theology: The Quest for God and Goodness*. Nashville: Kingswood Books, 2005.

Loyer, Kenneth M. "'And to Crown All': John Wesley on Union with God in the New Creation." *Methodist Review* 1 (2009): 109–25.

———. "Memorial, Means, and Pledge: Eucharist and Time in the Wesleys' *Hymns on the Lord's Supper*." *Proceedings of The Charles Wesley Society* 11 (2006–2007): 87–106.

———. "Progress and Possibility: Ecumenism at the 2006 World Methodist Conference." *Ecumenical Trends* 35, no. 9 (October 2006): 9–14.

Luby, Daniel. *The Perceptibility of Grace in the Theology of John Wesley: A Roman Catholic Consideration*. Rome: Pontifical University of St. Thomas, 1994.

Maddox, Randy L. *Responsible Grace: John Wesley's Practical Theology*. Nashville: Kingswood Books, 1994.

Malet, Antoni. *Personne et amour dans la théologie trinitaire de Saint Thomas d'Aquin*. Paris: J. Vrin, 1956.

Mansini, G. "*Similitudo, Communicatio*, and the Friendship of Charity in Aquinas." In E. Manning, ed., *Thomistica*. Recherches de Théologie ancienne et médiévale, Supplementa1. Leuven: Peeters, 1995, 1–26.

Maritain, Jacques. *Distinguer pour unir, ou les degrés du savoir*. 5th ed. Paris: Desclée, de Brouwer et cie, 1948. ET: *The Degrees of Knowledge*. Translated by Gerald Phelan. Vol. 7 in Ralph McInerny, ed., *The Collected Works of Jacques Maritain*. Notre Dame, Ind.: University of Notre Dame Press, 2002.

Marshall, Bruce D. "Aquinas the Augustinian: On the Uses of Augustine in Aquinas' Trinitarian Theology." In Michael Dauphinais, Barry David, and Matthew Levering, eds., *Aquinas the Augustinian*. Washington, D.C.: The Catholic University of America Press, 2007, 41–61.

———. "*Quod Scit Una Uetela*: Aquinas on the Nature of Theology." In Rik Van Nieuwenhove and Joseph Wawrykow, eds., *The Theology of Thomas Aquinas*. Notre Dame, Ind.: University of Notre Dame Press, 2005, 1–35.

———. "What Does the Spirit Have to Do?" In Michael Dauphinais and Matthew Levering, eds., *Reading John with St. Thomas Aquinas: Theological Exegesis and Speculative Theology*. Washington, D.C.: The Catholic University of America Press, 2005, 62–77.

Matthews, Rex D. "'Religion and Reason Joined': A Study in the Theology of John Wesley." Th.D. diss., Harvard University, 1986.

McCormick, K. Steve. "Theosis in Chrysostom and Wesley: An Eastern Paradigm on Faith and Love." *Wesleyan Theological Journal* 26, no. 1 (1991): 38–103.

Mealey, Mark. "Taste and See That the Lord is Good: John Wesley in the Christian Tradition of Spiritual Sensation." Ph.D. diss., University of St. Michael's College, Toronto, 2006.

Meeks, M. Douglas, ed. *Trinity, Community, and Power: Mapping Trajectories in Wesleyan Theology*. Nashville: Kingswood Books, 2000.

———, ed. *What Should Methodists Teach? Wesleyan Tradition and Modern Diversity*. Nashville: Kingswood Books, 1990.

Merriell, D. Juvenal, CO. *To the Image of the Trinity: A Study in the Development of Aquinas' Teaching*. Toronto: Pontifical Institute of Mediaeval Studies, Toronto, 1990.

———. "Trinitarian Anthropology." In Rik Van Nieuwenhove and Joseph Wawrykow, eds., *The Theology of Thomas Aquinas*. Notre Dame, Ind.: University of Notre Dame Press, 2005, 123–42.

Miles, Rebekah L. "Happiness, Holiness, and the Moral Life." In Randy L. Maddox and Jason E. Vickers, eds., *The Cambridge Companion to John Wesley*. Cambridge: Cambridge University Press, 2010, 207–24.

Moore, D. Marselle. "Development in Wesley's Thought on Sanctification and Perfection." *Wesleyan Theological Journal* 20, no. 2 (1985): 29–53.

Mühlen, Heribert. *Der Heilige Geist als Person: In der Trinität, bei der Inkarnation und im Gnadenbund: Ich-Du-Wir*. Münster: Aschendorff, 1988.

Nicolas, M.-J. "Théologie dogmatique." *Revue Thomiste* 47 (1947): 137–58.

Nygren, Anders. *Agape and Eros*. Translated by Philip S. Watson. Philadelphia: Westminster Press, 1953.

Oord, Thomas Jay and Michael Lodahl. *Relational Holiness: Responding to the Call of Love*. Kansas City, Mo.: Beacon Hill Press, 2005.

Orcibal, Jean. "The Theological Originality of John Wesley and Continental Spirituality." In R. E. Davies and E. G. Rupp, eds., *A History of the Methodist Church in Great Britain*. Vol. 1. London: Epworth Press, 1965, 83–111.

Osborne, Catherine. "The *nexus amoris* in Augustine's Trinity." *Studia Patristica* 22 (1987): 309–14.

Outler, Albert C. "A Focus on the Holy Spirit: Spirit and Spirituality in John Wesley." *Quarterly Review* 8 no. 2 (1988): 3–18.

———. "A New Future for 'Wesley Studies': An Agenda for 'Phase III.'" In M. Douglas Meeks, ed., *The Future of the Methodist Theological Traditions*. Nashville: Abingdon, 1985, 34–52; reprint: 1991, 126–42.

———, ed. and "Introduction." In *John Wesley*. New York: Oxford University Press, 1964.

———. "John Wesley: Folk Theologian." *Theology Today* 34 (1977): 150–60; reprint, 1991, 56–74.

———. *The Wesleyan Theological Heritage: Essays of Albert C. Outler*. Edited by Thomas C. Oden and Leicester R. Longden. Grand Rapids: Zondervan, 1991.

Owens, Joseph, CSsR. "Aristotle and Aquinas." In Norman Kretzmann and Eleonore Stump, eds., *The Cambridge Companion to Aquinas*. Cambridge: Cambridge University Press, 1993, 38–59.

Pelikan, Jaroslav. "The Doctrine of *Filioque* in Thomas Aquinas and its Patristic Antecedents: An Analysis of *Summa Theologiae*, Part I, Question 36." In Armand A Maurer, ed., *St. Thomas Aquinas, 1274–1974: Commemorative Studies*. Vol. 1. Toronto: Pontifical Institute of Mediaeval Studies, 1974, 315–36.

Penido, Maurílio T.-L. "A propos de la procession d'amour en Dieu." *Ephemerides theologicae lovanienses* 15 (1938): 338–44.

———."Gloses sur la procession d'amour dans la Trinité." *Ephemerides theologicae lovanienses* 14 (1937): 33–68.

Pesch, Otto H. "Existential and Sapiential Theology—The Theological Confrontation between Luther and Aquinas." In Jared Wicks, ed., *Catholic Scholars Dialogue with Luther*. Chicago: Loyola University Press, 1970, 61–81.

———. *Die Theologie der Rechtfertigung bei Marin Luther und Thomas von Aquin*. Mainz: Matthias Grünewald, 1967.

Pinnock, Clark. *Flame of Love: A Theology of the Holy Spirit*. Downers Grove, Ill.: InterVarsity Press, 1996.

Porter, Jean. "Right Reason and the Love of God: The Parameters of Aquinas' Moral Theology." In Rik Van Nieuwenhove and Joseph Wawrykow, eds., *The Theology of Thomas Aquinas*. Notre Dame, Ind.: University of Notre Dame Press, 2005, 167–91.

Powell, Samuel M. "A Trinitarian Alternative to Process Theism." In Bryan P. Stone and Thomas Jay Oord, eds., *Thy Nature and Thy Name is Love: Wesleyan and Process Theologies in Dialogue*. Nashville: Kingswood Books, 2001, 143–67.

Puglisi, James F. "A Catholic View of Methodist-Catholic Dialogue." *Ecclesiology* 2 no. 3 (2006): 268–83.

Quantrille, Wilma J. "Introduction." In Charles Wesley, *Hymns on the Trinity*. Facsimile reprint. Madison, N.J.: The Charles Wesley Society, 1998, vii–xiii.

———. "The Triune God in the Hymns of Charles Wesley." Ph.D. diss., Drew University, 1989.

Rack, Henry D. "Early Methodist Visions of the Trinity." *Proceedings of the Wesley Historical Society* 46 (1987–88): 65–69.

———. *Reasonable Enthusiast: John Wesley and the Rise of Methodism*. Nashville: Abingdon Press, 1993.

Rattenbury, J. Ernest. *The Eucharistic Hymns of John and Charles Wesley*. London: Epworth Press, 1948.

———. *The Evangelical Doctrines of Charles Wesley's Hymns*. London: Epworth Press, 1941.

Rieger, Joerg. *Christ & Empire: From Paul to Postcolonial Times*. Minneapolis: Fortress Press, 2007.

———, with John L. Vincent, eds. *Methodist and Radical: Rejuvenating a Tradition*. Nashville: Kingswood Books, 2003.

Rigl, Thomas. *Die Gnade wirken lassen: Methodistische Soteriologie im ökumenischen Dialog*. Paderborn: Bonifatius, 2001.

Rikhof, Herwi. "Trinity." In Rik Van Nieuwenhove and Joseph Wawrykow, eds., *The Theology of Thomas Aquinas*. Notre Dame, Ind.: University of Notre Dame Press, 2005, 36–57.

Rogers, Eugene F., Jr. *After the Spirit: A Constructive Pneumatology from Resources Outside the Modern West*. Grand Rapids: Eerdmans, 2005.

Root, Michael. "The Indwelling Spirit and the Agency of the Church: A Lutheran Perspective on the Catholic-Methodist International Dialogue." *Ecclesiology* 2, no. 3 (2006): 307–23.

Rousselot, Pierre. *Pour l'histoire du problème de l'amour au Moyen Age*. Münster: Aschendorff, 1908. ET: *The Problem of Love in the Middle Ages: A Historical Contribution*. Edited by A. Vincelette and P. Vandevelde. Marquette Studies in Philosophy, 24. Collected Philosophical Works of Pierre Rousselot, 2. Milwaukee: Marquette University Press, 2001.

Runyon, Theodore. *The New Creation: John Wesley's Theology Today*. Nashville: Abingdon Press, 1998.

Schlimm, Matthew R. "The Puzzle of Perfection: Growth in John Wesley's Doctrine of Perfection." *Wesleyan Theological Journal* 38, no. 2 (2003): 124–42.

Schockenhoff, Eberhard. "The Theological Virtue of Charity (IIa IIae, qq. 23–46)." Translated by Grant Kaplan and Frederick G. Lawrence. In Stephen J. Pope, ed., *The Ethics of Aquinas*. Washington, D.C.: Georgetown University Press, 2002, 244–58.

Schütz, Christian. "Die Heilige Geist—Liebe in Person." *Internationale katholische Zeitschrift "Communio"* 34 (2005): 333–40.

Sherwin, Michael, OP. "Aquinas, Augustine, and the Medieval Scholastic Crisis Concerning Charity." In Michael Dauphinais, Barry David, and Matthew Levering, eds., *Aquinas the Augustinian*. Washington, D.C.: The Catholic University of America Press, 2007, 181–204.

———. *By Knowledge and By Love: Charity and Knowledge in the Moral Theology of St. Thomas Aquinas*. Washington, D.C.: The Catholic University of America Press, 2005.

Shults, F. LeRon and Andrea Hollingsworth. *The Holy Spirit*. Grand Rapids: Eerdmans, 2008.

Smith, Timothy L. *Thomas Aquinas' Trinitarian Theology: A Study in Theological Method*. Washington, D.C.: The Catholic University of America Press, 2002.

Speaking the Truth in Love: Teaching Authority among Catholics and Methodists. Report of the Joint Commission for Dialogue between the World Methodist Council and the Roman Catholic Church. Lake Junaluska, N.C.: World Methodist Council, 2001.

Starkey, Lycurgus M., Jr. *The Work of the Holy Spirit: A Study in Wesleyan Theology*. Nashville: Abingdon Press, 1962.

Stevick, Daniel B. *The Altar's Fire: Charles Wesley's Hymns on the Lord's Supper, 1745*. Peterborough, U.K.: Epworth Press, 2004.

Suchocki, Marjorie. "Wesleyan Grace." In William J. Abraham and James E. Kirby, eds., *The Oxford Handbook of Methodist Studies*. Oxford: Oxford University Press, 2009, 540–53.

Thompson, Andrew. "From Societies to Society: The Shift from Holiness to Justice in the Wesleyan Tradition." *Methodist Review* 3 (2011): 141–72.

Tillard, J. M. R. "Commentary on 'Towards a Statement on the Church.'" *One in Christ* 22 (1986): 259–66.

Todd, John Murray. *John Wesley and the Catholic Church*. London: Hoddard & Stoughton, 1958.

Torrell, Jean-Pierre Torrell, OP. *Aquinas's Summa: Background, Structure, and Reception*. Translated by B. M. Guevin. Washington, D.C.: The Catholic University of America Press, 2005.

———. *Saint Thomas Aquinas*. Vol. 1: *The Person and His Work*. Revised edition. Translated by Robert Royal. Washington, D.C.: The Catholic University of America Press, 2005.

———. *Saint Thomas Aquinas*. Vol. 2: *Spiritual Master*. Translated by Robert Royal. Washington, D.C.: The Catholic University of America Press, 2003.

Towards an Agreed Statement on the Holy Spirit. Report of the Joint Commission for Dialogue between the World Methodist Council and the Roman Catholic Church. Lake Junaluska, N.C.: World Methodist Council, 1981.

Towards a Statement on the Church. Report of the Joint Commission for Dialogue between the World Methodist Council and the Roman Catholic Church. Lake Junaluska, N.C.: World Methodist Council, 1986.

Tuttle, Robert Gregory, Jr. *Mysticism in the Wesleyan Tradition*. Grand Rapids: Zondervan, 1989.

Unitatis Redintegratio. http://www.vatican.va/archive/hist_councils/ii_vatican_council/documents/vat-ii_decree_19641121_unitatis-redintegratio_en.html. Accessed March 12, 2010.

The United Methodist Hymnal. Nashville: United Methodist Publishing House, 1989.

Vanier, Paul. *Theologie trinitaire chez Saint Thomas D'Aquin: évolution du concept d'action notionnelle*. Montreal: Institut d'Études Médiévales, 1953.

Van Nieuwenhove, Rik. "'Bearing the Marks of Christ's Passion': Aquinas' Soteriology." In Rik Van Nieuwenhove and Joseph Wawrykow, eds., *The Theology of Thomas Aquinas*. Notre Dame, Ind.: University of Notre Dame Press, 2005, 277–302.

Vickers, Jason E. "Albert Outler and the Future of Wesleyan Theology: Retrospect and Prospect." *Wesleyan Theological Journal* 43, no. 2 (2008): 56–67.

———. "Christology." In William J. Abraham and James E. Kirby, eds., *The Oxford Handbook of Methodist Studies*. Oxford: Oxford University Press, 2009, 554–72.

———. *Wesley: A Guide for the Perplexed.* London: T&T Clark, 2009.

Wainwright, Geoffrey. *Doxology: The Praise of God in Worship, Doctrine and Life.* New York: Oxford University Press, 1984.

———. "Introduction." In *Hymns on the Lord's Supper.* Madison, N.J.: Charles Wesley Society, v–xiv.

———. *Is the Reformation Over? Catholics and Protestants at the Turn of the Milennia.* Milwaukee: Marquette University Press, 2000.

———. "Methodists and Roman Catholics: Bilateral Dialogue in a Multilateral Context." *Ecclesiology* 2, no. 3 (2006): 285–305.

———. *Methodists in Dialog.* Nashville: Kingswood Books, 1995.

———. "The Sacraments in Wesleyan Perspective." *Doxology* 5 (1988): 5–20.

———. "Trinitarian Theology and Wesleyan Holiness." In S T Kimbrough Jr., ed., *Orthodox and Wesleyan Spirituality.* Crestwood, N.Y.: St. Vladimir's Seminary Press, 2002, 59–80.

———. "Wesley's Trinitarian Hermeneutic." *Wesleyan Theological Journal* 36, no. 1 (2001): 7–30.

Walsh, Liam G., OP. "Sacraments." In Rik Van Nieuwenhove and Joseph Wawrykow, eds., *The Theology of Thomas Aquinas.* Notre Dame, Ind.: University of Notre Dame Press, 2005, 326–64.

Wawrykow, Joseph P. *God's Grace and Human Action: "Merit" in the Theology of Thomas Aquinas.* Notre Dame, Ind.: University of Notre Dame Press, 1995.

———. "Grace." In Rik Van Nieuwenhove and Joseph Wawrykow, eds., *The Theology of Thomas Aquinas.* Notre Dame, Ind.: University of Notre Dame Press, 2005, 192–221.

———. *The Westminster Handbook to Thomas Aquinas.* Louisville, Ky.: Westminster John Knox Press, 2005.

Weissbach, Jürgen. *Der neue Mensch im theologischen Denken John Wesleys.* Stuttgart: Christliches Verlagshaus, 1970.

Williams, A. N. *The Ground of Union: Deification in Aquinas and Palamas.* New York: Oxford University Press, 1999.

Williams, Colin. *John Wesley's Theology Today.* Nashville: Abingdon Press, 1960.

Wood, Charles M. "Methodist Doctrine: An Understanding." *Quarterly Review* 18 (1998): 167–82.

The Word of Life: A Statement on Revelation and Faith. Report of the Joint Commission for Dialogue between the World Methodist Council and the Roman Catholic Church. Lake Junaluska, N.C.: World Methodist Council, 1996.

Wynkoop, Mildred Bangs. "Theological Roots of the Wesleyan Understanding of the Holy Spirit." *Wesleyan Theological Journal* 14, no. 1 (1979): 77–98.

———. *A Theology of Love: The Dynamic of Wesleyanism.* Kansas City, Mo.: Beacon Hill Press, 1972.

Yong, Amos. *Spirit of Love: A Trinitarian Theology of Grace.* Waco, Tex.: Baylor University Press, 2012.

INDEX

God's Love through the Spirit: The Holy Spirit in Thomas Aquinas & John Wesley was designed in Minion and composed by Kachergis Book Design of Pittsboro, North Carolina. It was printed on 60-pound Natures Book Natural and bound by Thomson-Shore of Dexter, Michigan.